The Verb *'To Bird'*

by *Peter Cashwell*

Illustrations by Grant Silverstein

The Verb
'To Bird'

Sightings of an
Avid Birder

PAUL DRY BOOKS

Philadelphia   2003

First Paul Dry Books Edition, 2003

Paul Dry Books, Inc.
Philadelphia, Pennsylvania
www.pauldrybooks.com

Text and display type: New Baskerville
Composed by P. M. Gordon Associates, Inc.
Designed by Adrianne Onderdonk Dudden

3 5 7 9 8 6 4
Printed in the United States of America

Library of Congress Cataloging-in-Publication Data

Cashwell, Peter, 1963–
    The verb 'to bird' : sightings of an avid birder / by Peter Cashwell ;
illustrations by Grant Silverstein. – 1st Paul Dry Books ed.
        p. cm.
    Includes bibliographical references.
    ISBN 1-58988-000-5 (cloth : alk. paper) – ISBN 1-58988-001-3
(trade paper : alk. paper)
    1. Bird watching–United States. 2. Birds–United States. I. Title.
    QL682 .C38 2003
    598′.07′23473–dc21

                                                    2002152073

For my grandparents

Mama Lea, who gave me books

Papa, who gave me laughs

Mama Lou, who gave me words

Daddy Joe, who gave me birds

Contents

9 . . . And a Bird in Every Pot   132

Q ratings for birds–The clashing of symbols–Your legislators at work–I am amused by mockery–The Cardinal group–Identity crisis–I make my pitch to the voters

10 The Cardinal Sin   139

Establishment taste–What's in a name?–I study Catesby's paintings–Gaps in the historical record–I am in utter awe of Audubon–More gaps–I pray for indulgences–I realize I've been hunting

PART THREE *Birded*

11 Too Much Nature   165

Not in a New York State of Mind–Three Gothamites in a Boat (To Say Nothing of the Snake)–Scenes from the NY State Fish Hatchery–I delay gratification–Cold Spring Harbor–Clumsy gloves as a birding tool

12 The Mother of All Geese   179

I am startled by a gigantic goose–We encounter louder geese of more ordinary size–Snow Geese: Romance v. Reality–Flood of the millennium–Panic on the Rapidan

13 The Stoneless Land   188

There is a tide–All the bugs in the world–Painful and disgusting experiences with fire ants–Waders, big birds, and pointy white birds explained–I discover the one flaw in Peterson–Trying to be blasé–AOOOGA!–We discuss Low Country building materials–Www.BuBbasBaIT.cOm

Part One

Birding

1
The Verb *To Bird*

Yes, it's a noun.

I concede the point. The word *bird* is in fact a noun. You win.

. . . But the word *pen* is a noun, too, and here I am, penning these words. The word *look* is a noun—don't give me that look—and yet there you are, looking at these words. Ditto for *gaze, glance,* and *eye.* Any number of English nouns double as verbs.

"Any number," however, is not "all." I'm an English teacher, and trying to pass off certain nouns as verbs is guaranteed to set my teeth on edge. Whatever former Secretary of State Alexander Haig may have said, I do not believe it is grammatically possible to *back-burner* something, and though Madison Avenue may insist otherwise, I don't think there is an old way, let alone a new way, to *office.* My friends and I have long referred to this misuse of nouns as *haiging,* in memory of the man who verbed more nouns than any other verber in the history of verbing, and I would like to hate the practice of haiging completely, but try as I might, I can't. Even when faced with the horrifying specters of "This information strongly *impacted* on our understanding," or "We'll have to *paradigm* this differently," I have to allow for the possibility that some nouns, drafted into service owing to a real and pressing need, can make decent verbs. There is not, for example, a handy English verb meaning "to gain access to," so I can't get too upset when someone says, "I *accessed* the database." Even without these few examples of beneficial haiging, though, I still can't correct a haiger without wanting to bite my own tongue for my hypocrisy.

Why? Because I bird.

There it is; even as I draw pay for teaching grammar, my entire lifestyle is wrapped up in a form of haiging. "To bird" is a regular part of my vocabulary. Shall I conjugate?

***Principal parts of the verb "to bird": present:** bird;* ***past:** birded;* ***present participle:** birding;* ***past participle:** birded.*

The word *bird* itself comes from *bridd,* an Old English word whose archaic meaning is "the young of a feathered vertebrate." It's a circular definition, since the only feathered vertebrates are birds, but it shows that people have long considered the word *bird* to be a noun, period. This makes sense; words like *reptile* and *mammal* are exclusively nouns, and those few animal names that make it as verbs tend to do so as parts of idioms. You can *chicken out,* or *pig out* at dinner, but you can't really say "I was chickening yesterday," or "Did you pig?" Even these idioms tend to use only domestic animals; no one has ever, to my knowledge, *raccooned, possummed* or *deered* anywhere near me.

There is a way to make an animal name into a verb, however: use it to mean "catching (the animal)," as in *fishing, crabbing,* or *shrimping.* Such a meaning for *birding* has existed for centuries, but you'll rarely hear it nowadays. Instead, *birding* is used where most laymen would use the term *bird-watching.*

I don't think it's accurate, however, to say that people like me "bird-watch." The term suggests that we lie around waiting for birds to appear, and that when they do, we sit passively and stare at them. In reality, those who bird pursue birds, observing them, memorizing their names, learning their field marks and calls, chasing them over hill and dale, recording their voices, netting and banding them, photographing them, and, most importantly, arguing about them with other birders. I doubt that clock-watchers act this way around clocks.

Tenses of the verb "to bird": present: *I bird;* past: *I birded;* future: *I will bird;* present perfect: *I have birded;* past perfect: *I had birded;* future perfect: *I will have birded.*

Bird is not only a shorter and more accurate term for the practice of watching birds, but has also been included in Webster's New Collegiate Dictionary, where Webster defines *bird-watch* simply as "bird." *Bird* itself is an intransitive verb meaning "to observe or identify wild birds in their natural environments." This may get me off the hook grammatically—you can't haig with an official verb, after all—but the definition is a somewhat optimistic one. A lot of birding doesn't involve observing birds—it involves waiting for birds to make themselves observable. Even when birds do appear, you can't always identify them. Many an experienced birder has had to classify a bird as an "LBJ"— a "little brown job"—because it was so briefly glimpsed. Sometimes conditions such as bad weather or poor light prevent you from pinning down a bird's species.* It's also notoriously difficult to distinguish between some species,

---

*This common problem has led the Sill family, authors of two wonderfully tongue-in-cheek "field guides," to theorize in their second book (*Another Field Guide to Little-Known & Seldom-Seen Birds of North America*) the existence of the so-called "Silhouette Warbler," a flat black bird, most active in dim light, with no field marks whatsoever.

such as the Sharp-shinned Hawk and Cooper's Hawk, or the infuriatingly similar flycatchers of the *Empidonax* complex, even when you get a good look at them.

In addition, it's not true to say that birders always observe *wild* birds. It's hard to tell, sometimes, whether the mallard on that pond is a wild duck or a farm duck. And when you stumble across a full-grown peacock strutting across a dirt road in rural Virginia, as I did once, it's still an impressive event, even as the sensible part of your brain is sensibly telling you "This bird is *probably* not native to these woods." The thorniest part of the definition, though, is the part about observing them in their "natural environments."

Progressive forms of the verb "to bird": *I am birding today, I was birding yesterday, I will be birding tomorrow, I have been birding, I had been birding before, I will have been birding later.*

I am birding right now.

Yes, I'm sitting at a desk in a room with a computer in front of me, but I'm birding. If a Yellow-shafted Flicker flies into the room, I'm as primed and ready to observe and identify it as I would be out in the woods, its so-called "natural environment." Granted, Flickers aren't often seen indoors, but if one shows up here, I can damned well identify it.

I know this because I've seen one in a place about as unusual as my study would be: between the front seats of my 1991 Ford Tempo. It was much harder to observe the bird than to identify it, since it was a dark night and I had been concentrating on driving to the store, but after I had parked the car, reached down to set the handbrake, discovered a soft, feathery object lying under it, shrieked, and opened the door in preparation to run away, it was the work of a mere instant to look down and say "Oh. It's a Yellow-shafted Flicker." I noted the familiar field marks:

"Oh. It's a Yellow-shafted Flicker."

the red patch on the head and the strong, sharp bill, both typical of woodpeckers; the black "mustache" that marked it as a male; the brownish plumage and white rump common to all flickers; and the underwing feathers, the shafts of which are a pure gold-yellow and give this species its name. I could do all this because I am a birder—"one who birds"—and I am always, *always* prepared to observe and, with luck, identify any bird I encounter. To tell the truth, so prepared was I to identify its species, *so* focused on making the right call, that it took me a moment to note another key feature of the bird under my handbrake: that it was stone dead.

Piecing the events of its death together took a bit longer, but with daylight, it became apparent that the bird had flown through the open driver's window and smacked into the inside of the back windshield at a pretty high speed. Somehow it had somersaulted into the space between the front seats before giving up the ghost, and it managed to leave several distinctive purplish stains on the upholstery en route. I bear a strong liking for woodpeckers of all sorts, but I remain embarrassed by my funeral arrangements for this bird: I disposed of it in a nearby trash can, washed my hands, and tried not to use the handbrake for a few weeks. Birding is sometimes an ugly thing.

Nonetheless, I do it everywhere: on walks, at football games, on picnics, at soccer games, on the golf course, and in the car, where you can't help but see birds—most of them outside the vehicle. Even getting to the car can provide you with choice birding opportunities. As my family walked to our car one rainy March morning, preparing to drive to New York City for spring break, our rural Virginia farmhouse, which sits in sight of the Blue Ridge Mountains, was suddenly visited by a host of seagulls right out of a Mormon history book. They settled in the pasture next to our house, scores of Ring-billed Gulls, gray and white and raucous, while I scanned the clouds nervously for signs of divine intervention. I wanted to be sure that this event resembled a miracle only coincidentally, and that there was no need to cancel the trip and start building an ark.

I didn't start looking for gopher wood and deck sealant that day, but many birders would have considered doing so, because many seem to regard their birding as specifically ordained by God, much as Noah thought of his home woodshop work. And these aren't the yokels-abducted-by-aliens fringe of the birding world, either; these are respectable people. No less a figure than Roger Tory Peterson, the Saint Paul of the Church of American Birding, described the calling to seek out birds as "the Spark," usually fired by a particular vision of some bird at the right moment—a blinding light on the road to Damascus, so to speak. John Burroughs, patriarch of twentieth-century birders, said simply of his first glimpse of a Black-throated Blue Warbler, "It was a revelation." Even those who don't consider birding a religious calling cannot deny that the religious significance of birds is widespread and ancient, or that birds twitter around mankind's myths, legends, and holy scriptures in great numbers.

Some of these birds are mythical, such as the phoenix, the roc, and the jayhawk (which in Kansas qualifies as a holy bird), but some are not. Consider the raven: it was sacred to many Native American tribes, and far across the Atlantic, Odin, ruler of the Norse gods, acquired his great wisdom from the whispers of his two far-seeing ravens. His Greek counterpart, Zeus, took the form of a swan in order to ravish the beautiful Leda, from whose feather-bruised loins would spring Helen of Troy and her siblings. Worshippers of Zeus's wife, Hera, considered the peacock her sacred bird, while the owl was sacred to worshippers of Athena. The quetzal was revered by the Aztecs, and cranes are revered by many Japanese even today. Ancient European seers were said to gain their wisdom by observing the flight of birds, or by slaughtering birds and making indepth probes into their intestines. Some Egyptian gods even sported the heads of birds, Horus that of a hawk and Thoth that of an ibis.

Lest you think the religious significance of birds is limited only to pagans and polytheists, let us note the book of Leviticus, chapter 11, verses 13–19, which specifies the birds that are not kosher:

13   And these *are they which* ye shall have in abomination among the fowls; they shall not be eaten, they *are* an abomination: the eagle, and the ossifrage, and the ospray,
14   And the vulture, and the kite after his kind;
15   Every raven after his kind;
16   And the owl, and the night hawk, and the cuckow, and the hawk after his kind,
17   And the little owl, and the cormorant, and the great owl,
18   And the swan, and the pelican, and the gier eagle,
19   And the stork, the heron after her kind, and the lapwing, and the bat.

What do these birds have in common, besides being as inedible to an observant Jew as a pig, or, if you read on in Leviticus, as a chameleon, a snail, or a mole? The main attribute these fowl share is a carnivorous or insectivorous diet: every one of them eats live prey or carrion (including the bat, which is not a bird, but is sure as hell *trayfe*). Why should that matter? My own theory, untainted by any hint of actual research, is that the Hebrews believed not only that you are what you eat, but also that what *you* eat is what *it* eats. If a stork lives on snails, or a vulture on the corpses of pigs, your eating the bird means that the abomination in its gullet will end up in your own. In other words, I figure if you're going to eat ossifrage, you might as well just order a nice shrimp salad with bacon, or roasted chameleon with *escargot en sauce mole.**

What about Christians? Do they hold birds as important? Well, they consider the dove not only a symbol of peace but one long associated with the Holy Ghost. Saint Francis of Assisi was so renowned for his kindness to wild birds that his image is affixed to bird feeders around the world. Angels are usually portrayed with the wings of birds, not those of bats, dragonflies or moths, and it is often said of God that his eye is on the sparrow, demonstrating that the Deity Himself practices birding in some fashion.

Even secular humanism is based largely around the knowledge of birds: *The Origin of Species,* the book on which much scientific belief about human origins is founded, was inspired by Charles Darwin's observations of the various beaks of the Galapagos Island finches, and it opens with a lengthy discussion of pigeon breeding, which Darwin considered a good illustration of the elementary mechanics of selection. One of the first-discovered "intermediate" fossils, long sought by evolutionists to give hard evidence of transition from one form to another, was the first bird; for paleontologists, finding the fossil of *Archaeopteryx* ("a complex melange of reptilian and avian fea-

*If you're wondering what an ossifrage is, as I was when I first read this passage, it's the Eurasian vulture *Gypaetus barbatus aureus,* better known as the Lammergeier, and not, as you may have thought, a smaller bird which might appear in some way appetizing.

11

tures," as Stephen Jay Gould called it) was like turning up the Dead Sea Scrolls.

With so much of human history devoted to observing birds and their behavior, even to the point of worshipping them, why should it be surprising that modern birders treat their preferred activity with a reverence more commonly seen during Easter services at the Vatican? Is an argument over whether the bird in question had an eye-ring really so different from the debate over Adam's navel? Aren't migration-time visitors to Cape May basically acting like *hadjis* in Mecca? (And, given all this quasi-religious behavior among birders, shouldn't they, like Scientologists, get some sort of tax-exempt status?) Whatever their professed faiths, birders treat birding like yet another one. Read their writings and you'll see: The Bird is the Word.

Of course, not all words are the *right* words. A casual glance at the writings of many birders reveals a special insight, an unusual angle on the world. Birders, like writers, tend to believe that God is in the details. Unfortunately, this belief is sometimes coupled with a belief that birders who pick up pens are divinely exempted from the laws of taste. For every writer who finds true inspiration in the sight of a bird in the wild, there is another who lines the bird up in his cross-hairs and blasts it with every rhetorical trick he's got. And these writers include not only johnny-come-lately tree-huggers, but two hundred years' worth of scientists, writers, artists, and philosophers, men and women who might well have sat around Emerson's house trading life lists with Thoreau, or supped with Huxley and Darwin, hoping the latter wouldn't be holding forth on pigeons again.

The Romantic poets, in particular, sometimes seem possessed by birds, especially nightingales, and their quill pens, plucked—O Irony!—from the very wings on which they wax rhapsodic, e'er seem to fairly flow with a veritable Avon, nay, a mighty Amazon, of overblown language and hallucinatory imagery. Consider Samuel Taylor Coleridge's "Rime of the Ancient Mariner," wherein a gigantic white Albatross flies into the poem, saves the ship's crew from disaster, and is killed by the ungrateful Mariner. Coleridge even has the dead seabird slung around the Mariner's neck like a crucifix—a truly remarkable feat, given the albatross's three-meter wingspan.

Wordsworth and Keats come off a little better, though each has at least one noteworthy avian lapse. The former, more attuned to daffodils than birds, manages one spectacularly clunky couplet in "The Solitary Reaper": "A voice so thrilling ne'er was heard/ In springtime from the Cuckoo bird." Keats, an undisputed genius, has what is overall a worthy poem in "Ode to a Nightingale," but I still wince when I see him referring to the bird as "thou, light-winged Dryad of the trees."

Maybe some of you are thinking that this is a purely British problem. One look at the American poet William Cullen Bryant's "To a Waterfowl" should convince you otherwise. To begin with, there's the title; couldn't he have given us the species, or at least a field mark or two by which to help make the identification? "Duck" may be an inelegant word, but using the highfalutin "waterfowl" rather than the precise "teal," the graceful "swan," the un-likely "gadwall," seems a needless air to put on. And then there's stanza three:

> Seek'st thou the plashy brink
> Of weedy lake, or marge of river wide,
> Or where the rocking billows rise and sink
> On the chafed ocean side?

If there's not a rule against using "seek'st," "marge," and "billows" in the same stanza, I'm proposing one now. The word "chafed," meanwhile, seems borrowed from some other poem entirely, like perhaps a lyric of Kurt Cobain's that slipped through a time warp, and I don't know what I can say about "plashy" save to note that it sounds like one of those words a Madison Avenue type would dream up to describe cranberry juice or cheap perfume.

Finally, we must consider Shelley, whose "To a Skylark" is probably the nadir of avian Romance, even if it did provide Noel Coward with a title for a play. This poem not only claims that the Skylark isn't a bird, but also goes into metaphorical overdrive attempting to tell us what a Skylark actually *is*. According to Shelley, a Skylark is alternately a "cloud of fire," an "unbodied joy," a "star of Heaven," an "arrow," a "Poet hidden in the light of thought," or maybe even a "glowworm golden / In a dell of dew, / Scattering unbeholden / Its aerial hue / Among the flowers and grass, which screen it from the view," for crying out loud. When I look on such works of the mighty, I certainly despair.

Apparently, the thought of a bird can be enough to shake even the greatest of literary minds. What happens, then, when a less-than-great poet is told by his Muse to write on an avian subject? I could simply say "It's not pretty," but as evidence, I'd ask that you consider the following couplet from "Old Eagle," penned by one Fred Emerson Brooks near the end of the nineteenth century, and selected by editors Kathryn and Ross Petras to adorn the frontispiece of their outstanding 1997 collection *Very Bad Poetry*. As the opening salvo of a book containing such remarkably bad poems as "An Elegy to a Dissected Puppy"

and "Prophecy of a Ten Ton Cheese," the Petras siblings
selected a work which shows perfectly what happens when
a bad poet selects a bird as his subject:

> Fear not, grand eagle
> The bay of the beagle!

Despite the above examples, however, many great writers have discussed birds while maintaining control over
their packs of slavering modifiers. In his essay "Mr. Forbush's Friends," E.B. White manages to discuss the minutiae of birding in Massachusetts in the early twentieth century and yet remain, delightfully, almost terse. One of his
best-known books is *The Trumpet of the Swan,* which also
demonstrates that the topic of birds does not automati-
cally send one into a whirlwind romance with one's the-
saurus. T.H. White, who was no relation to E.B., shared
with him a love of birds, as can be seen in his marvelous
account of the migration of the wild White-fronted Goose
in *The Once and Future King.* In *Watership Down,* Richard
Adams creates a scene-stealing Brown-headed Gull named
Kehaar, while Roald Dahl constructs a straightforward
and grimly amusing morality play about the actions of
ducks and men in *The Magic Finger.*

As evidenced above, poets generally have had a bit
more trouble than prose writers in preserving their deco-
rum around birds, but when they succeed, astonishing
beauties are created. William Butler Yeats's "Leda and the
Swan" is a masterpiece of description, tucking into its
fourteen lines enough mythological and ornithological detail to satisfy any critic. Gerard Manley Hopkins's "The
Wind-Hover" is more of an acquired taste, using the European Kestrel, a small falcon that Americans would com-

monly call a sparrow hawk, as a vividly painted allegory for Jesus Christ. Dickinson's "Hope is the thing with feathers," the singing thrush in Whitman's "When Lilacs Last in the Dooryard Bloomed," Ted Hughes's cycle of "Crow" poems—these are admirable examples of bird poetry. I myself have always had a soft spot for Tennyson's fragmentary "The Eagle," which reads, in its entirety:

> He clasps the crag with crooked hands;
> Close to the sun in lonely lands,
> Ringed with the azure world he stands.
>
> The wrinkled sea beneath him crawls;
> He watches from his mountain walls
> And like a thunderbolt he falls.

I don't blame any casual reader for thinking that birding is just one more excuse for writers to spew out hot air; lord knows there's plenty of evidence to make that case. But still, I would hope that a more experienced student of literature would see that birds can draw something special out of a skilled writer's mind, not just flutter around a mad poet's fevered brow.

Fever is not, so far as I know, caused by birding, but I have seen it argued that the desire to bird is physiological. Symptoms may include involuntary tics and compulsions, such as swiveling heads, random attention deficit disorder, compulsive clutching of field guides, and, most shameful of all, the need to identify the species of every piece of roadkill on cross-country trips. (Or maybe this last is just me. I seem compelled to announce "Hmm . . . raccoon," upon spotting the telltale rings of tail fur jutting up from a pinkish mass of goo on the shoulder. I think it's a holdover from birding, a deep-seated need to justify staring at something by pronouncing its title, as if the identification were a matter of some controversy and a considered expert opinion were necessary for legal reasons.)

Birding may be as easily considered a medical disorder as a passion of the heart or an act of faith. Peter Scott said as much in *Morning Flight:*

> That I am not alone in this strange madness, I am sure; indeed, it is a catching complaint, and I hardly know any who have been able to resist its ravages, when they have been exposed to infection.

For those who are unafflicted, like my wife, Kelly, the idea that birding is a disease holds a certain appeal since it would provide an explanation of some otherwise baffling behavior. The diagnosis and study of Tourette's Syndrome has taken some of the stigma away from uncontrollable tics and curses, and no right-thinking person blames a dyslexic for having trouble with spelling. My wife would like to be able to similarly attribute many of the things I do to a physical or perceptual dysfunction. She could look at the photographs of our trip to the beach, some thirty of which are snapshots I took of seagulls from a quarter of a mile away, and blame my Birding Compulsive Disorder: "Oh, Pete's BCD must have really been bad that day." She could forgive my narrowly missing a fence post near the end of our driveway while I was peering up at a vulture by saying, tenderly, "Oh, honey, if your BCD is acting up, I'll drive."

I might like being an official victim of BCD, especially if it meant I got to take sick days at work during peak migration times. Maybe I'd get decent insurance coverage. I'm sure I could get written up in some human interest article:

> Pete Cashwell's head turns for a moment, then returns to its original position. It's a motion he will make dozens of times in the next hour. He is unable to keep his eyes trained on an object for more than a second or two. Inside his swiveling head is a normal human brain, with all the intelligence of a normal person, but tragically, he will never do normal things —read a book, drive to the store, or play outside with his children—without his head swinging around at the slightest perception of movement. Somewhere in his brain is a misfiring, a small electrical or chemical flaw, that will allow him no peace. He is caught forever in the prison that is BCD.

If I were birding purely as the result of a medical condition, however, I might be cured. If I were cured, I would no longer have any interest in the glossy backs of grackles, or the bounding flight of goldfinches, or the alert strut of the Killdeer. I'd give up walking in the woods before sunup and peering out at the seed scattered on the snow for the Cardinals. Falcons would become a matter of indifference to me, and the sight of a heron beating his wings against the sunset wouldn't even raise an eyebrow. If I were cured, I could get through the day without having my mind distracted from some demanding task by the sight of a bird.

Bring on the plague, I say.

In truth, my mind is less distracted by birding than inordinately pleased with it, probably because birding is as much an intellectual passion as an emotional one. A few days after his death, Roger Tory Peterson was celebrated in a column in the *Washington Post*, and its writer, John

Pancake, understood the cerebral nature of both birding and Peterson's contributions to it:

> What was special about Roger Tory Peterson was not his ability to paint. It was his ability to think. He could see the essential qualities of subjects . . . and organize those qualities with stunning simplicity.
>
> His *Field Guide to the Birds,* first published in 1934—and the 50 field guides published thereafter by Houghton Mifflin—democratized the wilderness. The province of experts was opened to amateurs.

This is an achievement on a par with the establishment of the state university or the community college: a way of encouraging the common man to experience and appreciate what had been before the province of an elite, a way of getting more people to use their brains. Birding is one of the few outdoor activities that demand more of your powers of observation and deduction than of your physical abilities. This doesn't mean birders are necessarily smarter than non-birders; the stereotype of the bookish, eccentric intellectual compensating for his shortcomings of character and physique by taking up birding is just that: a stereotype. It is demonstrably true that not all birders make or have made good grades. It's just that we like to correct other people.

Well, again, maybe it's just me. I like to be right. And if I'm right when everyone else is wrong, so much the better. Birding is something of a contest, after all; you can succeed or fail in your attempt to identify a particular bird, despite years of experience, proper equipment, or even all the skill in the world—that's what makes it interesting. In some ways it's like chess or bridge: the players ask, "How do these variables I'm observing affect my ability to understand the situation?" Nailing down an identification is like capturing a piece or winning a trick; getting a new species on your life list is like a quick checkmate, or a small slam.

It's even more satisfying, I think, because your opponent is no mere mortal. It's Mother Nature herself, and she plays for blood. She knows all the tricks: poor lighting, bad weather, thick foliage, muddy plumage, all kinds of ways to keep you from achieving your goal. She's a defense-minded player, usually content to frustrate her opponents' attacks, driving them home with empty count lists, frustrated and damp. Only rarely does she take a serious offensive posture, sending a birder over a cliff or into the jaws of a full-grown alligator, but, like a good power forward, she's not shy about getting physical in order to discourage you. She'll rub blisters on your heels, pour bacteria into your lungs, and fill your socks with wood ticks just as soon as look at you. When I get information out of an opponent like that, I don't feel as though I've merely pulled down an offensive rebound in traffic—I feel like I've made the highlight reel.

Birders therefore often see their life lists as testaments to their intellectual ability, much like a diploma on the wall or a copy of *Finnegans Wake* left conspicuously on the coffee table. This, as you'd expect, may mask a basic insecurity—the question *Can't my brain handle something more important?* echoes in many birders' minds—but like all loyal alumni, birders bristle when you fail to show the proper respect for their scholastic arena. I dislike criticism of my alma mater, the University of North Carolina, *especially* if it disparages Dean Smith, the Peterson of basketball; I'm equally caustic when teased about coots and titmice. It's a little like playing the Dozens, or writing letters to the editor; the object is to get the last word, but if you can't get that, you at least want, like Cyrano, to show a little panache.

The best birders, though—"best" judged in moral terms, not by the size of life lists—are not merely observing machines; they also have a strict sense of honor: If they're not sure of the identification, it doesn't go down on the list. If the smallish bird on the branch betrays no sign of white wing bars, or if it does not make the distinctive *pee-a-wee* call, or if it is wagging its tail, phoebe-like, it will not be recorded as an Eastern Pewee. For most official counts and contests, where accuracy and fair play are emphasized, an identification must be confirmed by a second person. When they're on their own, however, birders must weigh the hoped-for against the seen, with nothing to prevent them from padding out their lists except their own integrity. In the vast majority of birding situations, no one will be checking lists for consistency or administering random urine tests; there's no point. Sure, I could mark off a Kirtland's Warbler on my life list right now, but even if I had the call and the field marks memorized, even if I convincingly claimed that I'd been to the bird's northern Michigan breeding grounds, I'd gain nothing from it. There are no Nike endorsements, no soft drink commercials for birders; my amateur status will remain unthreatened for eternity. I can therefore afford to demand evidence when I see what appears to be an unusual bird, as much as I want to believe it's a new one for the life list.

Want to test a birder's integrity? Check his daily count list for *Empidonax* flycatchers. The National Geographic Society's *Field Guide to the Birds of North America* describes the members of this genus, accurately, as "the bane of birdwatchers." Even for experts, these small flycatchers are damn near impossible to distinguish from one another except by habitat, which may be shared by several species, and by song, which you'll hear only during breeding season. All are drab, the sort of neutral beige-ish colors that L.L. Bean would call *taupe, mushroom,* or *dun,* fading to *off-white, oatmeal,* or *ecru* underneath, and all have the same white eye-ring and two white wing bars. "Nondescript" is, ironically, the perfect description of an *Empidonax.*

And what sort of person is obsessed with these birds? Imagine a classical music lover who has a favorite composer—Beethoven, let's say—and a favorite piece by that composer—let's say the Third Symphony—and a favorite conductor—Herbert Von Karajan with the Berlin Philharmonic—and imagine that this music lover will happily discuss with you the reasons why these are his favorites; that's the personality type of your average birder. But a birder whose expertise allows him to reliably identify the various birds of the *Empidonax* genus is like the music lover who owns *all* of the three or four different Karajan recordings of each individual Beethoven symphony and will hold forth for hours on which *version* is the best and why. It's impressive that he can do so, but there can't be very many people with whom he can talk about it. The *Empidonax* genus is a topic of similar narrowness.

"And what sort of person is obsessed with these birds?"

So how will these paragons of dullness, these Babbitts with beaks, these tiny proles of the avian world help determine integrity? Easy. Over a period of years, an honest birder may be in a position to see any or all of the so-called "Empids," so five to ten different species may well appear on his *life* list. On a *daily* count, however, especially in the fall or winter, the odds of any but the most expert birder getting a firm ID on more than a couple of these species is slim to none. If such a count list says only "Empid—sp?" you can trust your life, your car, and your daughter to this person. If you see "Empid—(Acadian)," he'd better be from the Southeast, where the Acadian Flycatcher is the only breeding Empid; if not, the IRS probably wants to talk to him, though you as a private citizen can lend him books and expect to get them back eventually. If, however, you see a list from a daily count with an unbroken string of "Alder Flycatcher, Willow Flycatcher, Least Flycatcher," etc., beware! He may not swipe the silverware, but you can bet that he'll try to get you involved with Amway, or maybe put your name down to become part of his long-distance calling circle.

The way I figure, if you're going to lie about the birds you see, lie BIG. Why worry about fudging an indeterminate Empid into an Alder Flycatcher? Just go ahead and put down all the rarest birds: *Bachman's Warbler, Red-cockaded Woodpecker, California Condor.* Go nuts! You don't even need to leave the house! Why not include species from other continents? *Peruvian Cock-of-the-Rock, Egyptian Vulture, Galapagos Penguin!* Come on! Who's going to stop you? Put down *extinct* birds! *Dodo! Heath Hen! Passenger Pigeon!* Hell, make up your *own* species! *Lesser Scottish Hamster-catcher! Parallel Parkingbird! Gabardine Trouser-thrush!* Oh, like anybody's going to check. Go ahead! Have fun!

Just don't say you're birding.

What, then, *is* birding? A religious calling? A poetic Romance? A spreading plague? A complicated game? A test of morals?

I know what it is *not*:

It is not a hobby. I have hobbies; it's not as if birds were the only obsession open to me. I have a sizable CD collection, a library of mixed pop literature and *belles lettres,* and the experience-honed ability to spot a moving pick in any college basketball game you care to show me. I know who Robyn Hitchcock, Neil Gaiman, and Antawn Jamison are and why they're important. I can discuss the ideas of Stephen Jay Gould, Lao-Tzu, or James Madison with some degree of confidence. I can be fixated on a great many things.

It's just that none of them matter when there's a titmouse on my feeder.

So no, birding is not a hobby, any more than sneezing is, or Presbyterianism is, or liking the color blue is. It is not something one chooses to do so much as something one cannot help but do. It is an action that springs from the deepest parts of the human soul, uncontrolled by propriety or convenience. Its nature is as indefinable as the Tao, as elusive as the birds themselves.

Maybe it's divinely inspired, maybe it's a passion uprising in the breast, maybe it's simply a form of obsessive-compulsive disorder. All I know for sure is this:

1   *To bird* is a verb.

2   All English verbs require subjects.

Therefore I bird.

2
Wanton Freaks

Sometimes goldfinches one by one will drop
From low-hung branches; little space they stop;
But sip, and twitter, and their feathers sleek;
Then off at once, as in a wanton freak:
Or perhaps, to show their black, and golden wings,
Pausing upon their yellow flutterings.
—John Keats, "I Stood Tiptoe"

Having established the verb, and its subject, let's get to the modifiers: How does one bird? Where does one bird? When? In what condition? With what or whom?

Let's consider the last question first: a birder can obviously get along without equipment, but there are a few items that certainly make birding a whole lot easier. The first is a good pair of binoculars or a spotting scope, which will allow you to be distracted by birds over a mile away. Such devices are not strictly necessary for a birder, but a lack of them will limit you to observing birds that are large, close by, and in plain sight. Should you wish to examine a small bird perched thirty feet up in a broadleaf tree, or one particular shorebird in a large flock down the beach, the naked eye isn't going to do the job.

I should note that some birders eschew the eye altogether, preferring to bird by ear. Because many species have calls or songs that are at least as distinctive as their appearances, this method can be very effective, particularly if the bird in question is nocturnal or secretive in its habits. You can buy recordings of various birdcalls, but these will require no small amount of study if you want them to be as useful to you as a pair of binoculars. The auditory approach is also unwieldy in the field, as you can't easily flip through four hours of recorded chirps to find the bird you just heard, while a quick glance in a good field guide can immediately help with a visual identification. As a result, most birders I know use their ears to supplement their eyes, not to replace them.

The second item of birding equipment is a list. This can be a list of birds seen in a particular place (such as a yard, a park, or an official count area) or over a particular time (a twenty-four-hour period, a season, or a year), but the most common sort is the life list, a record of each different species of bird you have ever observed in the wild. Those birds on the list are commonly called "life birds" or "lifers," and knowing which lifers you have and which you don't have gives you two things: a sense of accomplishment and a clear knowledge of specific birds you can add to your tally. Let me be clear: it is perfectly fine to bird without such a list. I did so for more than twenty years. I found, however, that birding was more challenging and more interesting once I began listing. And why did I begin listing? I got item number three as a twenty-fifth birthday present.

This third item is Roger Tory Peterson's *Field Guide to the Birds,* which, as any veteran birder knows, will help you identify what you're observing better than any other book, period. Peterson's "field mark" system is head, shoulders, solar plexus, and abdomen above any other means of identification. Some guides may have nice color photographs or flashier paintings than Peterson's, but they don't always help you put a name to what you're seeing. I know many birders who use other field guides, such as the Audubon Society's photographic guides, the National Geographic guide, or the beautifully painted, exhaustively detailed, but somewhat unwieldy Sibley guide. I own several of these myself, but when it comes to identifying birds in the field, I use them only as supplements to Peterson. They're a way of narrowing down a difficult ID by using multiple sources, just as a student of the Torah will often consult the commentaries of dozens of rabbinical scholars in order to help him understand a particular point—*but only after he reads the Torah itself.* There's a reason why the Peterson guide is called "The Birder's Bible."

The field mark system, in Peterson's own words, is "in a sense, a pictorial key based on readily noticed visual impressions." In other words, it points to the distinctive and observable features of each type of bird, rather than those anatomical differences that you might notice only through in-hand study or dissection. The Peterson guide's paintings of the various birds are composed specifically to "show field marks to best advantage," usually through careful positioning of the bird and an arrow or two pointing to the most important features. For the Eastern Bluebird, for instance, arrows indicate the bird's overall blue color and rusty red breast; if you note those two features, you've seen everything you need to see in order to identify *Sialia sialis.* Beside it in the guide is the Mountain Bluebird, whose pale blue belly is noted as a field mark, thereby showing the main difference in these two similar species. If you can observe and compare the field marks, you can identify the birds.

In his 1996 appreciation of Peterson's life, the *Washington Post*'s John Pancake noted that "he was often celebrated as a painter and illustrator, but the truth is that the illustrations aren't very good art." I would both agree and disagree; true, the paintings in the guide aren't of a kind with Leonardo's *Mona Lisa,* but they are of a kind with Leonardo's technical drawings, artwork that had a specific purpose: to clearly state to the observer the exact nature of what was being observed. Sir Christopher Wren's blueprints for Saint Paul's Cathedral may not have been good art in and of themselves, but the cathedral they helped build certainly qualifies. If you want to construct for yourself a knowledge of birds that will be a source of beauty and enjoyment to you, Peterson is the only architect that matters.

The Peterson guide is not merely a collection of bird pictures, however; there are also brief, pithy descriptions of the birds, with especially noteworthy field marks in italics. After a long day of slogging through the verbiage of Bryant or Shelley, there is something bracing about a no-nonsense piece of writing like this:

NORTHERN MOCKINGBIRD
Mimus polyglottos   9–11″ (23–28 cm)
Gray; slimmer, longer-tailed than Robin. Note the *large white patches* on the wings and tail, conspicuous in flight.

In three lines, Peterson gives you everything you need to recognize the bird: an economic miracle, especially for a birder.

Of course, being a birder, Peterson is occasionally prone to more descriptive prose, but it comes off as effective—almost narrative, almost poetry. I think his word-picture of the Eastern Meadowlark would make a service-able piece of free verse:

> In grassy country,
> a chunky brown bird flushes,
> showing a conspicuous patch
> of *white*
> on each side
> of its short wide tail.
>
>> Several rapid wingbeats
>> alternate
>>> with short glides.
>
> Should it perch on a post,
> the glass reveals
> a bright yellow breast
> crossed by a
> *black V.*
>
>> Walking,
>> it flicks its tail
>> open
>> and
>> shut.

It's minimal, but complete in its suggestion, like the work of Basho. Indeed, I can envision an entire series of haiku based on Peterson:

WHIP-POOR-WILL
flushed by day, the bird
flits away on rounded wings
like a large brown moth.

GREEN HERON
a small dark heron
that in flight looks crowlike (but
flies with bowed wingbeats).

WILD TURKEY	BARN OWL
head naked; bluish	*white heart-shaped face.* A
with red wattles intensified	long-legged, knock-kneed, pale,
in male's display.	monkey-faced owl. *Dark eyes.*

And not a blithe spirit or a plashy brink to be seen.

The fourth thing a birder needs, at least some of the time, is a fellow birder.

Birding alone is peaceful, make no mistake, and a lone birder has the advantage of never having to debate whether the bird he has glimpsed is a Sharp-shinned Hawk or the similar but less common Cooper's Hawk—he can simply write down "Cooper's Hawk" on his life list and later dare anyone to deny it. Still, I have always enjoyed company when I am beating the bush for new lifers, and certainly there is no better way for a birder with a small-to-middling life list to see new species than to be taken around by a more experienced birder. My own growth from passive to active birder happened in Fayetteville, North Carolina, and it happened largely because of a fellow teacher named Mary Stevens.

Things began innocently enough. Soon after Mary and I discovered each other's interest in birds, I spotted a new life bird over Thanksgiving break. On our first day back, I sneaked into Mary's classroom before she arrived for first period and scrawled its name across her blackboard. She did the same to me after her next lifer, and the practice grew into a habit for us, a minor source of amusement that helped us prevent teaching from numbing our minds completely.

We did not, however, consider who else would be reading these messages. The first thing her Latin students saw that first Monday morning were the words "LITTLE

BLUE HERON" in my distinctive all-caps handwriting. This alone might have passed unnoticed, but my own students were later treated to Mary's retaliatory "WILSON'S WARBLER," and then a rapid exchange of "YELLOW-THROATED WARBLER," "ROUGH-LEGGED HAWK," "PIPING PLOVER," and so on. Soon, tongues were wagging about our torrid and ongoing affair.

The fact that said affair was totally nonexistent didn't matter. The kids didn't know a heron from a '74 Volvo, and assumed we were writing each other cute little terms of endearment from our passionate encounters, which they no doubt imagined taking place in the teachers' lounge, and sounding something like this:

HE: Oh, my little blue heron, how I have missed you!

SHE: No more than I have missed you, black skimmer of my heart!

HE: Am I still your piping plover, my darling?

SHE: Oh, no one has ever ploved me the way you do, *mon cher avocet*!

I have only two comments to make on the subject of this fictitious dalliance:

First, were I to have an affair, WHICH I'M NOT, I would not do so with another teacher. I'd constantly fear having my grammar, social behaviors, and/or angle of approach scrupulously corrected, perhaps even repeatedly until I got it right. Worse, I myself might be the one spoiling the mood by answering my partner's breathy demands with "That's unclear. What is the antecedent of the pronoun 'it,' anyway? And can't you use a more specific verb than 'do' here?"

But second, and more importantly, were I to have an affair, WHICH I'M STILL NOT, I would unquestionably compare my lover to something—anything—that did not have a needle-shaped bill, gnarly meter-long green-gray legs, and breath with the aroma of a thousand dead raw bullfrogs.

Having a fellow birder in the field is even more important when one's beloved, like my wife, is not a birder. Non-birders do not see birds in quite the way we do. While I may need a field guide to help me nail down a bird's species, I am, through long practice, almost always able to recognize the basic family—whether it is a songbird, or a vulture, or a heron, say. My wife, in her own words, divides all birds into two categories: "Duck" and "Not A Duck." There have been many times, however, when I have wished she could learn to appreciate the beauty and variety of birds, perhaps in the same way she appreciates the nuances of poetry.

English majors are much like birders; where one has a shelf full of field guides, the other has a dozen different Norton Anthologies. (I am both, which means that I have no shelf space at all.) But I hold out some hope that Kelly is not as immune to the pleasures of birding as she may pretend to be. I came home one evening to find her glowing with excitement over a bird she had encountered, and whose basic field marks she'd even noticed.

"The kids were playing on the slide and I was sitting on the front steps, reading," she said breathlessly, "and this hummingbird flew right up to me!"

"Wow," I said, in complete sincerity.

"It just hovered there, and kind of looked at me. It was green and white, and it just looked at me, and I didn't want to move, because I didn't want to scare it off or anything, but it flew down to where I couldn't see it because my book was in the way. But I could actually feel the wind from its wings on my leg!"

This last was delivered with such a shine in her eyes that it felt almost like a religious confession, and I realized that I had been selling Kelly short. For a long time, I had assumed that she found birds simply too mundane to care about, and that the only way a bird would impress her would be by winning a Nobel prize, marrying David Duchovny, or growing to a height of fifty feet and attacking downtown Tokyo. But now I realized that what gave her an interest in birds, this time at least, was quite simply proximity.

I grew up in a house where bird books were easy to find, and both sets of grandparents had them in quantity as well. When I was a toddler, my parents hung over my crib a mobile with small, brightly colored birds made of vinyl-covered cotton dangling above me. In fact, one of my mother's favorite stories is the one about the time she walked in on me and discovered that I had pulled the mobile down and was snapping the birds off it one by one, calmly identifying them as I worked: "This is a CARDINAL (yank) and this is a BLUE JAY (yank) and this is a GOLDFINCH (yank) . . ."

Birds were near me when I was young, and I was comforted by them, so I kept an eye out for them on trees, lawns, and feeders. Eventually I decided to seek them out on purpose. I wanted to have, and still want to have, the same kind of close encounter Kelly had with her hummingbird: to see the bird, to know the bird, and to feel its life against my skin.

A closer encounter with birds was exactly what Mary Stevens offered me once she found out that I was interested in them. She asked me to help her on a Christmas bird count organized by Raven Rock State Park outside Lillington, North Carolina. I took her up on the offer, and on the morning of that first count we wandered far afield in Harnett County, happily mistaking birds for other birds until the light got better, and generally wasting an entire morning of potential Christmas shopping. Until that trip, I had never known the fun of birding with a partner; well, honestly, it wasn't so much a sense of fun as a sense of relief.

I should explain that. Many birders are a bit embarrassed about the way we act. We do not really *choose* to stop paying attention to the road so we can pin down the underside markings of a passing hawk, or make a *conscious* judgment that the kids will be fine on top of the jungle gym while we inspect the shrubbery for towhees; it just happens to us. Unfortunately, these actions are often condemned by a society which neither knows nor understands the peculiar passions burning in the hearts of birders, who suffer in silent misery.

When I'm suffering, though, I'm pretty vocal about it, and I usually manage to inflict a certain degree of misery on those around me. My friends and family have suffered for me on many occasions, but surely the worst thing I have ever done to my loved ones is to dabble in golf. Not because I'm that bad a golfer—I don't hit the ball hard enough to be dangerous—but because a golf course is one of the prime places to spot birds. The varied terrain of most courses is a lure for birds of forest, grass, marsh, and, as I can attest, sand and water. The first Black-and-White Warbler I ever saw flew to the ground not ten feet from me as I searched gingerly among the pine needles for an errant three-iron shot on Southwick Golf Course near Saxapahaw, North Carolina; my reliable left-handed slice has also helped me put two species of kinglet, a fly-catcher, and an oriole on my life list. The payback for this bounty, however, is unrelenting abuse from my golfing partners.

"Jeez, Cashwell, will you *hit* the damn ball?" is the most frequent comment, usually heard while I stand over my ball, shading my eyes, peering into the stygian darkness of the forest primeval, wondering if that bird in the under-brush is a new and unusual species, like maybe a King Penguin. "It's a *bird*, dammit! There's plenty of 'em out in the parking lot!" It's ironic, of course, to get this treatment from friends who go ballistic if they hear you confuse one Pink Floyd song with another, but birders seem to attract more verbal abuse than your typical hobbyist, and those of us who bird begin to feel a tad isolated, like, say, the Man in the Iron Mask.

It is thus something of a relief to discover that you are not a freak, that others have borne your burden, too, that there exist intelligent people who are also wandering around wet fields at the crack of dawn with dog-eared field guides crushed against the granola bars in their pockets. That discovery in itself is a great feeling, but to be *invited* to share the experience, the intimate communion with na-ture, the uncertain probing of strange forests, the damp squelching noises coming from your shoes—this is true bliss.

Mary and I became regular partners on Raven Rock's counts, though we made a somewhat unlikely looking team; she stands almost a foot shorter than I, and she weighs less than half what I do. Nonetheless, while my stu-dents usually cooperated with my disciplinary demands only because they felt guilty about having gotten away with so much already, Mary's students feared her the way the turkey fears cranberry sauce. She has a sharp tongue and a savage sense of irony, and she holds a grudge in roughly the same way a wolverine grips a rabbit by the throat; I, on the other hand, am inclined to speak no hyperbole whatsoever, take everything literally, and am the soul of cooperation with all humanity. Despite these contrasts, we made a good team, because Mary was (and still is) far more knowledgeable than I about birds' calls and habitats, but I was at least as good as she at spotting them in the first place. If I could find them for her, she could identify them for me: a symbiotic relationship, something any naturalist can appreciate. She and I ventured out into Harnett County some half-dozen times, during spring counts and Christmas counts, accompanied by various friends and associates, through forest, fen, and pasture, and never once did I make fun of her for being the kind of small woman who drives a pickup truck bigger than her whole yard. I didn't feel that would lead to a productive count.

I now live in rural Virginia, far away from Harnett County, but still I feel the flocking instinct, that drive to join with others of one's kind that is observed not only in many species of birds, but in humans as well. That this drive is felt especially deeply by birders is only logical. Thus, when I moved from one school to another, I also moved from one birding partner to another—several others, in fact.

I can no longer recall exactly when it was that I discovered the truth about Tom Parker: not only that he, like me, wrestles verbs for a living at Woodberry Forest School, but that he, like me, is inclined to spend long hours staring at birds. Once we had discovered our mutual interest, we started telling one another about our recent sightings: "Did you see that Belted Kingfisher on the wires over the pond down near the end of Route 230?" "I was driving in today, and a Cooper's Hawk went right over the road and into a flock of Starlings!" "Ever see any of those Wild Turkeys down by the river?" It was a comfortable topic, unrelated to the demands of our teaching loads, and we explored it happily. When Tom asked me to come by his house, though, I sensed a new dimension in our friendship—you don't invite just *anyone* to come examine your new night heron carving, you know.

Tom collects woodcarvings of birds; not hunting decoys, but actual statuary. His most recent prize was a gorgeous carving of a Black-crowned Night Heron, one only about a quarter the size of the actual bird, but still pretty spectacular. A chunky, pearl-gray and black wader with blood-red eyes and two long white plumes sweeping back from its head is noteworthy even when it's only seven or eight inches high. Tom's face had an earnest glow as I examined the carving; he looked almost like Radar O'Reilly showing off a prized pet. The room was full of other small statues, too: ducks and songbirds, certainly, but mostly waders, plovers, sandpipers, and herons. I got the distinct feeling that, when Tom's at the beach, his wife and son must have to keep him focused on where he's walking in order to prevent him from stumbling into the surf. (It's a phenomenon I'm familiar with.) This was more than a look at artwork, however beautiful; it was a look into the soul of the collector as well. I felt as though I'd been offered a glimpse into a colleague's private world, and frankly, I was a bit apprehensive. What could I offer in response to this?

It took me a while, but I thought of something. Tom was still birding passively, as I once had: examining whatever happened to be around him, but not really seeking it out. He had never been on a count, or even done much active birding in the sense of going for walks or drives with the specific purpose of seeing birds. I might not know any more about birds than he, but I could at least give him a reason to go out and look for them. If I were to play Virgil to his Dante, or at least Mary to his Pete, I might be able to return the gift of trust he had given me. I told him we were going birding.

We agreed to meet at 6:30 on a Tuesday morning, a bit after sunrise, but still early enough for frost to be on the grass in the shady spots of the athletic fields. It was mid-March, the heart of our spring break, so we would be free to spend the morning digging up whatever we could on Woodberry Forest's sprawling grounds. Moreover, they were grounds about which I knew little at the time, but which Tom, as a fifteen-year veteran of the school, knew quite well. It seemed like another good, symbiotic partnership: I could offer knowledge of the birds, Tom could offer knowledge of the terrain.

This last was important because Woodberry's terrain is both plentiful and immensely varied, including as it does not only the parklike campus and the homes and yards of faculty members, but over a thousand acres of fields, woods, ponds, pastures, hedgerows, barnyards, and hills, including a stretch of the Rapidan River and a nine-hole golf course. Other than beach and mountainside, it's got pretty much every habitat a Virginia bird could want. Where does one start with such a smorgasbord? Thinking of early-morning duck sightings with Mary, I suggested that we march down the long hill from the main buildings toward what some call a water hazard. (Since it's technically not on the golf course, and sits behind a fence, I'm inclined to call it a pond not a hazard, but then again, anyone who hooks the ball off the second tee is going to get wet.) Even from far up the hill, we could see that there were birds on the water, and after a few moments, we could hear the brazen honks of a flock of geese.

Technically, the term should be "a *gaggle* of geese," for geese are one of the many birds whose aggregations are subject to what James Lipton refers to as "terms of venery." According to Lipton's classic *An Exaltation of Larks,* the huntsmen of medieval times went to great lengths to create descriptive and exclusive terms for groupings of any bird or beast they might be pursuing; thus, the word "venery" is simply the Anglicized version of the French *venerie* (to hunt), and not some sort of pun related to syphilis.* Terms of venery like "a school of fish" or "a pride of lions" are so well known as to pass more or less unnoticed, but any lover of language must take delight in the images of birds assembled not in flocks, but in far more subtle, precise, and descriptive terms:

a charm of finches	a siege of herons
a tidings of magpies	an unkindness of ravens
a descent of woodpeckers	a cast of hawks
a mustering of storks	an ostentation of peacocks
a parliament of owls	a murder of crows
a host of sparrows	a walk of snipe

The terms listed above are all established, in some cases from centuries ago, but Lipton should also be given credit for his creativity in adding to the list; anyone who has ever birded for even a moment can delight in the

*Of course, given that "venery" stems originally from the Latin *venari* (to hunt), "venereal" from *Venus* (Roman goddess of love) and "venerate" from *venerari* (to worship), the potential for rude and even blasphemous puns is immense.

thought of seeing a *shimmer* of hummingbirds or a *scold* of jays or (my favorite) a *gatling* of woodpeckers. Only in a few cases do I feel the need to comment further on Lipton's vigorous contributions to our language:

First, I must take issue with his creation of the term "a clutter of starlings," not because I find it at all inaccurate or ugly, but because the existing term is so spectacularly apt: a *murmuration* of starlings. Those who have seen a large group of starlings taking off from a field can attest to the shiver of sound produced by countless primary feathers beating against the air; sometimes the vibrations can even be felt. Luckily, we have an elegant solution available: like geese, who form a *gaggle* on water and a *skein* in the air, starlings can be assigned to a *clutter* on the ground and to a *murmuration* when in flight.

Second, I would like to suggest a term for a bird left high and dry by the venereal linguists of the Middle Ages. Lipton rightly points out that the fifteenth-century technical term for swans is "singularly colorless for so inviting a subject," being simply "an Herde of Swannys." Even spelled "herd," it hasn't got a lot of zing to it, nor does the more recent "wedge of swans" seem much of an improvement. I would instead propose a term which I think is distinctive and appropriate, and which makes reference to another classic work of literature: a *trumpet* of swans. There is, after all, an entire species known as the trumpeter swan, and I can think of no better way to honor birder-author E.B. White than to appropriate for official use the title of his book *The Trumpet of the Swan*.

Finally, I must quote a passage of Lipton's regarding a term I had never seen or heard before reading his book:

A MUTATION OF THRUSHES
A Mutacyon of threstyllys *in the* Porkington MS. *On June 1, 1867, a letter from William Dodgson in* Science Gossip *provided*

the "recognized fact amongst naturalists that thrushes acquire new legs, and cast the old ones when about ten years old."

I don't have anything especially clever or worthwhile to say about this except that (a) I love the term and plan to use it at every opportunity, and (b) I have the distinct feeling someone has been pulling someone else's leg, regardless of when it was acquired.

As we can see from even our very language, the flocking instinct is such a part of a bird's makeup that it should come as no surprise to learn that there is a similar instinct in birders. It was that, I suppose, that drove me to find another person with whom to bird, and though I am never averse to doing so alone, I must admit that birding in company has a certain inherent energy; somehow you feel as if you're actively *doing* something, rather than just goofing off and staring at the trees.

That energy, moreover, has begun to spread: since our morning's exertions, Tom and I have discovered other faculty members and students who share our interest in birds. So what do we call this group? Clearly such an aggregation requires its own term of venery: a *guide* of birders? A *listing* of birders? These would work well enough, but frankly, I think the only appropriate term for a group of academics with binoculars around their necks is a *school of birders*, but that's just my opinion, and it's merely one of a host. Or a flock. Or a covey. Or a clutter.

The first avian sound I ever heard with Tom Parker was the chaotic honking of a gaggle of geese, but the most important to me, by far, was the clear *to-wink* of the Rufous-sided Towhee we heard a bit later that morning.

We were strolling down a muddy farm road when I caught a glimpse of white tail spots as the bird ducked into a stand of running cedar. I said, "Oh! Towhee," or something equally innocuous, to which Tom immediately cried "Where?!" with a bit more enthusiasm than I'd expected. He explained that despite a wealth of shrubbery around his house, he'd never had a towhee come visit, nor had he managed to spot one skulking in the dead leaves before.

I brought the walk to a halt for several minutes as we stooped and stretched and wandered along the cedar for a while, occasionally inspiring the bird to give a *to-wink* to prove he was still there. Finally he gave up and exposed himself on an outer branch for a moment: white breast and belly, rusty-red sides, black back and head, set off by brilliant red eyes. Satisfied that we'd seen him, he darted back into the undergrowth. I think I may have been happier than Tom that our pursuit of the bird had been successful, because I was on the way to paying Mary Stevens back: for the first time, I'd helped someone else get a lifer of his own.

And that, perhaps more than anything else, is what I love about birding in company: everybody wins. In July of 2000, I took a guided birding trip through the Meadows of Cape May, New Jersey. There were roughly twenty of us on the tour, varying in experience from expert to tenderfoot, and we had logged forty species in just under two hours. Our guides had helped us nail down a number of birds, including a Least Bittern, a diminutive wading bird that I wouldn't have spotted for myself with a seeing-eye dog and a GPS readout, but they weren't the ones who spied the weird bird flying in over the pond to the west—that honor fell to me.

I didn't know what it was, mind you, but I could see that it was a small sandpiper with an unusually long bill. "What's that coming over the water?" I cried. "Is it a Snipe?" It was moving at a good clip, and I had trouble

keeping it fixed in my binoculars. My Aunt Linda, however, was also along for the day, and though she is a less
active birder than I, she has a talent for patiently keeping her eye on a bird, even in flight. I lost sight of it several times, but with Linda's help, I was always able to
find it again, noting as I did that it had a large triangular
white patch on its rump. I called the field mark out even
as Linda called out the bird's location over the water, and
eventually Karl, one of our guides, found it in his glasses
and cried, "Short-billed Dowitcher!" A quick look in my
Peterson guide confirmed it (and showed that the bird's
unusually long bill was short only in comparison to that of
the Long-billed Dowitcher). We had another lifer, for me,
for Linda, and for several others in the group. I could take
pride in having spotted it first, but I couldn't take the bird
away from anyone else who'd seen it.

It's a small act of kindness, helping someone get a new
life-list bird, but such are the acts we remember long after
we've forgotten who won the golf match, or the bridge
game, or the coin toss. Like the list itself, it's the accumula-
tion of the acts that matters, not the smallness of the individual components. If Saint Peter really is keeping a list of
all our worldly actions, he of all people should appreciate
a lifer shared.

3
Counting Crows

. . . once you start counting the milestones you may count on till a
speckled haze dances before your eyes . . .

–Nikolai Gogol, Dead Souls

If you've never been on one, you're probably wondering: What happens on a bird count? Well, for the first hour
or so, very little. This is because counts always start long
before dawn, and persuading the coffee pot to function is
the top priority. For Raven Rock counts, I usually managed to wake at about 4:30 A.M., stagger to the car, and barrel the thirty-odd miles from Fayetteville to Mary's home
in Lillington without benefit of caffeine, but an entire
morning in the field without the life-giving ministrations
of coffee would have left me useless to the count. Upon
my arrival, Mary would get a pot going, usually before
opening her eyelids. While the coffee was brewing, a two-
hundred-piece Scarlet Macaw marching band could have
formed the letter "M" on her front lawn while blaring out
a medley of Jimmy Buffett favorites, and the only comment it would have gotten from either of us would be "I
swear I've got 'Cheeseburger in Paradise' stuck in my
head."

Once we were really awake, the planning began. The count leader was Park Ranger Paul Hart, an enormously skilled birder; if an unseen bird makes a call near him, it might as well be handing him a copy of its high-school yearbook. Paul and his cohorts at Raven Rock had divided Harnett County into about a dozen count areas, within which teams of two or three birders would be free to move about as they saw fit. Counters were to mark down both number and species, providing a statistical picture of both the population and the diversity of the area's bird life. Each team was given an official map, an official clipboard, and an official photocopied checklist of the eastern American birds that might be seen during the day.

Mary would affix the list to the official clipboard, which seemed to hold all the power of an olive branch or a diplomatic passport. Whenever we went onto private land, we tried to notify whoever was in charge of it, but some of the unfenced fields and woods we inspected probably belonged to someone whose hobby was filling the butts of trespassers with buckshot. We were wandering about before six on a Saturday morning, so there wasn't always a person around to ask for permission, but no matter where we went, as long as Mary had the clipboard, I felt reasonably sure that no one would shoot us, at least not without a warning blast across our bow first.

The clipboard properly prepared, she would check me for sufficient alertness by asking me for a pen. Since I am required by the laws of my guild* to have a pen at all times, my only excuse for not finding one somewhere on my person is unconsciousness. Once Mary had gotten the pen (or forced more coffee down my throat), she would

---

*The Most Ancient and Sacred Order of Sentence Diagrammers and English Teachers, Local #839

look over the map and consult her memory banks; she had a remarkable knowledge of which birds she'd seen in which places, and had driven the back roads of the county many times. Until I began counting with Mary, I had never realized just how large a part specific location plays in spotting birds; I had just assumed that if you were within the breeding range or winter range of birds, they would be evenly sprinkled throughout that range like pepperoni on a pizza. In fact, they are concentrated very much according to terrain: Rufous-sided Towhees and Carolina Wrens don't go where there's no cover; Common Yellowthroats and Prothonotary Warblers appear only in damper scrub and woodlands; Field Sparrows and Eastern Meadowlarks, unsurprisingly, don't go into heavily forested areas. You can live in a county populated by any number of Belted Kingfishers, but unless you go down to the waterside, you'll probably never see one. Mary knew not only what birds were around, but exactly where most of them were likely to be.

Finally, once clipboards, pens, drinks, and snacks were properly loaded, once field guides were placed in easily accessible pockets and binoculars hung carefully around necks, we were ready; yawning but excited, we took to the road.

Invariably, we would arrive at our first count site before dawn. This was intentional. An early start gives a birder the chance to get situated in a comfy viewing spot before most of the birds are awake and about; shy species can thus be spotted more easily. It is also a lot easier to hear birdcalls before dawn, when there are comparatively few human-made noises to compete with them. And if you want to get an owl on your count list, you'd better do it before the sun is high.

We never did get an owl, but it wasn't for lack of trying. Mary did a passable imitation of a Screech Owl's wavering cry—something that the sound effects people for the old *Scooby-Doo* cartoons should have latched onto, but never did—but it was never answered. Usually our first stop was in a forested area north of Lillington, where a boggy creek flowed down a cutting for some power lines. The pre-dawn air was always full of mist, and small chirrups and clucks came from the water's edge, whether from birds, frogs, or insects we were never sure. The vague shadows of branches and pylons over the roadway were enough to make you thoroughly paranoid about what might try to drop onto your neck from above. Add into this strange and shadowy picture Mary's tremulous whistle, even without an answering owl, and you had a scene worth remembering.

No owls ever answered Mary, but her calls certainly had an effect. Screech Owls are not large—a foot is about as long as they get—but they are one thing that all sensible birds respect: *carnivorous.* Hearing the cry along the roadway gave a lot of sleepy birds good reason to wake up and pay attention. Flickers would poke out of their nestholes, eyes still bleary from a long night of beating their heads against tree trunks. Red-winged Blackbirds would straggle to the tops of cattail stalks in half-awake alarm, letting loose the occasional *queerp?* in hopes of finding out what all the fuss was about. Even tiny Ruby-crowned Kinglets would appear, usually in my peripheral vision, checking out the scene from the branches and then silently departing. (Kinglets have always reminded me of the sort of non-plused cartoon character best personified by Droopy; they're small, they're nondescript, they betray no particular concern about anything, and they're darned near

THE VERB *TO BIRD*

everywhere.) Once the lack of owls became clear to them, they would vanish, but somehow we felt sure that the kinglets were still out there, and moreover, that they had taken down our license plate number.

The first lifer I ever saw on a Raven Rock count was a close relative of the kinglets, a Blue-gray Gnatcatcher, evidently flushed from its nest by its fear of owls. The Gnatcatcher is only about four inches long, a small slate-gray bird that might be easily overlooked, but it boings around the treetops so much that you can't help noticing it; unfortunately, it moves fast enough that in most cases the only way to pin down its species is by its call. Luckily, every time Mary started in whistling, several Gnatcatchers would begin their hyperactive treetop dances, hopping from limb to limb like pinballs and filling the air with their *zee zee zee zee*s, but for the most part, all I ever saw of them were glimpses of the white edges of their black tails.

More satisfying, even spectacular, results of Mary's calls usually came from the surface of the water, for the creek was popular with Wood Ducks. The name is rather drab, admittedly, and the female Wood Duck is not pretty— a small, mottled gray-brown duck with a pale eye-ring and a barely noticeable crest—but she manages to attract the drake, and unlike his mate, the male Wood Duck is a thing of beauty.

It is not stretching things to call the drake the gaudiest waterfowl in North America. To imagine one, start with the common duck outline familiar to most people, but shrink it down to about twenty inches in length. Make the bill a bit smaller, too, then color it from tip to base: black, white, and flaming red, with a thin line of yellow where it meets the head. The plumage of the duck's crown sweeps back and down in a great Presleyan wave, ending in a thick crest of iridescent green striped with white. The face is a

"No owls ever answered Mary."

harlequin mix of dark glossy purple-green and white, with a gold-rimmed red eye. Below the white throat, the breast is a rich chestnut, flecked with white, while the sides are a golden bronze. The legs, which you won't often see, are not only a rich yellow, but bear sharply clawed feet strong enough to help the duck perch in trees. In short, this duck has everything it needs to be an American icon: the hair of Elvis, the makeup of KISS, and a love of trees stronger than John Denver's.

It is also a duck with a strong survival instinct, so when Mary made her owl call, any Wood Ducks on the water nearby would shoot up like Polaris missiles, whistling off into the mists. Less fearful were the Mallards that would also appear in the same creek, but we considered them unremarkable: larger and more obvious ducks than Woodies, and worse, common. The sad truth is that birders are strongly prejudiced in favor of rare birds. Thus, the handsome Mallard drake, his rich green head throwing off iridescent purple highlights in the pearly, diffuse light of a Carolina dawn, got very little of our attention—just enough for us to note the sighting and move on. It is both utterly human and awfully sad that, merely because of its abundance and availability, such beauty is taken for granted by an observer who should know better.

Looking, though, was only part of the job for Mary and me; we also had paperwork. Once the owl-inspired action was over, we would take out the checklist and make sure we recorded (a) the correct birds, and (b) the number of each kind we had seen: "Northern Flicker—2, Swamp Sparrow—1, Wood Duck—2, Mallard—3, Blue-gray Gnatcatcher—4," and so on. (We tried to be accurate, but I think once, while looking at a huge flock of grackles, we lost our patience and wrote down "A googol and six.") From there, we would move on to a variety of other spots to record the bounty found there. Happily for me, Mary knew where to find good birds; we often managed to find new lifers for me (and sometimes for her) in the process of checking the local populations. Altogether, in the course of our counts from 1992 to 1995, the following birds were added to my life list:

Blue-gray Gnatcatcher	Bobolink
Common Snipe	Grasshopper Sparrow
Yellow Warbler	Savannah Sparrow
Common Yellowthroat	Black-throated Blue Warbler
Prairie Warbler	Rough-winged Swallow
Solitary Vireo	Northern Parula Warbler
Red-eyed Vireo	Prothonotary Warbler
White-eyed Vireo	Hermit Thrush
Rusty Blackbird	Ring-necked Duck

Counting with an experienced partner is a great way to pick up lifers, but how does this happen? Let's look at an example: warblers.

The New World birds we call warblers are technically named "wood warblers," as opposed to the true warblers of the Old World, but our warblers (the family Parulidae) also differ from the drab Sylviidae of Eurasia and Africa in that American warblers tend to be quite colorful, at least in breeding plumage. Warblers are therefore the passion of many birders. Because most warblers are small and inclined to stay in the treetops if possible, and because some are among America's rarest birds, they can provide a real challenge for the veteran. On the other hand, some species are common enough that, given a good pair of field glasses, the right time of year, and a little luck, you can easily turn at least a few of them up.

Warblers are also sort of a dividing line among birders. Think about drivers: you can certainly be a good driver without knowing how to use a stick shift, but the best drivers want to know how to work one. As the stick is the dividing line between drivers, the warbler stands between what I call the *passive* birder and the *active* birder. A passive birder is happy to sit and watch the birds of home, garden, and feeder, but since warblers are mainly insectivores, few ever visit a feeder. If you want to see one, you almost have to become an active birder: you must go and seek the little buggers out. And when you do, you've got to be lucky.

Only once have I gone looking for a specific warbler and been rewarded. While driving around on the morning of my first spring count, Mary and I had been playing a favorite birder's game, "What Haven't You Seen Yet?" This one makes everyone feel better because there's almost always some familiar bird on your life list that, astonishingly, isn't on your partner's. Mary, for example, confessed to never having seen a Black Skimmer, a coastal bird I'd first seen almost twenty years before. As for myself, I tried to be vague, confessing that the big gap in my list was the warblers; I'd seen "only a few."

"Any examples?" Mary replied. I'd momentarily forgotten I was talking to another teacher, and our profession's motto, after all, is *Be More Specific! Minus Five Points.*

"Uh—let's see, Redstart, Black-and-White, Yellow-rumped . . . uh, and Louisiana Waterthrush," I allowed. To appreciate the paucity of this list, consider that there are over forty species of warbler in the eastern United States alone. I was pretty much letting her measure my manhood.

Luckily, Mary passed up the chance to humiliate me forever and simply asked, "You don't have a Pythagorean Warbler?"

This brought me up short for a second, until I realized she must mean a *Prothonotary* Warbler. I'd at least heard of that one.

$$\sqrt{(a^2+b^2)}$$

a

b

"You don't have a Pythagorean Warbler?"

"No, I don't," I said cautiously.

"Then we've got to go to this lake I know. There's a cypress swamp and Pythagoreans all over the place." She hit the gas and left me back at square one.

During the drive, I considered breaking down and asking Mary what she meant, but instead, I surreptitiously looked at the index in my Peterson guide and found no entry for "Pythagorean" Warbler. Scoping out the entry for the Prothonotary, however, I discovered that it is, in fact, a swamp dweller; circumstantial evidence, to be sure, but evidence nonetheless.

We drew to a stop where the road ended. Ahead of us lay a good-sized lake, with a fair number of cypress trees poking out of it and a small wooden hut beside it, with a sign listing the prices for fishing privileges, boat rentals, and bait. Mary poked her head inside the hut and waved her official clipboard at the counterman, who nodded silently and gestured that we should walk around the lake counterclockwise. I climbed down stiffly from the cab of Mary's truck, a vehicle larger than some of the count areas I'd seen on the map, and fell in behind her.

The path led around the bait shop and down to the shore, where a most remarkable landscape caught my eye. On the left was the lake: big, round, wet, with a small island or two toward the middle. While it was entirely pleasant to the eye, it was unsurprising, utterly lake-like. It was also man-made; I can say this with some certainty because the path on which we walked lay atop the earthen dam forming it. The spillway was just ahead of us, spanned by a large plank and pouring down maybe ten or twelve feet into a dark green pool. Picturesque, sure, but again, not unexpected.

On the right, though, below the dam and surrounding the pool, was cypress swamp. Pure, unadulterated swampland, the kind which had covered the basin of the lake before the dam was built. (A cypress swamp isn't hard to describe: Take some ground. Cover it with black mud. Cover that with about eight inches of black water. Insert cypresses. Ta daaaa.) The pale gray of the tree trunks and the green of the cypress needles offset the dark waters, which were highly reflective and almost entirely opaque. The trees' shade added even more darkness, as well as a welcome coolness, though like most coolness in the

South, it was relative. The water probably should have disgusted me, but instead it filled me with a sense of purity, as if clean, clear water had been poured over leaves to brew; I might have been gazing on a gigantic pitcher of black iced tea.

And sailing from branch to branch over this flooded forest were Prothonotary Warblers.

Nothing else is that yellow. Even the Yellow Warbler isn't that yellow. The head, neck, and breast of the male Prothonotary are a yellow so intense it could only be produced by the controlled fission of a goldenrod atom: a rich, searing yellow, too deep for lemons and too bright for butterscotch. Contrasted with his olive back and blue-gray wings, the yellow is even more vivid; you wonder how the bird's jet-black eye can function surrounded by all that glare.

There weren't many birds, three or four at most, but I was happy to stand and stare for many long minutes. I have seen both birds and places that I consider more beautiful, but rarely have I seen one set the other off so perfectly: a pool of deep green stillness, dark and slippery, and above it, the warblers, like dandelions freed from gravity.

"There we go," said Mary with satisfaction. "Pythagorean Warblers."

"Uh-huh," I said, checking off *"Prothonotary* Warbler" in my Peterson guide. "You, my friend, have spent too much time studying the ancients."

I complimented her on leading me to a specific warbler so precisely. Usually they turn up when you're looking for something else, like a golf ball or a Common Snipe. We were after the latter on one cold morning, standing in the middle of a cow pasture whose owner had long ago given the count organizers permission to bird there. Mary was fairly sure we could turn up a Snipe there, and we gamely began circling the large pond that lay at the center of the field. On the surface we saw a Pied-billed Grebe and a few Canada Geese, and a Great Blue Heron or two stood impassively on the shore. We were still snipeless as we came across the earthen dam at the far end of the water, but I noticed a lot of activity in the fruit trees along the edge of the pasture: Yellow-rumped Warblers were there in great numbers, flitting from limb to limb. I had seen them before, but not often; their gray bodies contrasted nicely with the yellow patches on the rump and sides, as well as with the inverted U of mottled black the males wear across their white breasts.

I was cheerful, having spotted an unexpected bird, if not a lifer, and was already back to concentrating on the promised Snipe when something yellow flickered by on my right. For no good reason, I wandered off toward the blossoming orchard, and atop an apple tree I saw him: a Yellow Warbler.

There are some bird names that are just plain appropriate, and "Yellow Warbler" is one, for there was no doubt that this one was determined to warble away the morning, and he was yellow from stem to stern, save for the small red streaks on his underside, just barely visible to my eye, though clear through my binoculars. I have only seen a few Yellows since then, never so close by, and never so unexpectedly, but the sight and sound of that first one, clear in the morning light against a misty blue sky, surrounded by the smell of apple blossoms—well, it's the kind of thing that makes getting up early worthwhile.

(And, a little later on, we successfully spotted a Snipe. Yes, they really exist. Those of you who were told to hunt them with a bag were the victims of a cruel hoax on the part of your camp counselors, but they're real birds, I swear.)

The Northern Parula Warbler was another accidental sighting. We had driven to a construction site in northern Harnett County where the old bridge across a swampy stream had been torn down and the new one was still unfinished. As far as birds went, it was a darned active site. At the top of a sycamore in a meadow beside the stream was a Yellow Warbler, almost invisible without binoculars; his sudden disappearance puzzled us until we saw, gliding swiftly over the treetop, a full-grown Cooper's Hawk, gray and menacing, which circled the sycamore a few times, no doubt looking for our warbler, before soaring back over the swamp. A Great Crested Flycatcher appeared next, flying from branch to branch along the roadside while I followed it along, making sure of its field marks; it is a bird of somewhat subtle colors, though the cinnamon-red tail is a good identifier if you can see it in good light. Soon afterwards, at the end of the half-bridge, Mary and I spotted my first Rough-winged Swallows—swift, brown, unspectacular birds engaged in what seemed a perpetual chase. We watched them for a time and then turned back toward the car—and saw a Parula Warbler sitting in a cypress not thirty feet from us.

Like most warblers, the male Parula has some yellow plumage, but it is dressed mainly in pale blue and olive green, an unlikely combination which otherwise occurs only on the uniforms of the Tulane University Green Wave. This Parula was quite cooperative, posing on the cypress branch long enough to remove any doubts about its field marks. I marked down another lifer and looked smug; Mary looked smug, too. We were becoming insufferable and we liked it.

No sooner had our heads begun to swell than Mother Nature decided to remind us who was boss. As we drove away from the bridge, both of us spotted a small hawklike bird on a power line across a pasture, and I almost put the car into a barbed-wire fence trying to bring it to a halt. We slapped our binoculars to our eyes and were rewarded with the sight of the flashing white wing patches of—the Northern Mockingbird, of which we'd seen some two dozen already.

Hawks were a bit of a weakness for Mary and me. Even early on the first day we ever counted together, slogging around the same pasture where we eventually got sniped, this was obvious. We were as yet a bit uncomfortable with each other. I still felt very odd birding with another person, let alone one who knew Snipe habitats and could imitate a Screech Owl; Mary still had no idea of my level of expertise. My only real contribution to the count so far had come when we parked the car beside this pasture. As I climbed out, I had spotted a Green Heron winding its way through the pine trees across the road.

"Green Heron," I said at once, keeping my binocs on it and pointing.

"Really?" said Mary, with the birder's natural skepticism; I wasn't offended.

"Chestnut neck, white on the throat, about crow-sized," I observed aloud. "Just lit on that pine branch next to the big knothole."

Mary eventually found and confirmed it, but I'm sure she still didn't know how to rate my birding skills. Then, as we tromped across the pasture a half-hour later, both our heads practically turned in stereo when we noticed a large, dark bird flapping along the trees to our left. Neither of us could have seen it for more than an instant before we turned, and without another thought, both of us pointed and cried out, "Hawk!"

The bird called out, "Caw!" and flew on, black against the trees. Crow-black, in fact.

Both of us burst out laughing. "I think we *may* have missed that ID, Pete," cackled Mary.

"Oops," I replied. Wonder of wonders, my solo identification hadn't especially impressed her, but she could respect me for making the same idiotic mistake she did. That, I think, was the moment when we became partners.

Our mutual competence was never in question; our mutual acts of incompetence are somehow easier to remember. One early spring morning we chased a small brown and yellow warbler over half a Lillington subdivision, hissing different species at each other for a good fifteen minutes:

PETE: *(Squinting.)* Yellow-rump?

MARY: *(Focusing binoculars.)* Too brown. And it's got yellow on its tail. Magnolia?

PETE: Naw, no black. *(Desperately.)* Could it be a Yellow-breasted Chat?

MARY: *(With certainty.)* No, they're *way* bigger than this thing.

PETE: *(Flipping through Peterson frantically.)* Uh . . .

MARY: *(Consulting National Geographic Society guide.)* Ummm . . .

Some time later, it occurred to me that we might not be looking at an adult male bird, which launched us into a thorough investigation of juvenile warblers, all of which looked suspiciously like *Empidonax* flycatchers and led me to believe that someone, either God or Peterson, was having a good laugh at our expense. Nothing matched our bird, though, until I was hit with another revelation: not only are there adult male birds and immature birds, there are also adult *female* birds.

And there it was, of course: one of the most distinctive warblers in the hemisphere, the American Redstart. Female.

Mary, as strong a supporter of women's rights as I've ever met, was aghast. Embarrassed as I was, I was in no way inclined to rub her nose in it.

I only rubbed Mary's nose in it once, masking my perceived inadequacy as a birder with excessive glee on the one occasion when I identified a bird and she didn't. It was a spring count, and that morning she and I had stopped near the turnoff to our cypress swamp and were peering around the fields, hoping to spot a Bobolink. Also known as Ricebirds, they aren't common in North Carolina by any means, but they do migrate through on their way to the northern and central United States, so we had reason to be hopeful. For the moment, though, they weren't around. It was nine o'clock on a Saturday; the regular crowd shuffled in: bluebird, meadowlark, sparrow.

Overhead I heard a whistle, rising and falling, and spotted a small dark bird heading toward us, bounding up and down in its flight—and I caught my breath. This might be it: a lifer, and a gorgeous one at that. In the autumn, the male Bobolink is much like the female: brown, streaky, not much to look at. In the spring, though, the male's breeding plumage emerges, and it is utterly distinctive: face, breast, belly, wings, and tail all black, with white shoulders and rump, and a buttery yellow nape. This bird was certainly the right size, and from underneath, it was the right color. I called out "Bobolink!"

Mary was having none of it. "By itself?"

"Bobolink!" I repeated, stupidly pleased with myself, even though it was still little more than a black outline.

Still, the word "Bobolink" itself is such fun to say that I would happily have repeated it even if I'd decided the bird was a Canada Goose.

"Pete, they're gregarious. You'll see them in flocks, not one at a time. It'd be like seeing one Starling. Or one sorority girl."

"Bobolink!" I insisted, reading her Peterson's lovely description: "'Song, in hovering flight and quivering descent, ecstatic and bubbling, starting with low reedy notes and rollicking upward.'"

Mary blinked. "And this proves what?"

"Didn't you just hear that happening?"

"It's not a Bobolink, Pete. Let's go."

For once, we were driving my car, rather than Mary's monster truck, so I controlled our movements. I relied on this advantage and began walking up the road toward the power line on which the bird had just settled. Unfortunately, it was facing us, still black and featureless. Suddenly another bird landed near it: brown and streaked— a female!

"Aha!" I cried, training my binoculars on the pair.

"I see 'em, too," said Mary, whose glasses were already trained on them, "And I'm betting that's a House Sparrow."

All at once the first bird hunched down, hopped up very slightly, and pivoted around like a lawn sprinkler. The back of its head was clearly yellow.

I'll spare you the details of my triumphant glee, except to say that Mary was entirely gracious in admitting she'd been mistaken, and that it was the only time I ever got her a lifer, as compared to the dozen and a half she found for me.

I'm now living five hours from Raven Rock, so I no longer get to spend the odd Saturday morning poking

THE VERB *TO BIRD*

around Harnett County, but I still remember most of those days clearly. Nor have I forgotten how much those counts meant to both Mary and me; instead of colleagues, we became friends. I was drawn farther and farther into the world of birding, my lifelong fascination midwifed by Mary until it became a hunger to seek out birds wherever I went; Mary, for her part, developed a more personal and emotional attachment, an ever-increasing desire for companionship, romance, and then finally marriage—to Paul Hart, Raven Rock park ranger.*

Since my own long-suffering spouse was stuck at home with the kids when I was gallivanting about with clay all over my pants, I always left the count after lunch, which was, by mutual agreement, at the Burger King south of Lillington. The count teams would straggle in two or three people at a time, boots and heavy shoes stained and covered with burrs, hair gone askew from dampness and the random pressure of hats, and faces lit up with a peculiar joy usually seen only on the faces of fathers outside maternity wards. Muddy hands passed count lists around and carried fries up to voracious mouths; the air filled with the damp odor of cold human skin growing warmer; occasional imitated whistles and chirps emerged from booths. Within thirty minutes, some twenty volunteers would have taken over the dining room, complaining about blisters or rhapsodizing over sparrows, while other customers looked on warily, finishing their coffee in a few quick gulps.

Paul, meanwhile, would frantically tally the morning's numbers with a stub of pencil. Mary would sit beside him, checking his addition, or gleefully announcing that she and I were the only ones who'd seen a Black-throated Blue Warbler that day, and I would smile at her. I wasn't from

*Who did you think? Jeez, y'all are as bad as my students . . .

the Lillington area; she and Paul were the only two people I knew there. The satisfied camaraderie in the room was clear to me, but the friendship, for the most part, was something I could only observe, rather than feel. But still, I smiled because I was a part of the larger effort, doing what I loved with others who loved it too. I had been playing pickup ball on the blacktop all my life; now I was on the team.

4
Hang Down Your Seed and Cry

And He that doth the ravens feed,
Yea, providently caters for the sparrow,
Be comfort to my age!
  —William Shakespeare, As You Like It, II, iii

Mountaintop, city street, desert, ice shelf, open sea, rain forest—birds can turn up damn near anywhere. A birder has got to be ready wherever he travels, or a lot of opportunities will be missed. But what if you don't travel much? Suppose you haven't got a lot of spare income for vacationing elsewhere or don't have friends and relatives to stay with all over the country; what then? What if you're physically unable to get around easily, and spend most of your time in your house or yard? How can you be ready to bird in these circumstances?

One of the best ways to show your readiness is a yard list. Unlike a life list, the yard list is concerned only with the birds one sees in a particular place—usually the yard, but you could as easily do it for the workplace, a vacation spot, or the Red and White Grocery parking lot at Front & Myrtle; expect a lot of Starlings and House Sparrows at the latter, though.

A yard list is also a terrific way to renew your birding spirit. Once your life list already includes the easily seen birds of your area, you may find yourself in a period of frustration. At such a time, the appeal of common birds like the Cardinal or the Tufted Titmouse may wane a bit. Making a yard list, though, means that all birds are once again fair game—even a species you're sick of seeing in the field can make you happy simply by coming into your yard. I remember the surprisingly intense pleasure I got from putting down on my yard list the Common Grackle, arguably the most abundant bird in the eastern United States; for some reason, none came into my yard for the first six months we lived in Virginia, and the sight of one actually became welcome when I realized it would be another bird for the yard list.

(This may be hard for the layman to understand, but I'll try to put it in perspective: a birder's saying "Oh, boy! I saw a grackle!" is akin to a TV viewer's exclaiming "Oh, boy! I saw a commercial!")

I first got the idea of keeping a yard list from two friends of mine, Gilly and Brenda Macknee, who used to live outside of Chapel Hill, North Carolina, near Jordan Lake. They had begun keeping a yard list when they lived near Saxapahaw, but their newer house's rural setting—yes, even more rural than Saxapahaw—and the nearness of open water combined to make their yard a tourist spot for almost every feathered creature in the region. In only sixteen months, from May 1995 to August 1996, Gilly and Brenda spotted some sixty-nine species in their yard, a number which is almost a third the size of my *life* list.

Over time my yard didn't do all that badly by comparison; between August 1995 and August 1999, sixty-seven species of birds came into or flew over my yard:

Eastern Meadowlark	Eastern Pewee	Barn Swallow
Yellow-shafted Flicker	Mourning Dove	American Crow
European Starling	Eastern Bluebird	Eastern Goldfinch
White-breasted Nuthatch	Eastern Kingbird	Chipping Sparrow
Baltimore Oriole	Tufted Titmouse	Ruby-throated Hummingbird
Carolina Chickadee	Chimney Swift	Northern Mockingbird
Turkey Vulture	Blue Jay	Eastern Phoebe
Pileated Woodpecker	Tree Swallow	Northern Cardinal
House Finch	Downy Woodpecker	Red-Tailed Hawk
Screech Owl (voice only)	Slate-colored Junco	Winter Wren
Red-bellied Woodpecker	Carolina Wren	Cedar Waxwing
Blackburnian Warbler	Rusty Blackbird	Canada Goose
White-throated Sparrow	American Kestrel	American Robin
Yellow-rumped Warbler	Song Sparrow	Ring-billed Gull (!)
Brown Creeper	Common Grackle	Yellow-bellied Sapsucker
Brown-headed Cowbird	Killdeer	Rufous-sided Towhee
Red-winged Blackbird	Indigo Bunting	Brown Thrasher
Cooper's Hawk	Rock Dove	Blue-gray Gnatcatcher
Great Crested Flycatcher	Hairy Woodpecker	Great Horned Owl (voice only)
Black Vulture	Belted Kingfisher	Common Bobwhite (first seen by Kelly)
Blue Grosbeak	Field Sparrow	Common Nighthawk
Orchard Oriole	Ruby-crowned Kinglet	Sharp-shinned Hawk
Empidonax flycatcher (most likely Acadian)		

Is this list a little excessive? Yes. The house sits in a rural area and has pastures on three sides, all of which are full of Meadowlarks and Bluebirds, and one of which contains a pond on which I've seen such uncommon birds as the Hooded Merganser. The house is also less than a mile from a good-sized river, which attracts Belted Kingfishers and herons of all sorts, and is often visited by large flocks of geese as well. Though we have since moved to another house nearby, the local fields and river still provide a wide variety of native birds in most seasons. In addition, our region gets a lot of peculiar species in migration. We live close enough to the Blue Ridge Mountains to see them on all but the haziest days, and the pseudo-northern climes on the Appalachian heights are favored by many birds; as a result, all sorts of species migrate through the area, and a lot of them pass overhead or stop by my feeder en route to their wintering and/or breeding grounds.

Not all houses, alas, are going to have this natural bounty. I lived for a year in Manchester, England, and my place there would have had the following yard (and I use the term loosely) list:

House Sparrow	House Sparrow	Feral Pigeon
House Sparrow	House Sparrow	House Sparrow
House Sparrow	House Sparrow	House Sparrow
European Starling	House Sparrow	House Sparrow

On the other hand, my house in Fayetteville, a slightly less urban and far less Victorian city than Manchester, would have had a yard list of probably about two dozen birds:

Brown Thrasher	House Finch	Northern Cardinal
Northern Mockingbird	Blue Jay	Common Grackle
Yellow-rumped Warbler	American Robin	Red-tailed Hawk
Carolina Wren	Gray Catbird	Mourning Dove
Chipping Sparrow	Chimney Swift	American Crow
Ruby-throated Hummingbird	European Starling	Rock Dove
Rufous-sided Towhee	Downy Woodpecker	House Sparrow
Slate-colored Junco	Tufted Titmouse	Carolina Chickadee

67

That's all I can recall, since I didn't keep a list in the four years we lived there, but even this partial list shows that places not graced with spectacular scenery (a category for which Fayetteville would certainly qualify) can hold a fair amount of birding pleasure, even if you don't do anything much besides look out the window at a feeder.

Feeders themselves are topics of great debate and discussion in the birding world, and whole books have been devoted to the question of how best to build, fill, and place them. Possibly the most exhaustive of these is the National Audubon Society's *North American Birdfeeder Handbook* by Robert Burton. Not only does Burton give you information on feed, plus instructions for building feeders, nestboxes, and birdbaths, he also gives about eighty pages to identifying the most common birds of yard and garden. It's a wonderful supplement to the basic field guide, with a clarity of design that is both beautiful and satisfying, like a perfectly made bed. The ugly secret of bird feeders, though, is this: no matter what the official line is, every birder runs his own show. To wit:

Every birder is hoping to attract different sorts of birds. With the combination of our usual seed mix and our style of feeder, we've pulled in White-breasted Nuthatches, Downy Woodpeckers, House Finches, Goldfinches, Chipping Sparrows, Tufted Titmice, Carolina Chickadees, Blue Grosbeaks, and, I'm happiest of all to say, Indigo Buntings on a fairly regular basis, depending on the time of year. The spillage has largely been cleaned up by Cardinals, Mourning Doves, Brown-headed Cowbirds, White-throated Sparrows, Northern Juncos, and Yellow-Shafted Flickers, most of which are too large or too terrestrial to use the feeder itself. All these birds appeal to me, but deep down, I'm a woodpecker fan, so I've also put out a commercially available suet mix. Those hoping to attract Cedar Waxwings or Baltimore Orioles, however, will probably have to plant berry bushes or put out a lot of fruit, and the birds still might not show up except in winter.

Every birder has a preferred food mixture. I usually use the commercial mixes, figuring the pickier birds will still show up even if I'm not serving their absolute favorites, and I augment that with occasional table scraps or suet. On those occasions when I've used pure sunflower seeds, which are more expensive, the Cardinals seem to have come around more often, but not by an enormous degree. Thistle seeds, also not cheap, are reputed to be a sure way to attract Goldfinches and Pine Siskins; Burton specifically mentions that thistle is "especially popular with Goldfinches," but when I've tried it, I've seen only the usual crowd at the feeder. One suggestion of Burton's that worked well, however, was putting out half of a fresh coconut; he recommends hanging it from a wire, but I just bolted it to a tree trunk. It greatly pleased the local nuthatches, and also brought in a number of Red-bellied Woodpeckers. I'm also not shy about setting out table scraps; fruit seems to go over fairly well, while leftover spaghetti and bread crumbs have taken a while to disappear.

Every birder has a favorite type of feeder. For seed, I once used a converted plastic two-liter soda bottle, which dangled upside-down with an attachment on its mouth to hold the feed inside. It was very inexpensive—since the attachment was a gift from Gilly and Brenda, it was all but free—and held a lot of seed. Unfortunately, circumstances (see below) have recently forced me to replace this with a new and more expensive seed feeder, a plexiglass cylinder with four metal perch/dispenser attachments. (On the plus side, there's at least one male Indigo Bunting who's very happy about the new arrangement and now shows up much more regularly.) I've also hung up a wire cage that holds cakes of suet and seed in winter (which the Downies, in particular, seem to enjoy) and grapes and table scraps in warmer weather; this last I do because suet just won't stand up to a Southern summer, and there's nothing like the smell of rancid sun-baked beef fat to wreck a perfectly good July morning.

Every birder has a "Damnedest Bird I Ever Saw At A Feeder" story. Mine involves a half-dozen Baltimore Orioles, decidedly migratory birds, hanging around Mary Stevens's feeder in Lillington in the middle of December. When this kind of thing is brought up, non-birders should listen politely and feign interest by nodding.

Every birder has a "Damnedest Thing I Ever Saw A Squirrel Do At A Feeder" story. And sadly, these may be more numerous than their stories about birds.

It's bad enough that those who feed birds should have to put up with squirrels, but it's even worse that squirrel problems have become clichés. Even people who know nothing about birders or squirrels know that the former are locked in an eternal conflict with the latter. Squirrels are now like the gang of "darned kids" in the *Scooby-Doo* cartoons, the ones who not only solve the mystery and disprove the existence of anything vaguely supernatural in the "haunted" resort hotel/Old West town/amusement park, but who do so in a manner both intensely irritating and mind-numbingly dull. And worse, both kids and squirrels are always successful. Every time the Mystery Machine stops for an investigation, someone goes to jail, usually the caretaker who warned them about the ghost in the first place; every time you put up a feeder, a squirrel gets to it. Squirrels are just as single-minded as Freddy, as foolish as Shaggy, as creative as Velma, as hungry as Scooby, and as likely to stumble into something painful as Daphne, but they always get their seed.

Robert Burton, more inclined to understatement than I, says simply that the trouble with squirrels "is that they are extremely acrobatic and resourceful," and recommends that all feeders be placed at least ten feet away from any branches, trunks or structures that a squirrel might climb. His advice is good, but I will never be fully convinced that any feeder is squirrel-proof; then again, I believe that a squirrel would have claimed the Nobel Prize in physics by now, if only it were edible. They're just too relentless.

If you've watched squirrels for any length of time, you know that they occasionally make mistakes. If you watch them for a few seconds afterward, you'll know that when a tree-dwelling mammal makes a mistake, there is usually only one form of payment accepted, and that gravity charges interest at the rate of thirty-two feet, compounded per second. Squirrels fall from ridiculous heights, but somehow, like Wile E. Coyote, they walk away. I have often seen one drop from well over ten times its own length, scramble to its feet, look about frantically for a minute, and then leap back onto a tree trunk and begin ascending. Not two days ago, I was conversing with a student on a brick walkway on our campus when a squirrel missed its jump from the walnut tree on the south side of the walkway to the Japanese ornamental on the north side. It fell probably fifteen feet, hitting the bricks with a *thwack* loud enough to interrupt our conversation. Nonetheless, by the time we had turned our heads to look, it was on its feet and moving back toward the trunk of the walnut tree. It didn't look especially eager to be doing so, mind you, but no human could survive this kind of abuse. Even if we could, most of us wouldn't go back up a tree except at gunpoint. Squirrels, though, spring back into the branches with a will, clearly invulnerable to all harm.

If there is a squirrel equivalent of kryptonite, however, it will be discovered by a birder, and I for one will cheer. Why do I have a vendetta against squirrels?

They stole my bird feeder.

Not the seed—the *feeder*. It's gone. On a night several years back, we had just returned from a trip and begun unpacking the car when I noticed something strange: the inverted two-liter soda bottle, with its special green plastic hanger and dispenser attachments, was no longer hanging from its length of clothesline in the Norway maple in our front yard, nor was it on the ground under the maple.

It was pretty dark by the time we unloaded, so my further investigations were performed with flashlight in hand, but I was able to confirm two things: the clothesline was not the culprit here—the feeder's hanging attachment was damaged, but still hung from the intact clothesline; and the feeder was not only absent from the ground under the maple, but from the entire yard.

What we have here is not merely an act of nature—a full bird feeder does not just vanish from a yard without help. Could it be, then, an act of some human agency? I suppose so, but boy, that's a petty theft. It's also possible that my feeder was kidnapped like the garden gnome in *Amelie,* and that it will reappear someday, along with a stack of Polaroids showing it sitting in front of the Taj Mahal, Mount Rushmore, and South of the Border, but I doubt it. The culprits are squirrels.

I'm not just showing a birder's prejudice here, either. The classic elements to consider in a whodunnit are motive, opportunity, and method, and all three point to the same conclusion: *Sciuris carolinensis.*

Motive? Start with a simple multiple-choice question: Who would have any use for two liters of birdseed and a bottle with a feeder attachment?

a Birds, obviously, but this job isn't their style—besides, they wouldn't take the source of their year-round food supply, they'd just take the food. And even if a nuthatch wanted the feeder, a five-ounce bird could not carry a two-liter bottle full of seed.*

b A sociopathic birder. He might have use for the seed, but it's not *that* expensive. Even if he were desperate to feed his birds and had an empty feeder himself, the Food Lion in Orange is open twenty-four hours a day. What's more, the house is in the middle of nowhere on a dead-end road—very few people would have had the opportunity to see our feeder, let alone covet it.

c Squirrels. They did get some regular benefit from the food's presence, but they also had good short-term reason to capture it: they knew it was not meant for them, and by stealing it they could hoard a large supply of seed for the winter, rather than sneaking away a bit at a time. The bottle itself, being waterproof, might make an excellent storage bin for the winter.

Opportunity? We know they could *get* to the feeder; they can get to anything not currently in orbit. Their main reason for not climbing onto the feeder in the past had been the watchful presence of our dog, who would have been on them in a flash if they were to slip from the feeder, but who was being kenneled while we were out of town. The timing, in other words, points to the squirrels, the primary beneficiaries of the dog's absence.

Method? Consider the damage to the hanger attachment: as plastic goes, this is pretty tough; it had lasted a

*Not even two of them using a strand of creeper held under the dorsal guiding feathers.

good four years. Certainly it's tougher than the plastic of the soda bottle itself. Yet when the feeder "broke," it was the tougher plastic that "gave way." You don't find that suspicious? Yes, and you probably believe Oswald acted alone, too. Squirrels could easily gnaw through the hanger attachment, for which they'd have no particular use, and several squirrels together could roll or haul the bottle away once it had fallen. In a robbery scenario, it would be quicker to haul off the whole bottle than to have each individual squirrel—I'm assuming several perps, here—fill his cheeks with seed and run.

Moreover, the telltale cunning of the squirrel is displayed in the fact that the clothesline was untouched. A damaged cord would have been an obvious indicator of squirrel attack, since rodents have been gnawing through ropes for generations—from Aesop to *The Lion, the Witch and the Wardrobe*. The squirrels, aware that any reader of C.S. Lewis would spot the clothesline approach as a dead giveaway, used a little misdirection here by attacking the hanger attachment—a tougher substance, true, but a bit thinner, and less likely to point directly toward the squirrel community.

In other words, the only suspects with the desire, the opportunity, and the ability to attack, detach, and hide the feeder are the squirrels. QED.

Now I'm on to them. I'll keep investigating. I'll find that feeder. And when I find it, I'm betting I'll find the answer to a lot of other mysteries: Dealey Plaza. Roswell. The Tunguska blast. Black helicopters. The truth is out there. And it's furry and gray.

5
Great Unexpectations

We can never surprise Nature in a corner.
–Ralph Waldo Emerson, "The Method of Nature"

It's sad but true: some birds live only in far-away places, inaccessible to those without airline tickets, up-to-date vaccinations, and more money than they will ever deserve. You will see the Nene only in Hawaii, the Arctic Three-toed Woodpecker only in the far northern climes, and the South African Jackass Penguin only in South Africa.

As a quick look around will tell you, however, there are birds everywhere, and by "birds" I don't mean just pigeons. Even the most uninviting locales are surprisingly full of birds, and the variety of species in them is often surprising as well. I have stood in the middle of Manhattan, in Central Park, and watched a Red-tailed Hawk doing his best to get back to Jersey before the two local crows on his tail could catch him and get medieval on him. I have seen a Blue Grosbeak sitting happily on the guard railing of the Central Business District Loop in a decidedly non-rural part of Fayetteville. I have even seen a Brown Creeper in my parents' wood stove.

The stove, luckily, was not operating at the time, but the creeper was nonetheless in great danger. I say this because its brain had allowed it to crawl down a creosote-choked chimney pipe under the impression that it was a hollow tree, yet not to notice that the way out was identical to the way in; this is not the kind of brain that will keep a bird safe for long. The creeper was hopping about in the ashes, no doubt puzzling over the lack of insect life inside the average American woodstove, and making enough noise to tell my brother David and me that there was some small animal loose in our home. After a thorough search of all the closets at that end of the house, we eventually tracked the sounds to the stove and peered through the ventilation slots; all we could tell was that the creature within was small and ashy brown.

"Rat," said my brother. "Definitely a rat."

"Oh, sure," I replied. "How would a rat get down the chimney?"

"I'm telling you, it's a rat. They can go anywhere."

"It's too small," I said. "Maybe a mouse."

"There are small rats, too," Dave argued. "They're not born big."

I couldn't beat that logic, so I looked into the stove again, this time catching a glimpse of a bright eye and a small beak, curving down.

"It's a bird!" I cried.

"Oh, sure," said Dave. "How would a bird get down the chimney?"

I held off telling him about the Chimney Swift, which nowadays lives almost exclusively inside chimneys, and pulled one of the stove's doors slightly open. Even given the thoroughness with which the creeper had festooned itself with soot and ash, the identification was easy; there simply aren't that many small birds with thin decurved bills in the eastern United States, and what coloration I could see was pure creeper: white underside, streaked brown back. More difficult was answering the question "How do we get him out of here?"

Birds are not, for the most part, dangerous animals, but something about having them loose indoors often turns otherwise reasonable people into quivering idiots. Pine Forest Senior High, where Mary Stevens and I taught together, often left its doors open during warm spells to keep those inside from dying of heatstroke. Fayetteville is, as any resident will assure you, the warmest town in North Carolina by several degrees, perhaps because of all the tarmac on the runways at Fort Bragg, which soak up the heat of the day like a big sticky solar cell. It's not a comfy spot for schooling in warm weather. The open doors did provide a sluggish breeze through the halls of PFHS, but they also gave House Finches access to the building's interior.

The House Finch is a small sparrowlike bird with relatively little fear of humans, and the male's bright orange-red and brown plumage is attractive enough to encourage most people to tolerate its presence.* Unfortunately, the name "House Finch" is all too appropriate; the birds will build nests on and around buildings with no hesitation whatsoever, and they habitually populated the open stairwells at the ends of the building at Pine Forest, which put them in perfect position to fly through an open door.

---

*Despite this, the House Finch doesn't really belong in this neck of the woods; it's a bird of the West Coast, transplanted to New York City by pet dealers in the 1940s and released, according to Robert Burton, because said dealers were trying to get rid of the evidence that they had been selling the transplanted birds as "Hollywood Finches." Like the Starling, the House Finch has spread explosively, and in some places it seems to be taking over the territory of the similar but less aggressive Purple Finch.

Thus, every spring, I would find myself holding a gym towel in my hand, climbing up a ladder, and closing in on a House Finch trapped in one of the school's skylights. After a short battle, which would usually involve my climbing down and moving the ladder to the other end of the skylight at least twice, I would either terrify the finch into flying down past me, in which case it stood about a three-to-one shot of getting trapped in another skylight, or I would successfully net it in my towel, after which I could gently carry it down the ladder and out the door for release. Like baseball and hayfever, this became one of the rituals of spring for me.

But only for me. Everyone else in the school seemed to be terrified of these birds, though there's nothing about them being carnivorous in my Peterson guide—under "Food" it says quite clearly only "seeds, insects, small fruit" —and my copy of *Man is the Prey* is, perhaps surprisingly, devoid of any mention of finch-induced fatalities. Nonetheless, when one flew down the hallway, or, as invariably happened with doors and windows open, into a classroom, the students acted as if the bird was a five-inch yellowjacket with rabies. Girls would shriek, boys would drop books, and people would duck and cover like those in a civil defense instructional film from the '50s; if the Soviets had really wanted to immobilize our forces and demoralize our populace, they could have saved a bundle of money by selling off their ICBMs and letting loose a horde of Siberian Tits into our nation's public buildings.

But I was there, and as long as I had a towel handy, I was unafraid. Calmly, I would net the bird and return it to nature's loving bosom, inflicting only a mild scolding for its audacity in daring to interrupt my carefully-devised lesson plan. And where had I learned this netting technique?

In front of my parents' woodstove, with a dim-witted Brown Creeper to wrangle.

I had actually used a bedsheet on the creeper, since it made for a larger net, but the principle was the same: Advance on the bird when it's in an enclosed area, and throw the fabric over it before it can get its bearings. Once it's down, wrap the cloth around it and carry it off. My technique doesn't exactly provide the triumphant feeling of landing a marlin, but it does keep things calmer in the classroom.

This kind of unexpected call to arms is what makes birding a verb, rather than a hobby: a birder is *always* birding, like it or not, and doesn't have to make any elaborate preparations to do so. Hobbies like fishing, needlework, or collecting comic books require enormous outlays of time, money, and equipment; these hobbies simply don't exist unless you own fishing tackle, needles and thread, or a whole pile of comic books.

It's good that birding requires little preparation time, because birds have a way of appearing where you least expect them; in fact, these kinds of surprises are largely what drive me to bird. To understand what I mean, consider my first sighting of a Painted Bunting. Most birders would probably suppose this was one of the top pleasures in my birding life, and there is good reason to suppose this; the male Painted is unquestionably one of the most beautiful birds in America. It is certainly the most brightly colored. It looks, in fact, rather like something you would see on the cover of a Grateful Dead album: a small finch with a rich blue-violet head, contrasting with a bright red eye-ring, a rich scarlet belly and rump, and a yellow-green back, with slightly less vivid green wings and tail. When you blink, it leaves an afterimage.

Birds of this pseudo-tropical plumage are not common in the United States; their page in Peterson seems to glow in comparison to, say, the pages showing sparrows or wrens. As a result of this gaudiness, most birders I know would love to have the Painted Bunting on their life lists.

This should come as no surprise; the most popular birds have almost always been the most brightly colored. Look at the nicknames of professional sports teams and consider which birds are used. (I'm counting the National Hockey League's Pittsburgh Penguins as a reference to cold and ice, rather than to birds.) Birds of prey, which have enough panache and aggressiveness to appeal to fans, can be dull in color and still make the cut, but only if the team abandons the bird's real colors. I hate to break it to the laymen out there, but you will not see a lot of green and silver Eagles, black and silver Falcons, red and yellow Hawks, or blue, green, and silver Seahawks (better known as Ospreys) when you're out birding. Consider, though, the few songbirds for whom teams are named—all major league baseball teams, strangely—and you'll see how bright colors go with popularity: Cardinals, Blue Jays, Orioles. Notice any subtlety on those palettes? If that doesn't prove my point, consider the meager merchandising dollars you'd make hawking caps and jackets in the dun and beige of the Saint Louis Song Sparrows.*

Given the carnival colors of the Painted Bunting, then, no one should be surprised that birders want to see one. It's not all that common, however; if you live near the south-central United States or the Atlantic coast south of

---

*"What about the Ravens?" I hear some of you Baltimoreans objecting. "They're black and purple and named after a glossy black bird!" I say the Baltimore Ravens were named after Poe's poem and not the bird itself since Poe lived in Baltimore and ravens don't.

Cape Fear, you may get a few of them in the summertime, and some do winter in south Florida, but most people have to travel to spot them. My parents' house in Beaufort, South Carolina (pronounced "BYOO furt," as opposed to Beaufort, *North* Carolina, which is pronounced "BO furt"), is well within the summer range of the Painted, and once I had heard from my dad that he'd spotted some just down the road from the house, I resolved to do some traveling of my own.

Well, no, actually, I'm not yet so far gone that I'd drive the nine hours to Beaufort solely to see a single species of bird; I'd have to be sure of seeing at least, oh, maybe eight lifers before I'd expend that kind of effort. I did, however, resolve to go looking for a Painted when we went to visit my parents during summer vacation.

The morning of my hunt for the Painted Bunting dawned bright and clear, and I was already outside, binoculars around my neck, field guide crammed into a pocket of my shorts. I walked slowly down Cat Island's main riverfront road, trying not to make any sudden motions. From time to time I paused to look at a darting bird, but it was always a Chickadee or a Cardinal. The sun peeped up over the horizon, pinkening the sky faintly, and I walked on. I was less than half a mile from my parents' driveway when I heard a twittering up ahead.

The sun was now high enough to shine over the young pine trees along the east side of the road, but the light was still rosy and warm. Its beams struck the branches of a small mimosa tree that stood in a clearing beside the blacktop, lending the feathery pink flowers an extra degree of color. Gently waving in the cool breeze of early morning, the mimosa's leaflets dappled each other, and the smooth gray bark seemed almost golden-brown. I slowed to a stop and put my binoculars to my eyes. Warbling from a perch about seven feet up in the mimosa was my first Painted Bunting.

The scene, as I think about it, was lovely to a degree I can't describe: the hour, the weather, the light, the bird, the tree—all gorgeous. Even the type of tree was just right for the colors of the male Painted, like the perfect china on which to serve a delicious meal: a small and delicate tree of the warmer climes, with lovely, gaudy, fragile flowers.

I stood and watched him singing in the mimosa for perhaps three minutes, at which point he flew across the road and into the branches of a live oak, still singing. Then, flit by flit, he worked his way up and into the forest, like a Cheshire cat, leaving only his song. Well, that and the afterimage burned into my retinas.

I returned to my parents' house. The entire trip had taken twenty-five minutes. I took off my dew-soaked shoes and sat down on the sofa to flip through my Peterson guide. Making the obligatory check mark next to the Painted Bunting's name, though, I felt both curiously unsatisfied and mystified by my lack of satisfaction. What more could I want out of the scene, after all? I had almost immediately found the bird I'd been after, in as beautiful a few moments as I could have asked for. Why wasn't I grateful?

I was grateful, really, and I still am. It was a lovely morning, a gorgeous lifer, an entirely successful birding experience. But I can compare it to other moments on other mornings and still find it wanting in one quality: surprise.

As much beauty as I saw in that mimosa, I've found surpassing beauty by stumbling across it. On our honeymoon, for instance, driving along the coast of western Scotland, my wife and I came around a peninsula and along the shore of a small sheltered bay, upon which floated, in a scene I can only describe as ethereal, a pair of utterly serene Mute Swans and their cygnets. I brought the car to a sharp halt, climbed out, and staggered down to the shore, quite honestly amazed. I had seen Mute Swans before, but always as imported ornaments, tamed birds with clipped wings paddling around the ponds of plantations and country houses. These were birds as wild as the weather, huge, strong, fearless, uncontained by anything, least of all the treeless hills and cool mists around us. Neither the wind, the waves, our car, nor our camera attracted their interest in the slightest. I was very close to awestruck. Even Kelly barely breathed. We were rushing to catch the ferry from Mallaig to Skye, so we couldn't have lingered there more than five minutes, but in that time, we stood absolutely still, and the parents made no motion save the gentle sculling of their feet, keeping themselves close to their downy children. I find myself sometimes imagining that they are sitting there still, a work as beautiful and eternal as Keats's Grecian urn.

Another bird I first saw in Scotland surprised me once by turning up close to home—my home, that is. My feelings on introduced species are usually pretty negative, but I'll confess that there is one bird of Asian descent that I'm quite glad to have in the United States, and if you've ever seen one set off against a background of golden grainstalks, you'll know why: it's the Ring-necked Pheasant. I first saw one scuttling across a road in Scotland (where it was also introduced, albeit at least a millennium beforehand, thanks to the Romans), but I had never caught sight of one in my native land until one turned up, quite to my surprise, at Bombay Hook National Wildlife Reserve in Delaware.

It was hard to miss. Unlike our native quails and partridges, which are also members of the family Phasianidae, pheasants are neither small, nor round, nor unobtrusive, nor brown and gray and streaky. They are among the world's most flamboyant birds, combining colors that make most parrots look dull and wan by comparison, and they are bred and shown by people all over the world. The meter-long male Ring-neck is a veritable drag queen of a bird, bearing a glossy green-violet head equipped with feathery "horns," large red wattles around and below its eyes, a clean white ring around its neck, a bronze back and breast, and a pointed golden tail longer than the rest of the pheasant. It is also, at least on my Peterson guide's map, confined to the New Jersey side of the Delaware River, which explains why I was so surprised to see it at Bombay Hook.

Tom Parker, who saw it at the same time, told me of a birding acquaintance whom he'd met in Massachusetts. Tom had spotted some shorebird or other there and was telling his new buddy how surprised he'd been, since his guidebook indicated the bird didn't live in New England. The friend had given him a measured glance and drawled in a Yankee accent, "Ayup. But then again, most birds don't read those books."

A more prosaic, though equally unexpected, sighting occurred during another family visit to Beaufort. (Are you pronouncing it correctly, O Best Beloved?) We had all gone to Hunting Island State Park, one of the better public beaches I've visited, and decided to stop at the Shrimp Shack on U.S. 21 on the way back. Highway 21 is the only road which links the sea islands—Fripp, Hunting, Harbor, Saint Helena, and Lady's Islands—to the mainland, so the Shack's owners get a lot of business from the beach crowd and don't seem to mind patrons dining in flip-flops and wet swimsuits. This is probably why the Shack doesn't have tables, exactly; they're more like picnic benches that have been linked together and boxed in with wire-mesh screens to keep the bugs out.

We were sitting on such a bench waiting for our shrimpburgers—fresh and delicious, but if you don't like horseradish, avoid the cocktail sauce—when I saw a peculiar-looking bird alight on the shoulder of the highway across from us. It was dove-shaped, with the dove's small head and pointed tail, but it looked a bit too long, with tail feathers that looked a bit too white. I pointed it out to my dad, a birder of longer experience, if less active habits, than I, and he too thought it might be a dove, though a bit on the odd side. I had deliberately left my binoculars behind while we went to the beach, because I can't tend the kids with shorebirds nearby and field glasses around my neck. I was content to let the matter rest until I finished eating, an entirely pleasant experience that involved hush puppies which had been removed from the fryer at precisely the right moment—just after cooking all the way through, but before the crust became too leathery or too crunchy. Birds, for the moment, were a secondary pleasure.

When we left the restaurant, however, the reality of my obsession once again intruded on me. As we approached our cars, I strolled across the parking lot to see if the bird was still on the shoulder across the road. It was. It had an unusually long and pointed tail with a thick white border on each side, a white rump, large white wing patches, a gray back, a yellow head and crest, orange cheek patches, and a thick, hooked bill adapted for tearing fruit.

It was a Cockatiel.

Seeing parrots in the wild is not something North Americans are particularly used to. The only parrot native to our country, the Carolina Paroquet, became extinct in

1918, and I was about 180 degrees of longitude away from where I might reasonably expect to spot a wild Cockatiel: it is native to Australia. This particular bird was obviously an escapee from a cage somewhere, but its ability to fly was intact, for as soon as I was close enough to confirm its identity, it zoomed off into the palmettos with a most dove-like flip of its wings.

Of all the sightings I've had in the field, this is the one that puzzles me the most in terms of how to record it—well, this and the Peacock on the dirt road outside of Locust Dale, Virginia. It was certainly not caged, so I suppose it counts as a wild bird, though "feral" might be a better term, in which case I should be able to log it on my life list. On the other hand, it's highly unlikely that Cockatiels are breeding in Beaufort County, so the *species* is not really established. I therefore left the Cockatiel off my life list, figuring that should convince all the Bachman's Warblers out there that I'm an honest guy who'll keep their location a secret if they'll just come out and let me look at them. Promise.

I had never before seen a parrot in the wild, nor am I all that likely to again, so this is one experience I'll treasure for its novelty and its rarity, as well as the beauty of the bird itself. In short, it is the *unexpected* birds that I remember, in the same way that I remember rainbows: a misty bow over Loch Lochy in Scotland, a fat tropical one over the water as we traveled to Hanauma Bay on Oahu, a spectacular double bow that drew everyone out of Breadmen's Restaurant after a thunderstorm in Chapel Hill, a colossal horizon-to-horizon double bow that filled Woodberry's eastern sky at sunset in early June. It's not that I disapprove of chasing rainbows from time to time—that's the whole *raison d'être* of most liberal arts majors, when you get down to it—but if you *expected* them to appear in Breadmen's parking lot, you probably wouldn't abandon your omelet to go look at one. The greatest beauty of the rainbow, and by extension the bird, is that whether you're in Kansas, Key West, or Kennebunkport, you can always be surprised. They can turn up anywhere, at any time.

In fact, one has turned up right now; yes, as I sit here, my fingers tapping away, I am in mid-bird. My wife has just run up to me with a hastily scrawled sign saying "LARGE BIRD IN BUSH—HURT?" As a rule, Kelly and I communicate through spoken English, but I often listen to music on my headphones as I work. (Brad's *Shame* CD is on right now, if you're wondering.) A sign is the most effective means of getting my attention.

Once we're outside in the evening light of summertime, Kelly tells me that our dog has been barking at a boxwood for ten minutes. Since these shrubs have never bothered him before, she assumed it was something *in* the bush, and pulled some foliage aside to look in; the feathers she saw were black and glossy, and there was a fleeting instant when she thought they might be the coils of a snake. Now that she's sure it's a bird, my job begins: find out its species, find out what the heck it's doing crouched in a boxwood, and then find out whether it can be persuaded to do it elsewhere.

I squat down and pull a small branch aside. In the dim evening, it takes a second for my eyes to adjust to the darkness within the leaves, but whatever it is, it's definitely black. My first diagnosis, therefore, is "American Crow." They're as common as hydrogen around here, and this is the right color, after all. On second thought, I realize that what I'm looking at is a wingtip, and the primary wing feathers have got to be at least six inches long—way too big for a crow. A brief "Northern Raven?" flickers into my head, met by an immediate "Stupid idea!" Some ravens *do* live in Virginia, but only in the higher altitudes—I saw my first one at about 3,000 feet on Old Rag Mountain—and this feather is too big even for a full-grown raven.

Then I think of what I saw three days ago: just east of U.S. 15, in a pasture I drive by on my way to work, I saw two Wild Turkey hens and at least two chicks. This bird is a bit low to the ground for a hen, let alone a tom, but could it be a young one? I'm almost ready to say "Wild Turkey" when the bird finally turns around, tired of my intrusion, and shows me its head, a tiny object that squats on its great squared-off shoulders like the hood ornament on a limousine. The head is smooth, naked, a sickly-looking red. The beak is hooked, whitish, unfriendly.

In other words, what we have here, folks, is an adult Turkey Vulture.

This is a bit unexpected. Vultures are almost always seen soaring far overhead, or sometimes perching atop large trees, surveying the landscape for carrion. Nonetheless, they are ground-nesting birds. If this one is nesting, though, it's picked a pretty dumb spot: a bush not thirty feet from a crazed dog's house, and a bush which is, moreover, right next to a driveway down which heavy farm equipment moves with regularity. A vulture that tries to raise a brood in this environment is going to get a pointed lesson in natural selection very quickly.

So, my guess is that it's hurt or ill, which brings us to the question: what now?

Hmm.

Boxwoods are notoriously thick shrubs; they have lots of spiny branches packed close together, so simply reaching in and pulling the bird out is not an option. Moreover, this vulture is tucked well down into the branches, so I don't think I could even get a grip on him without using a Bushhog to cut through some greenery first.

And even if I did get a grip on him, how would he react? Would he be likely to cooperate, understanding my concern for his welfare, or just to panic and try to make it a fight? I don't know how well vultures understand anything, but considering the amount of brainpower needed to outwit a dead possum, I wouldn't expect much. Too, vultures' wingspans can reach six feet, which would make us about even, as the tale of the tape goes. I have the advantage of superior intelligence and an opposable thumb, but the bird has a nasty hooked beak and a pair of nasty hooked claws, and is in a superior defensive position to boot. I've read enough about the Civil War to know what happens when you attack an entrenched opponent, as the Union did at Fredericksburg and Pickett did at Gettysburg; I believe the technical term used by military historians is "ass-whupping."

And even if I could wrestle him out, why would I *want* to? This is an animal, after all, which eats liquefying meat from animals who have long since rung down the curtain and joined the choir invisible. This bird has no doubt put its entire head inside some animals whose *outsides* I find too unpleasant to touch. Yes, it performs a vital function in the ecosystem and it's sadly misunderstood and it's not an evil creature but *I am not about to give it a hug.*

My young son Ian notes that "Turkey Vultures are a little bit beautiful" and I nod, agreeing with the "little bit" part. I put a cold chicken frank on the driveway near the bush and hope that will lure it out. The family returns indoors.

In observing this bird, however, I have made a very interesting discovery. From the moment I began looking at it, it did its best to keep its head close to the trunk of the boxwood and its tail toward me; this is, I suppose, a sensible defense mechanism, since the tail feathers are not nearly as vital to survival as the head. No surprises there. But as I moved around the bush, looking into it first from the yard side, then the driveway side, the vulture seized upon a new strategy:

It buried its head in the leaves.

I'm completely at a loss to explain how the vulture picked up this trick. There are a handful of domesticated Ostriches in the area, but the vulture couldn't have learned to do this from them because Ostriches don't actually bury their heads; that's one of the many bird-related myths handed down from antiquity, including the mistaken beliefs that swifts don't have feet and that the chicken came before the egg. (Eggs turned up a *lot* earlier; think about all the caviar produced before *Archaeopteryx*'s first appearance in the fossil record.) Apparently, this behavior is simply Turkey Vulture instinct: metaphorically putting its fingers in its ears, closing its eyes, and chanting "This is not happening! This is not happening!" I must say, though, that this kind of denial does not become a scavenger; if there's any creature that ought to have a fatalistic streak, it's a vulture.

Reality throws curve balls, no doubt about it; the key is to approach the plate *expecting* a curve. This is what makes birding a pleasure, after all: the belief that, through observation of any situation, no matter how weird, you can deal with it. So it's a gigantic black beast in a bush—big deal! Look it over, see what it wants, and cope. The wisdom of Tao Chi'en may find its perfect application in birding: "Drift on the Stream of Infinite Flux."

In the time it has taken me to record all this, the bird has managed to extricate itself from the bush, leaving

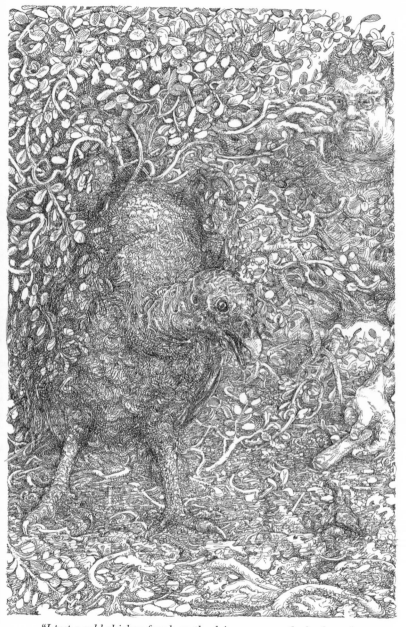

"I put a cold chicken frank on the driveway near the bush . . ."

nothing but a faintly upsetting odor and an uneaten chicken frank, which our dog obligingly dealt with. If this vulture was wounded, it certainly wasn't wounded too badly; I'm now beginning to wonder if it wasn't temporarily intoxicated from eating a particularly ripe haunch of groundhog, or if it smelled something equally yummy under that shrub. In any case, it has departed and we're now sitting down to dinner; I'm sure the bird is fervently hoping that when we next meet, the reverse will be true.

Part Two

Birds

6
Schieffelin's Starlings

For there is an upstart crow, beautified with our feathers, that with his tiger's heart wrapped in a player's hide, supposes he is as well able to bumbast out a blank verse as the best of you . . .
—Robert Greene, The Groatsworth of Wit

You may by now have the idea that all birders are wonderful people. That we all love nature and its little critters with an unearthly wisdom and benevolence. That our understanding of birds and their lives is so penetrating that we would doubtless make the best possible conservators of our planet's precious resources. That, to this end, we should all be supplied with large sums of money and positions of great power.

This is not the case.

Who, then, are the villainous birders? What evils have they committed? How do their acts match up with those of the birders we love and admire? In short, if Audubon is birding's Bach, if Peterson is its Mozart, what are we to do for a Salieri?

I have a nomination.

The name *Sturnus vulgaris* just reeks of trouble, doesn't it? If your Latin is past its expiration date—lord knows mine went sour some years ago—you may not recognize the species of bird to which it refers, but you can still appreciate the name by considering the bird's behavior: imagine great crowds of loud, drab, surly birds gathering in fields, forests, and towns in order to whistle and shriek at one another in preparation for a long trip south each winter. Now imagine that each bird's attitude is similar to yours before *you* take a long trip south, only make the situation even worse: you have to travel under threat of death, because you'll freeze or starve if you don't get going; you have to make the trip without benefit of a car, propelling yourself thousands of miles; you have to caravan with several thousand of your relatives, all of whom are, like yourself, loud, drab, and surly, and dangerously inbred to boot; and every meal along the way will be like the whole group's pulling into a single fast-food restaurant drive-through, knowing full well that there aren't enough fries ready.

Congratulations: you're a Starling.

Now you know, don't you? You're probably familiar with the unappealing squeaks and croaks they use for songs. You've been around in the fall when the great flocks of birds settle in to dine like huge feathered locusts. You've dodged the vast quantities of guano dripped from great heights. You know the avian plague that is *Sturnus vulgaris*. Was Linnaeus accurate with this one's nomenclature or what?

I am, admittedly, a bigot where the Common (or European) Starling is concerned. It is one of over a hundred Old World species in the family Sturnidae, which includes many useful and beautiful varieties of starling, but it is the only member to make it to these shores—and therein lies the problem. I resent it more because it's *here* than because it's so much more awful than any other bird. It's not evil; it's arguably not even as distressing to other species as our native Brown-headed Cowbird, which routinely slips its eggs into other birds' nests at the expense of their own young. The Starling's song is no more grating, its appearance no duller, and its personal habits no more unseemly than those of the Common Grackle. When the bird is in its breeding plumage, it's reasonably attractive; its bill turns lemon-yellow, contrasting nicely with its dark feathers, themselves shot through with green and purple highlights, iridescing brightly in the summer sun.

There's actually a lot to admire about the Common Starling. I once saw one saying "Hello" on a local news show, and was reminded that in Welsh mythology, the goddess-witch Rhiannon had a Starling with whom she sometimes spoke; I had assumed this was due to her supernatural powers, but now I wondered if she hadn't just trained her Starling well. As birds go, they're pretty smart, ranking just behind jays and crows, and their mimicry is good enough to rival that of their cousins, the mynahs.

I have thus on occasion been impressed by the sounds they make, but only once can I recall enjoying the sight of Starlings. In truth, I should have been enjoying the sight of my son playing teeball, a variant of baseball for kids too young to handle the difficulties of the real game, but my attention had wandered. I noticed a number of birds soaring over the diamond, nabbing insects in mid-flight. This is a common sight at baseball games, especially night games, where the lights attract a gigantic buffet of bugs for the dining pleasure of swifts, swallows, and night-hawks, but it was a bit unusual on this occasion. The Orange County Booster Fields are unlighted, and all games must be over by nightfall, so there were no clouds of insects to attract birds, only the usual airborne bugs of late afternoon. Nor were these the tiny, darting sorts of birds epitomized by swifts and swallows, but instead birds that were larger, darker, and more powerful, if a bit slower. I saw one whirring over the home dugout and noticed its long, sharp bill just in time to see it close on a sizable bug, which might have been a bumblebee or Japanese beetle. With a graceful midair twist, the bird was off over the outfield, making for the trees beyond the fence. Once I saw it in direct flight, I recognized the wedgelike silhouette: it was a Starling.

Intrigued, I looked around for others. There were a couple of them soaring around, triangular wings tucked back like those of an F-14, short tails spread to aid maneuverability, and every time I saw one make a sharp turn, a large bug appeared in its beak immediately thereafter. It was remarkable. They were Starlings, but they were beautiful, they were precise, they were deadly; they were in their element. I had never seen anything in them worth marveling at, but on this night, marvel I did.

No less an authority than Edward Howe Forbush saw much to praise about *Sturnus vulgaris:*

> The Starling's physical fitness for the struggle for supremacy is seen at once on an examination of its anatomy. It is a very hardy, muscular, and powerful bird. . . . It is exceedingly tough and wiry, and the bill, its principal weapon of offense and defense, is superior in shape to that of the Crow. It is nearly straight, long and heavy, tapering, and nearly as keen as a meat ax, while the skull that backs it is almost as strong as that of a Woodpecker. . . . [W]hile brave and active in the face of any foe that it can master, it shows the acme of caution and intelligence in its relations with man or any other creature too powerful to master. While it is comparatively fearless

where it is unmolested, it is always on guard, and if hunted becomes more wary than a Crow.

They're also hell on insects, at least in Europe. Forbush tells of their fondness for destructive land snails and other pests, but seems most impressed by their performance during the 1889–91 invasion of the spruce moth into Bavaria, when "great flights of Starlings, which were credibly estimated to contain as many as ten thousand in a flock," gorged themselves on caterpillars and pupae, no doubt doing the European spruce forests a fair amount of good in the process. I myself have seen Starlings strolling along the backs of reclining cows like oxpeckers on rhinos, helpfully picking engorged ticks and biting insects off the great bovine smorgasbord underfoot.

Despite all these positives, however, Forbush pointed out over half a century ago:

> The Starling can give no service here that cannot be equally well performed by our own Blackbirds, Meadowlarks, Bobolinks, Sparrows, and other birds. . . . Already, however, the Starling has begun to show a capacity for harmfulness which may be expected to become more prominent as its numbers increase.

Crops of cherries, apples, strawberries, corn, peas, and grapes, among others, have been attacked by Starlings, offsetting the agricultural benefits of their insect eating. Wild berries and even hickory flowers are susceptible to their appetites, leaving fewer nuts and fruit for the native thrushes and waxwings. Worse, Starlings drive out other birds that nest in holes, such as woodpeckers and bluebirds (who, due to DDT's ravages, had a hard enough time surviving the last century), and will relentlessly rebuild nests even after the other birds have destroyed their first efforts. They have even been implicated in the spread of histoplasmosis, a fungal infection of the lungs to which farmers are subject.

They also make a godawful mess. Oliver L. Austin, Jr., reports that in the early 1930s, Washington, D.C., was visited by a plague of Starlings:

> Wintering flocks that fed by day over the surrounding countryside streamed into the heart of the city from every quadrant late in the afternoon. The birds lined the ledges on the government buildings, swarmed into the trees on Pennsylvania Avenue, and perched in noisy windrows in every nook and cranny in the foyers of theatres and department stores. Their droppings soiled the buildings, and the streets and pedestrians below them as well. In residential districts their night-long wheezing and chattering kept people awake.

In short, they are at best an enormous nuisance, and at worst a natural disaster, an uncontrolled virus that has wreaked havoc on America's ecosystem, driving other species to the brink of extinction. I consider them apocalyptic: to me, they fly alongside War, Pestilence, and Famine. Yet their presence here is not the work of a savage nature, a vicious deity, or a cruel fate—for once we know who did the dirty deed, who planted the bomb, who fired the revolver in the conservatory.

Blame the Common Starling on Eugene Schieffelin.

There is some debate as to facts surrounding the introduction of the European Starling to our shores; among the facts disputed are the number of unsuccessful attempts to introduce the species to the United States, the number of birds released in the first successful attempt, and even the spelling of the perpetrator's name, but the basic facts are well-established: a wealthy drug manufacturer named Eugene Schieffelin (or Schiefflin, or Scheiff-lin) released sixty (or eighty) birds in Central Park on March 6 (or 16) of 1890, and forty more on April 25 of the following year. There are now over 300 million Star-lings in North America, according to the *Washington Post* of May 14, 1997, and most authorities believe that every one of those 300 million is descended from this original group of five or six score. This concept demands at the very least respect for the bird's sexual drive, but it simulta-neously calls up reasonable expectations of Starling hemo-philia and dementia, at least among the noble houses.

Not that inbreeding has hampered the Starling—not much of anything has. The first nest was found in the eaves of the American Museum of Natural History in the summer of 1890, but the birds didn't stay in Central Park's environs for long. According to Forbush, by 1908 the birds had spread "over the first forty miles of Long Island, up the Hudson River to Ossining and beyond, through much of eastern New Jersey and into Pennsylvania and Delaware." In another twenty years, they had covered the Midwest; by the 1940s, the first birds had reached Califor-nia, and by 1952, they were breeding in Alaska, Canada, and Mexico. If the original colony of English settlers had experienced even mildly comparable success, the group that vanished from Roanoke Island after arriving in 1587 would have instead kicked out the natives, swept west-ward, and controlled the Louisiana Territory by about the time the Pilgrims arrived on Plymouth Rock. Europeans of all sorts overran North America with ruthless efficiency, but for sheer speed of conquest, the Starling is rivaled only by Cortes and his microscopic ally against the Aztecs, the smallpox virus.

Human history is full of this sort of thing: the intro-ductions of the cane toad to Australia, the mongoose to

Hawaii, and kudzu to the American South are just a few of the horrific jokes we have played on nature. Usually, though, these gaffes have been due to some equally bad joke nature was trying to play on us; the cane toad was brought in to combat the grubs that were decimating sugar cane crops, the mongoose to combat the accidentally introduced rats that were ravaging Hawaii's native species, and the kudzu vine to control the ferocious erosion of topsoil that threatened farmers below the Mason-Dixon line in the 1930s. Still, accidents will happen; the zebra mussel, which now menaces the fresh waters of eastern North America from the Saint Lawrence to the Mississippi delta, was probably just dropped into the Great Lakes by a European ship discharging its ballast water. (Interestingly, this story is detailed in the same edition of the *Washington Post*—May 14, 1997—which lists America's Starling population at 300 million; moreover, Tom Wilkinson, the author of "Zebras Musseling In," describes this zebra mussel invasion as "a prime example" of what an introduced species can do, and goes on to list as another example "the purposeful release in the 1890s of 40 [*sic*] Starlings in New York City and the resulting millions of their progeny.")

Unlike the zebra mussel, however, the Starling was brought into the Americas for a reason, albeit not a particularly *good* reason. John L. Long's *Introduced Birds of the World* gives a table for every family of birds and explains when, where, how, and why they were introduced to each new area. The "reason" column may say something like "cage bird" or "insect control" for most birds, but for the Starling's introduction to the United States, perhaps uniquely, the reason is given simply as "aesthetic." It's a reason so bizarre, so unbelievable, that at least one person who read this manuscript accused me of making the whole thing up for a cheap laugh. I only wish I had. Alas, it's a reason supported by a number of other authorities, including Long, Edwin Way Teale, and Annie Dillard.

Why did Schieffelin bring Starlings to New York?

Shakespeare.

This is not a case of political correctness demanding that we blame Eurocentric culture for every disaster; yes, Shakespeare is a Dead White Male, but in this case the Dead White Male at fault is Schieffelin, who apparently envied the British both their literature and their avifauna, and even worse, was in a position to do something about it.

Resurrecting the Bard of Avon in Brooklyn was beyond him, but birds were another matter. Seizing upon the idea that Shakespeare's England was the proper model for all right-thinking countries, Schieffelin also seized upon the corollary that the birds mentioned in Shakespeare's works were the proper birds for all such countries. He no doubt took careful stock of America's species and realized that while we might have a lot of Shakespeare's birds, we didn't have them all. In *Henry IV, Part 1,* Hotspur, who is hoping to have his captured uncle, Mortimer, ransomed out of prison by the unwilling King Henry, conceives the following plan to persuade the king:

> . . . I will find him when he lies asleep,
> And in his ear I'll holla "Mortimer!"
> Nay,
> I'll have a starling shall be taught to speak
> Nothing but "Mortimer," and give it him,
> To keep his anger still in motion.

This tells us that even Elizabethan England (or at least a certain well-read native of the West Country) was aware of the Starling's powers of mimicry. It wasn't a lot of praise, but it was enough. If Good Will had seen fit to mention the bird, then it was clear to Eugene Schieffelin that America, its eons of Starling-less life notwithstanding, could not survive without its presence.

He also imported Skylarks, Chaffinches, and Nightingales, which did not establish themselves in New York, but Schieffelin's release of Starlings was enough to alter forever the ecosystem of the Americas. The descendants of these birds now swarm over every state in the continental United States. (In Hawaii, their cousin, the Common Mynah, has gained its own foothold.) They have probably done more damage to the birds of our continent than any other species—excepting, of course, the one that brought them here.

If you're an American, your can-do spirit is no doubt bubbling over by now, filling your head with ideas for ridding the country of Starlings. You're probably saying to yourself, *Hey, if we can put a man on the moon, it'll be a snap to get rid of a few birds.* This is a popular and widespread opinion. Unfortunately, as any episode of *Family Feud* will demonstrate, a popular and widespread opinion is not necessarily a sensible opinion.

The occasion of the first attempt to eradicate the Starling is known with less certainty than the occasion of its American release, but there have certainly been a staggering number of such attempts. In California, where patience with nature seems to be a way of life, the bird was given about twenty-five years (after its 1942 arrival there) before it was targeted for extermination, but I suspect the temporary reprieve was too long for the state's own good. A three-year program to kill Starlings in Solano County saw nine million birds destroyed between 1964 and 1967, but over five thousand still remained there by its end.

That's a reduction of 99.944475 per cent, but it still left too many birds. Since the Starling may breed two or even three times a season, producing from two to eight eggs every time, those five thousand could easily become a million within three years, eight million within four. Even if the survivors themselves didn't breed, however, thousands of Starlings would likely enter the county from other areas. In 1966, a single roost in another part of California was calculated at some five *million* birds, and the overall population in the United States is well into the hundred millions.

Aside from their sheer numbers, the birds are hard to kill, or even scare away. They're not protected by law in many places, but they can reach speeds of up to fifty miles an hour, making them a tough target; if they didn't travel in massive flocks, they'd be almost impossible to shoot. In places where gunfire is frowned upon, however, other methods have been used, and have, for the most part, failed miserably. In Washington, D.C., live wires were strung atop the columns of the Capitol, which got rid of the Starlings—and sent them to roost on the ledges of other buildings nearby, such as the Library of Congress buildings across the street. On the grounds of the White House, loudspeakers were once employed to broadcast recordings of Starlings in distress, which sent them all the way to the sycamore trees along Pennsylvania Avenue before they worked up the nerve to return. In Providence, Rhode Island, fireworks were lit in an attempt to scare off the birds, but to no avail. In Englewood, New Jersey, the city cut off its nose to spite the Starling, removing many of its shade trees. Alexander Wetmore lists the following methods of exorcism, all of which have failed:

> . . . rattles, balloons, whistles, fireworks, blank shells, fire hoses, stuffed owls, and other bogies. They also pay little heed to supersonic sounds. . . .

How this last fact was determined I do not know, but if nothing else, it shows the lengths to which America has gone to extirpate the Starling from our shores, all without success. Meanwhile, during the same century, we wiped out the Passenger Pigeon, the Carolina Paroquet, and the Ivory-billed Woodpecker without even trying. Since *Sturnus vulgaris* arrived here in 1890, diseases like polio and smallpox have been all but eradicated, the atom has been harnessed for both military and scientific purposes, and the microchip has put a world of information at the fingertips of the world's population, all through the ingenuity of the human brain—but in spite of every offense the bird commits, in spite of all our creativity, in spite of decades of effort, we can't get rid of Schieffelin's handiwork.

What makes Schieffelin's act doubly foolish is the fact that he had a model to work from. A species of European bird had already been introduced into the Americas with results that can only be described as disastrous. For this introduction, however, the culprits are not known; only the results are.

The House Sparrow, *Passer domesticus,* also known as the English Sparrow, was brought to America in the middle of the nineteenth century. T. Gilbert Pearson reports that eight pairs were brought to Brooklyn in 1850 and released in the spring of 1851; Wetmore says the initial group, imported in order to control cankerworms in the borough, did not survive, but that later groups did; Austin gives the date of release as 1852 and the specific release point as a Brooklyn cemetery, a location wholly appropriate given the bird's effect on native species.* Whatever the

*At least one version of the story claims that the House Sparrow was imported to help deal with the horse droppings that littered New York's streets. The theory was that the bird would pick through the dung in search of undigested seeds and help break down the various piles. Yes, according to this tale, some thoughtful soul actually *wanted* a bird to come spread shit evenly over the city.

details, it seems clear that, like the Common Starling and the House Finch, the House Sparrow began its conquest of the East Coast in the Big Apple, but the Sparrow's tour of world domination has also seen it establish itself in Canada, Cuba, South Africa, South America, Australia, New Zealand, and Hawaii. (Adding insult to injury, Schieffelin imported House Sparrows of his own in the 1890s.)

The House Sparrow has been introduced in several places *un*successfully. That one of these is Greenland is hardly a shock; even the introduction of humans to Greenland has barely been successful. A more interesting (or even ironic) failure took place in the Philippines, where the bird was driven to extinction by another introduced species, its cousin the European Tree Sparrow.

As introduced birds go, the Starling gets the majority of my ire, but that's personal. I could certainly understand the point of view of any authority who found the House Sparrow more offensive, because in many ways the two birds have had precisely the same effect on both our farmers' crops and our native wildlife. Pearson's list of the Sparrow's offenses is almost identical to Forbush's list of the Starling's ravages: House Sparrows have destroyed cherries, grapes, pears, peaches, flower buds, tree buds, peas, lettuce, and wheat, among other crops, while their nesting behavior (and willingness to attack other birds' eggs) has hampered the reproductive success of the House Wren, the Purple Martin, the Tree Swallow, the Barn Swallow, and the long-suffering Eastern Bluebird. Indeed, the Starling comes off looking benign in comparison to the House Sparrow, at least in Pearson's description:

> The filthy habits of these birds are most annoying. They gather in immense flocks to roost, and generally select cornices, ornamental work about the eaves and gables of houses,

window-cappings, and the vines which cover the walls of buildings. These they defile with their excrement. Great and serious damage is often caused by their carrying nesting materials into rain-spouts, gutters, and similar places about houses, so that cisterns are defiled, or pipes overflow, causing destruction of or injury to property. . . . The English Sparrow among birds, like the rat among mammals, is cunning, destructive, and filthy.

Pearson is a scientist, make no mistake, but in this case he seems to have objectively examined the available evidence and come to the eminently logical conclusion that the House Sparrow is a waste of protoplasm. I see no reason to disagree.

Where my anger diverges from Pearson's, however, is at the point where Schieffelin decided to release the Starling—only forty years after and less than ten miles away from the point where the sparrow was released. Here we have a situation where a man is stepping in to rearrange nature—a decision fraught with hazard in the best of circumstances. Worse, he is doing so for what we have already seen to be less-than-adequate reasons. Worse yet, he has no official authority and no means of redressing any problems caused by his actions.

And somehow he didn't notice that some bloody fool had committed the exact same idiocy just across the bridge!

The notion that those who are ignorant of history are doomed to repeat it has rarely had such a clear and concrete example. Even as Schieffelin's hand was reaching toward the Starlings' cage, preparing to lift the latch and turn *Sturnus vulgaris* into a part of the American landscape forever, surely he must have noticed a House Sparrow or two. He was in Central Park, after all—there must have been at least a couple of them in the vicinity, terrorizing a Robin or defacing a statue with guano. In that moment, a birder of good will might have done something to stop Schieffelin—made a sudden cry of protest, slapped a temporary restraining order on him, or nailed him and his birds with one well-placed hand grenade—but no one did. No one mentioned the House Sparrow fiasco, or perhaps they did; we'll never know if Schieffelin acted out of ignorance or obstinacy.

Whatever the case, though, I cannot picture that scene in Central Park without a shiver; I see the Starlings rustling in their cages, like the rats in Winston Smith's cell, and the Sparrows hopping about the sidewalks, watching, waiting for the next wave of invaders to join them in their work, driving the weak, the unfortunate, the different, the unique, into oblivion. When I picture the spectators, I see faces filled not with hatred, but with cheer, a supreme confidence that their actions are right, an utter lack of concern for any consequences. I see a self-righteous certainty that utterly chills me. It is the same certainty I sometimes see on people's faces in photos of book burnings.

And then I picture myself standing beside a bonfire earlier in the nineteenth century. In my hands I hold a thick volume, a gift for young Master Eugene Schieffelin, who's just learning to read: *The Complete Works of William Shakespeare.*

And I simply don't know what to do.

7
Cool

. . . As a skate's heel sweeps smooth on a bow-bend: the hurl
*   and gliding*
Rebuffed the big wind. My heart in hiding
Stirred for a bird,–the achieve of, the mastery of the thing!
    –Gerard Manley Hopkins, "The Windhover"

Once in South Carolina, at the end of a long birding session, I saw something that stirred my heart: a flock of Starlings scattering from the crown of a nearby pine tree. This wouldn't ordinarily make me happy, but in this case I knew that what had scattered them was probably eating one of them. It was a large Red-tailed Hawk, and it was hunching atop the pine directly between me and the sun.

Gary Larson was right: birds of prey *do* know they're cool. (Indeed, their collective name, *raptors,* was considered so hip that it was snagged for use as a name by Toronto's NBA team. Granted, the mascot chosen was a dinosaur, but *Velociraptor* was named after the birds, not vice-versa.) This particular raptor perched unconcerned atop the tree just long enough for me to trudge up and catch a glimpse of its tail—a magnificent burgundy, much less rusty than is usual for a Red-tail—and its beak—a vivid yellow, almost canary-colored—before it decided that I wasn't cool enough to be watching it. With obvious disdain, it dropped off the pine and skimmed out of sight below the treetops.

You might not think that social cachet and birds would be so intimately involved, but in fact it's a long-standing tradition where birds of prey are concerned. In medieval times, both in Europe and Japan, hunting with hawks and falcons was a pastime of the aristocracy, and rigid hierarchies existed even within the sport itself. In Japan, the birds themselves were ranked like martial artists; their jesses, or leg coverings, were colored according to the size of their largest kill. Only a bird that had brought down the revered white crane was worthy of the purple jesses. In Europe, the hierarchy involved the humans who hunted with the birds. Only royalty could fly the great Gyrfalcon. Earls were restricted to the smaller Peregrine Falcon, clergymen to the still-smaller Merlin. Commoners could not hunt with raptors at all.

Even discounting centuries of human social stratification, birds of prey have inherent qualities that make them cool. Within the order Falconiformes are found avian superlatives of all sorts, whether in speed (the Peregrine Falcon, which can dive at speeds of 175 miles per hour), size (the Andean Condor, most massive of flying birds, with a ten-foot wingspan and a weight of up to twenty-five pounds), or ubiquity (the Osprey, which has been recorded on every continent and almost every island on earth, with the exception of New Zealand). Indeed, there are even bird-of-prey wannabes, as I found out not long after being blown off by the Red-tailed Hawk.

I had given up pursuing the hawk and had turned toward home when I noticed a gang of birds chattering furiously in a sapling by the edge of the woods. They were immature Red-winged Blackbirds, their glossy feathers still streaky and brown, but showing a few red epaulets on the shoulders of the males. There was also a Mockingbird in the tree, and within a moment or two, I thought I saw its mate arrive as well; all in all, it was a pretty crowded tree.

Suddenly a chorus of raucous cries broke out, and the flock abruptly departed the sapling. After a few moments, the Red-wings rustled to a stop on the grass below. Then, with a peculiar flutter, the second Mockingbird flew down to join the flock—and once again every bird in it went scattering. A closer look revealed why: the "Mockingbird" was a Loggerhead Shrike.

Shrikes are birds of prey, but no one except the prey gives them credit for it. They're too small, for one thing, being roughly Robin-sized. They're also more closely related to the Cedar Waxwing than to the Bald Eagle; they belong to the order Passeriformes, or perching birds, rather than the Falconiformes. Maybe this handicaps them, keeping them from being quite as cool as hawks and falcons. Nonetheless, they'll kill and eat anything smaller than they are: lizards, insects, mice, even other birds. I doubt a lone Loggerhead could take on a mature Red-winged Blackbird, let alone a whole mob of them, but I feared for these Red-wings, which were young and far too disorganized to form a mob, which is, let's face it, about as disorganized as you can get. The shrike had smaller prey on its mind, however, and it promptly seized some hapless insect from the turf and flitted into the sapling to hang it up.

That caught my attention; shrikes are sometimes called butcherbirds due to their flamboyant habit of hanging their kills on thorns, or even barbed wire. Whether they do this to store food for later, to age and tenderize the meat, or to display their hunting prowess to the neighbors, I don't pretend to know, but it sounded like a pretty cool activity, and one I'd never observed, so I peered intently into the tree. The shrike was gamely whacking the bug against the base of a branch that had broken off, but either the short spur of wood was too dull or the bug was too tough—no impalement resulted. Eventually, fed up with itself or its prey, or perhaps embarrassed by its inability to impale smoothly, it darted off into the forest, suggesting that so far, at least, shrikes don't have the necessary attitude to qualify as birds of prey. We'll have to wait and see if they can evolve a coolness gene.

One thing that makes America cool is the fact that our national bird is a raptor. (And America is very definitely cool. It isn't always suave, urbane, respectable, dapper, courteous, sensitive, mature, pensive, safe, or even sanitary, but it's *always* cool.) Part of the bird's coolness is that it is not at all common, except in parts of Alaska. Sightings of it are still events of some import in a birder's life. Despite decades of birding experience, I can count on one hand the places where I've seen Bald Eagles: North Carolina's Jordan Lake, South Carolina's Coosaw River, Virginia's Caledonia Wildlife Area on the Northern Neck, Virginia's Rapidan River, and Bombay Hook National Wildlife Refuge in Delaware. There's something inherently memorable about spotting a bird with the size, the symbolic power, and the *clarity* of a Bald Eagle; once you've gotten close enough to see the bird, its very eagleness seems to fill your eyes. When you look at most birds, there's usually a nagging doubt in the back of your mind that maybe, just maybe, you've slipped up in your identification, or confused your field marks or your habitats or something. Maybe that gray bird on the fence *isn't* really a

Mockingbird, but a Loggerhead Shrike with a very pale mask, or a partially albino Catbird, or a species of thrasher from out west that you just don't know yet. But when the bird in question has a six-foot wingspan and a head and tail of pure white, there's not much else it could be besides a Bald Eagle.

Happily, the eagle is a good deal easier to see in many parts of America today than it was a few decades ago. In 1963, when I was born, there were fewer than a thousand left, and I can remember from my childhood a feeling that it was a bird I would probably never see in the wild; by 1996, however, its numbers had increased tenfold, and the Bald Eagle was once again established in central North Carolina. Much of this increase can be traced to a single event: on June 14, 1972, the pesticide DDT was banned in the United States, and soon ceased to be absorbed into the systems of carnivorous and insectivorous birds across the country.

The Bald Eagle was just one of the raptors that benefited from this particular environmental law; two others were the Osprey (now up to over fourteen thousand pairs after dipping below eight thousand) and the Peregrine Falcon, which came so close to the brink of extinction that it might well have peered over it and gotten dizzy. In 1975, there were only thirty-nine breeding pairs of Peregrines left in America, and none of them were in the eastern part of the country. Now there are three times that many pairs in the East alone, and about a thousand pairs overall.* Even the Eastern Bluebird has become more common

---

*In fact, Peregrines are even colonizing Eastern cities; one pair has gone so far as to nest atop Kodak's corporate headquarters in Rochester, New York. The company, recognizing a good photographic opportunity, installed a camera near the nest and displays the pictures on a website at birdcam.kodak.com.

since the ban on DDT, though it has doubtless also been helped by the popularity of bluebird houses, which protect its nests from attack and usurpation by House Sparrows and Starlings.

The Bald Eagle remains the most obvious standard in measuring the effects of environmental law on an endangered species. There are those, however, who question the wisdom of the DDT ban, and indeed of almost all environmental legislation. Some think that DDT has been a convenient scapegoat, despite studies showing that when birds ingest DDT-tainted food they tend to lay eggs with shells that are either absent or too thin to protect the chicks inside. They believe instead that the decline of the Bald Eagle has been due to other factors. Ignoring the fact that many of these other factors, such as the spread of humanity and the destruction of habitat, are also subject to environmental legislation, we can at least examine some inferential evidence regarding DDT and the Bald Eagle:

➤ My 1936 edition of Pearson's *Birds of America* mentions the distribution of the eagle in several places: "United States to southern Lower California and northern Mexico, breeding in suitable location throughout its range." The various times of egg-laying for eagles in Florida, the "Middle States," and "districts further north" are given. Except for the note "rare and local in California and the arid interior," which makes perfect sense for a bird whose diet is primarily fish, the eagle is nowhere described as rare, and there is absolutely no mention of its being in decline.

➤ In 1939, Swiss scientist Paul Muller discovered a practical use for the compound DDT, first isolated in Germany in 1874, and won a Nobel Prize for his work. The prize was in medicine, not chemistry. Why? Because for controlling disease, DDT seemed like a godsend. For sev-

THE VERB *TO BIRD*

eral decades it effectively destroyed the insect vectors of malaria, yellow fever, typhoid, and even bubonic plague. Its use in World War II probably saved thousands of soldiers' lives, while the destruction of malaria-carrying anopheles mosquitoes in India is credited with extending the life span of the average Indian from thirty-two to forty-seven years. In the United States, malaria cases dropped from a quarter-million per year in the 1930s to fewer than ten cases per year.

➤ In 1961, Oliver L. Austin wrote the following in *Birds of the World:*

> While the Bald Eagle breeds throughout North America, it has become quite rare in most of its range and is plentiful today only in Alaska and in Florida. In Florida its numbers have declined markedly in the last two decades; just why is not certain, for the species is protected and is seldom shot. Though it is long-lived and lays two eggs, it is not rearing enough young to replace the annual mortality. . . . Destruction of nesting trees as the human population expands is partly blamed for its decline. Suspected, but not as yet proved, is poisoning by air-sprayed DDT ingested with poisoned fish the eagle eats.

➤ In 1962, Rachel Carson published *Silent Spring,* in which the theory that DDT was laying waste to bird populations first became widely publicized. Less publicized but no less important was Carson's observation that the pesticide wasn't saving human lives anymore, because its overuse had led to the proliferation of DDT-resistant insects.

➤ In 1963, there were fewer than five hundred breeding pairs of Bald Eagles in the United States.

➤ In 1972, DDT was banned in the United States, though its use continued in other countries (such as China, where by 1975, DDT resistance had become so widespread among mosquitoes that the nation had nine times more malaria cases than in 1961).

➤ In 1996, there were over five thousand breeding pairs of Bald Eagles in the United States.

In other words, between 1936 and 1961, something ravaged the population of Bald Eagles in America, and between 1963 and 1996, whatever it was, it stopped. This timeline alone does not prove the involvement of DDT, but if "environmental extremism" is intended to describe the sort of pressure that brought the Bald Eagle and the Peregrine Falcon back from the edge of extinction, perhaps it is not so extreme after all.

People may have stepped in too late to save one of our native raptors—the California Condor, which hovers near extinction—but at least America is not faced with the embarrassing prospect of having wiped out our national symbol. Yet.

8
An Owl for the Moping

. . . from yonder ivy-mantled tow'r
The moping owl does to the moon complain.
*   —Thomas Gray, "Elegy Written in a Country Churchyard"*

There are traditions, and then there are holiday traditions. There is stress, and then there is holiday stress. There are birds, and then there are holiday birds. And it was one of the latter that saved Christmas in 1996.

The interrelations between tradition, stress, and birds take a while to explain. They are rather complex, and one reason they are complex is that the religious backgrounds of my extended family are complex. My father's father was an Episcopalian who late in his life attended a Baptist church, while my mom was raised Jewish, but now she and my dad both attend an Episcopal church. My mom's brother married a Catholic (who converted to Judaism), while my mom's sister married a Quaker (and converted herself). My wife started out as a Methodist but now is a member of a Presbyterian church. The family's Christians range from Pentecostal to Catholic, the Jews from Orthodox to Reform, but the gist of the matter is that my relatives worship in close to a dozen different churches, representing almost all the world's major religions except Islam and Hinduism.

What does all this make me? Tolerant.

Please note that "tolerant" does not equal "relaxed." The holiday season at my house begins with a surge of anxiety right before Thanksgiving, moves into a brief calm as Hanukkah settles in, and picks right back up into full-throttle panic as Christmas moves closer. (This is probably why we've never bothered doing much for New Year's Eve; we're too exhausted to do more than watch a few bowl games and eat black-eyed peas.) Certain traditions, however, are always observed, even if their observation is sometimes unlike that of any other family.

One such tradition is the opening of the Christmas season. The retailers of America have made the Friday after Thanksgiving the *de facto* beginning of the holiday season by starting their holiday sales on that day, when our resistance is low from overconsumption of turkey, but I see this as the top of a slippery slope. If you let the nation's merchants tell you when to start celebrating (or shopping, which to them is the same thing), then all I can say is "Ho ho ho! Merry Labor Day!"

For years, though, my wife's holiday season began with a solemn event: the first televised appearance of the Norelco ad featuring the Claymation Santa riding an electric shaver. Even after she married and left home, my wife would call her father, or vice-versa, as soon as either spotted the commercial, and holiday cheer would follow. Yes, dammit, we're Americans, and as a result, even our most basic family rites revolve around that glowing box in the living room.

Admittedly, our family is a little fanatical where animated Christmas specials are concerned. The dogma:

That whatever you may think of the live-action movie version, Chuck Jones's masterful *How the Grinch Stole Christmas* is without question the best Christmas special ever made; that *A Charlie Brown Christmas,* for all its flaws, is still terrific, even if considered on the basis of its Vince Guaraldi soundtrack alone; and finally, that try as we might, we can't look away from *Rudolph the Red-Nosed Reindeer.*

I and many other members of my generation became fixated on *Rudolph* during our childhoods, and I think it's partially because of the horrific freakshow called the Island of Misfit Toys, where all the toys judged unsuitable for Christmas morning are banished by Santa. It's an appalling injustice to be cast into an Arctic limbo because you're unconventional, an injustice that even a young child can perceive. Of course, I also think the whole "misfit toy" thing is ridiculous for ornithological reasons. One birdlike toy complains, "How'd you like to be a Bird That Can't Fly? I *swim,*" and leaps into a fishbowl to demonstrate. Well, what's wrong with that? Isn't it normal for some birds? Penguins, say? Plenty of birds are more able in the water than on land—loons and ducks, in particular. The Ruddy Duck is flat-out unable to walk, but it swims perfectly well, and I dare say other birds (like grebes or anhingas) are more at home in the water than in the air, too. After all, you can float without a lot of effort, but staying aloft requires some serious energy expenditures. The Bird That Can't Fly is no misfit.

Indeed, such a bird would probably fit in well at our house; we cling tenaciously to our holiday traditions, but the overall combination of these traditions may seem like an odd mixture. We light candles on Hanukkah, for example, but I didn't start doing that; my wife did, bless her little *shikse* heart. We always read Clement C. Moore's "A

Visit from Saint Nicholas" the night before Santa comes. Most importantly, we have a tree, a tradition which is probably as central to my feelings for the season as anything else. My mom has long been in the habit of buying a Christmas tree ornament for each family member every year. I now have dozens of these, as does my younger brother, plus over a dozen for my wife, and almost as many for my sons. This does not include ornaments we have bought, or been given by other people, or made ourselves. As you can imagine, then, the Cashwell-Dalton Christmas tree is chock-full of ornaments, and not a few of them are birds.

The first ornament I ever got was a bird. It still hangs on the tree every year, a small wooden die-cut bird, no more than three inches long, painted silver, with its eye, feathers, details, and the words "P.C. 1964" added in black. How my mom knew I'd be a birder I have no idea. She claims I was already identifying species when she bought the ornament, but since I wasn't yet two, I have to wonder.

In any case, birds festoon my Christmas tree: I have a Ring-necked Pheasant, a shaggy-headed Mallard, a Gray Partridge, a Mute Swan, and any number of other birds of fictitious species: velvety songbirds in red, yellow, and blue, lacquered hummingbirds, parrots and doves, even nesting birds with straw wrapped around them. I'm very proprietary about them; no one else gets to put them on the tree, and I'll selfishly move any ornament that gets in the way of my placing them in the perfect spot.

For me, decorating the tree is the pivotal moment of Christmas; the lights, the carols playing in the background, and the sounds and scents of family all play around me, and each ornament has a significance of time and place.

But for Christmas 1996 there was no decorating.

Abandoning any Christmas tradition is stressful for me, but abandoning the tree was especially bad. We did actually *have* a tree, yes, but we couldn't get it to stand up; when we came home with it, we discovered that our old stand, the traditional four-threaded-bolts-mounted-in-a-circle kind, was missing one of the bolts, and the tree couldn't be made to stand upright. It was Monday, December 16. We leaned the tree against the wall, filled the basin of the stand with water to preserve the foliage, and promised the kids we'd find a new stand and decorate the tree before we left for their grandparents' on Friday the 20th.

On Tuesday the 17th, we began our search for a stand.

"Why not earlier?" I hear some of you sniffing. "We get our tree done by Thanksgiving." You probably have a Merry Labor Day, too, don't you?

Orange, the town closest to us, doesn't have a lot of places that stock Christmas tree stands, but I checked them all. Faulconer's Hardware on Madison was sold out. The Western Auto store in the same shopping center didn't sell them. The florist just past the railroad bridge didn't sell them. The Madison-Orange Farm Co-op down toward Gordonsville had had some, but they were sold out now.

And that was that. There was no time for long-distance searching. If we were going to leave for Fayetteville on Friday, we couldn't have a tree for Christmas.

I felt thoroughly grinched.

Kelly's family has long held its main celebration on the Saturday night before Christmas. That year, however, things were fairly grim. Kelly's dad had died in May, and this would be the first Christmas without him. Her mother, Ruth, had also lost her best friend to cancer, and Hurricane Fran had badly damaged Ruth's summer place at

White Lake. Finances demanded a slightly scaled-back celebration. We knew all this, but we tried not to think about it. We would be driving into it from five hours away, frenzied, disorganized, cut off from our memories of Christmases past, and not yet in the holiday spirit—but first we had to pack. Packing is never fun for anyone at our house, but it was worse this year, because of the rabbit.

Back in November, Kelly had carefully arranged for our dog to be kenneled over Christmas. Unfortunately, neither she nor I had remembered that we'd also need kenneling for our newer pet: Grassy Carrot, a black-and-white English Spot rabbit (of dubious pedigree) that we had obtained at the Orange County Volunteer Fire Department's benefit fair in June, but that was not entirely integrated into the family yet.

Worse, the rabbit, in its cage, took up an inordinate amount of room in our car, so we had to place it behind my wife, who had to scrunch up uncomfortably against the dashboard. This meant that I got to do all the driving, since I couldn't fit in front of the rabbit and Kelly couldn't drive crammed into the dash. There wasn't much space in the back seat for the kids, either.

There we were, fretting, panicking, and contorting ourselves and our belongings in order to drive three hundred miles with two small children and a surly lagomorph, which incessantly grunted and nipped at me. Moreover, we did so knowing that we hadn't had time to properly celebrate the season at our house and that we wouldn't really be having much of a celebration at Ruth's house. We hadn't done any Christmas shopping yet, either.

Oh, did I mention that it had snowed the night before? The roads were mostly clear by the time we set out, but ice was a concern for me on bridges and curves until we got south of Richmond.

We arrived in Fayetteville early Friday evening and collapsed; Saturday was taken up with cleaning, shopping, and preparing for the family gathering that night, which was pleasant, if subdued; and given that my wife has four brothers and eight nieces and nephews, three of whom were engaged and all of whom were hungry, it should come as no surprise that Sunday was largely taken up with cleaning again. It hadn't exactly been an old-fashioned holiday.

And then came Monday the 23rd.

We had wanted to leave for my parents' house in Beaufort early that morning. Unfortunately, we still hadn't found any presents for my dad, which meant that before we could leave, a short trip to Sears would be necessary. But when you talk about Fayetteville traffic during Christmas shopping season, no trip is a short trip, especially not near Cross Creek Mall.

Cross Creek Mall is the center of—at least according to the natives—the nation's largest single swath of acreage devoted to retail establishments; there are over a dozen separate shopping centers and strip malls surrounding it, with any number of independent businesses and stores wedged in and around them. Entering this area two days before Christmas is like entering the jaws of Consumer Hell, and Virgil can't help you because he's pinned down behind the counter ringing up Tickle Me Elmos and Whitman's Samplers. The surrounding roads were choked with the honking vehicles of the damned, so there wasn't room to park in the Inferno proper. We put the car into a space somewhere on the far side of the Styx and made for the entrance.

We were going into Sears in hopes of turning up the kerosene lantern Dad had requested; he had gotten sick of having no light source during the not-infrequent power outages on Cat Island. It would have been a simple enough job in ordinary circumstances, but as you may have noticed, this was not an ordinary Christmas. Inching through the traffic, I'd been grinding my teeth hard enough to create sparks, and the situation in Sears wasn't doing much to lower my blood pressure. We couldn't find any kerosene lanterns, only some battery-powered fluorescent lamps and a Coleman camping lantern that ran on butane. Ruth asked the counterman if she could use the phone to call a local hardware store; he graciously allowed this, but he said he was surprised that Sears didn't have kerosene lanterns. In disbelief, he took us back to the shelves we'd just scoured in order to see for himself. Satisfied, he recommended that we try Roses, where he had bought such a lantern himself several months ago, and then, all at the exact same moment:

Ruth reported to me that Hope Mills Hardware didn't have lanterns but that she would call Roses and see if they had any, if that was what I wanted;

and Kelly suggested that maybe the fluorescent lantern was the way to go even if that wasn't what Dad had asked for, if that was OK with me;

and the counterman suddenly realized that we were looking for a *kerosene* lantern rather than the *butane* lantern he'd bought at Roses so he wasn't sure what to do next, what did I think;

and Ian, who was five at the time, reached out for a boxed volleyball game which was standing on end in a display and set off a chain reaction that knocked over that box *and* the fifteen boxes that were standing behind it in a strikingly domino-like array.

When I had stopped shrieking, I was led to the car, lanternless, and we drove back to the house. There we spent what felt like a week and a half packing, though it was

really only about two hours, and got on the road sometime after two-thirty, by which time I was developing a pronounced tic in my left eyelid. Ruth, ever gracious, volun-
teered to keep the rabbit while we were in Beaufort. That
was a relief, but the relief was tempered by the knowledge
that we still had at least four hours of heavy driving ahead
of us.

We drove swiftly, efficiently. We cared nothing for comfort or scenery, only for speed. We didn't tell jokes. We
didn't count cows. We stopped once for a bathroom break.
The sun went down. We turned off I-95 near Yemassee
and took the shortcut past Old Sheldon Church. Its walls
had been burned away in the Civil War. Over the river and
through the woods we drove. Minimally. Like Hemingway.

By the end of the trip I was gripping the steering wheel
hard enough that I could easily have taken it with me into
my parents' house. Instead, I pried my fingers off and
took the kids inside, putting off the unloading of the car
for a while. I didn't know it yet, but that decision would be
an important one for me.

After a short visit with my folks and a few Christmas
snacks, I felt strong enough to go back out to the car for
the luggage. Kelly was upstairs putting the kids to bed,
since it was after eight by then. I walked out the side door,
down the deck stairs, and along the sidewalk to the end of
the driveway. I had just touched the trunk of our car when
I stood bolt upright, arrested by a sound.

Hooo, hooo, hoo-hoo-hoo, hoooooo.

I managed not to move quickly, though part of me
wanted to run back to the house to grab Dad's binoculars
and Peterson guide; I don't know why I felt I needed
them, though, because there's only one thing in the Southeast that makes that sound: the Great Horned Owl. No
barking, like the Barred Owl, or shrieking, like the

Screech Owl. For honest-to-god hooting, there's only the Great Horned, and I had never seen one.

I stood by the car for a moment, trying to decide on a course of action. I was sure of the call, but where was the bird? Not far off, certainly; that hooting had been *loud*. I moved slowly down the driveway, peering toward the brush on the other side of the road. The night was clear, and the moon was already beaming brilliant white light over the live oaks and scrub; it would be full on Christmas Eve.

Hooo, hooo, hoo-hoo-hoo, hoooooo.

It was very close. It was also one of the few birdcalls I felt pretty sure I could imitate. I'm not a great whistler, but I can hoot pretty well, especially when the bird is large enough for its voice to drop into the baritone range. I decided to try a hoot of my own. If it scared the owl off, I'd probably get at least a glimpse of it in the moonlight, and all you need to ID a Great Horned Owl is an idea of its size; there's simply no night bird anywhere near as large in this part of the world. I covered my nose and mouth with my hands to muffle the direction of my call:

Hooo, hooo, hoo-hoo-hoo, hoooooo.

Nothing moved. For a moment I was sure I had scared it off and that it was winging off through the shadows. Then came the reply:

Hooo, hooo, hoo-hoo-hoo, hoooooo.

Now I knew I could track it down. If it would keep calling, I could triangulate the spot where it sat. All I had to do was keep moving slowly and get it to talk to me from time to time.

We exchanged hoots repeatedly, and I soon had its basic location: the next-door neighbors' front yard, full of locust trees, which lose their leaves in the winter. My parents' yard, by contrast, is full of live oaks, the traditional spreading shade trees of the south, which stay green and lush all year. Had the owl been one lot over, I would never have had even a chance of spotting it.

For all their leaflessness, the locust trees did have one thing which presented a problem: Spanish moss. It is not true that absolutely every tree in the South is draped with this stringy gray stuff, but near the coasts and swamps, you'll find it on nine out of ten, sometimes in flimsy strands, sometimes in great bushy clumps. The locust trees had entirely too many of the latter, dozens of clumps which were large, dark, and annoyingly owl-like.

Temporarily stymied, I moved slowly back toward the house. My binoculars were still in my suitcase, but Dad's were, I knew, right there in the living room. I eased back around the garage and out of sight of the owl, then sprinted inside, seized the binoculars from the mantel, and sprinted back out, terrified that during my brief absence the owl had flown away.

There are those birders who are content to put a bird on their life lists when they've only heard, not seen, the bird in question. I am not one of them. This is largely due to my ineptitude with calls, but even so, I don't feel entitled to list what I haven't even caught a glimpse of. (I have the Whip-poor-will on my list because I'm sure I've heard their calls and have seen birds that at least *might* have been making the call.) In other words, though I knew perfectly well that I'd heard a Great Horned Owl, it was not yet a lifer for me; I had to get at least a quick look at it.

Hooo, hooo, hoo-hoo-hoo, hoooooo.

It was still there. I replied in kind, putting the binoculars to my eyes. The trunks of the locust trees glowed silver in the moonlight. Slowly moving down the driveway, I continued my chat with the owl, scanning this way and that, up and down trunks and limbs, waiting for movement. I

"I . . . seized the binoculars from the mantel."

began to get the fear peculiar to birders that the binoculars were narrowing my field of vision too much, that I'd have them trained on a small area of a tree branch while the owl was taking off from a completely different place, and that I would lose it.

And then a clump of Spanish moss moved.

She wasn't huge, as Great Horned Owls go, probably a little less than two feet in length, but she sat on the locust branch in full glory, her brown feathers black-

". . . she sat on the locust branch in full glory . . ."

ened and grayed by the moon and the shadows, her horns
clearly outlined against the deep blue of the northwestern
sky. She called again, and this time I heard, from across
the marsh, another fainter series of hoots answering it—
a slightly different pattern, a male. She replied, and the
two owls sat quietly, contentedly, and talked.

I stood in the moonlight in the December night under
a crystalline sky and listened. After a while, I went inside
and brought my mother out to see the owl, and when the

kids were finally asleep, I brought out my wife. She stood in the darkness, looking at a bird-shaped shadow that was doing nothing more than hooting, and by doing so both gave a present to me and received a present from me. She looked because it was important to me, not yet knowing she would see something strange and magical; and she looked because she could tell from my face that the worst was over; there was no holiday stress that could take from me the vision and sound of this owl moon. It was a gift beyond words.

We stayed a week, during which I saw another lifer, a Forster's Tern, but it was almost anticlimactic. We drove back to Fayetteville for New Year's Eve, which was Kelly's father's birthday, and helped her mom get through the night. We got back to Virginia late on New Year's Day, and I removed from the trunk the new Christmas tree stand we had bought in North Carolina. On January 2nd, we put up our tree, with its pheasants, partridges, and nameless songbirds, and near the top I hung my tiny silver bird with "P.C. 1964" on it. Christmas had come at last.

Peace on earth. Good will toward men. And owls.

9
. . . And a Bird in Every Pot

Beauty will not come at the call of a legislature . . .
—Ralph Waldo Emerson, "Art"

Some birds have broad appeal, some don't. Rarely, if ever, will you find anyone other than a hardcore birder waxing eloquent about the appeal of the Rough-winged Swallow or the Eared Grebe. They just don't have much of a Q rating.

There are birds that have entered the awareness of the average American. Most people know that it's a sin to kill a mockingbird, that what's good for the goose is good for the gander, that ugly ducklings grow up to be swans, and that the swallows return to Capistrano. Others may recognize that the albatross is a bloody seabird that doesn't come in any bloody flavor, that a swallow reputedly has to beat its wings forty-three times per second in order to maintain air-speed velocity, and that when you're on a highway and a Road Runner goes *beep-beep*, you'd best step aside or you might end up in a heap (especially since the only way a Road Runner will go *beep-beep* is if he's driving a car). Those of a musical bent may well know that there'll be bluebirds over the white cliffs of Dover, that blackbirds are only waiting for this moment to arrive, that all the little birds on Jaybird Street love to hear the Robin go *tweet tweet tweet,* and that Chestnut-brown Canaries and Ruby-throated Sparrows would sing a song, not be long, and thrill you to the marrow—if only they existed, which, whatever Stephen Stills may claim, they do not, at least not without chemical assistance.

Certainly every red-blooded American knows the falcon is swift, the dove peaceful, the eagle powerful.* Many Americans have also heard that Benjamin Franklin favored as our national symbol the striking, wily, and eminently useful Wild Turkey, but I, like the members of Congress who rejected it in favor of the Bald Eagle, have a number of reservations about the idea. There's something disturbing about the symbolism of sitting down every Thanksgiving and tearing into the carcass of our national bird, though I freely admit it would be even worse if we were eating Bald Eagle.

We choose symbols for a reason, after all—to represent qualities we find valuable, or in some cases to link ourselves to those qualities in an almost shamanistic fashion. When those symbols fail to satisfy us, controversy results. In the Washington area alone, for example, the names of two professional sports franchises have caused arguments for years. In the mid-1990s, local NBA fans began a public debate over whether the name "Bullets" was appro-

*How powerful is subject to debate. The Bald Eagle is actually something of a coward, usually preferring to eat dead fish rather than something more likely to put up a fight, but in March 2002 one ambitious eagle in Maine did attempt to fly off with a thirteen-pound dachshund. After carrying the dog three hundred feet through the air, however, the bird reconsidered and dropped its would-be prey. The dog survived the attack.

priate for a city with one of the nation's highest murder rates; eventually Abe Pollin, owner of the team, decided it wasn't. He renamed the club the Wizards, but not before a few people objected that the new name had connections either to Satanism or the Ku Klux Klan. The football team's name, meanwhile, has caused an even greater uproar. The continuing national debate about the use of Native American names has been fiercest around the name "Redskins," considered by many not just an inappropriate name for a team, but a direct ethnic slur. One court even ruled that the team's trademark on the name, because it is a slur, is invalid.

Perhaps the people of Washington are caught up in these controversies because of their proximity to the one occupational group that best recognizes the power of symbols: politicians. Look at our legislators, whose primary job sometimes seem to be selecting official symbols for their states. That these symbols are often bizarre, useless, and occasionally downright offensive is not the issue right now; no, it is simply enough for us to recognize that the Great State of North Carolina, home of my ancestors and cradle of my youth, has officially named a State Mammal (the gray squirrel), a State Seashell (the Scotch bonnet), a State Tree (the loblolly pine), and even a State Rock (granite). There may be states with State Plaids, or State Poisonous Mushrooms, or State Hangover Remedies, but other than songs, there seem to be only two symbols considered significant enough to be chosen by every state in the union: a State Flower and a State Bird.

A look at the list of State Birds reveals a few things of interest about our country. First, legislators sometimes bring a sense of history to their choice of bird: Utah, for instance, chose the seagull in recognition of its bravery in coming down into the middle of a plague of locusts and eating millions of the insects; South Dakota recognizes that the most successful attempts to introduce the Ring-necked Pheasant into the United States were made in the Plains states; and Delaware and Rhode Island both picked breeds of chicken that were developed in their states, the Blue Hen and the Rhode Island Red, respectively. Second, if there is no particular history involved, legislators will often consider the bird's particular habitat and the state's geography: thus California has the California Quail, Hawaii the Nene (aka the Hawaiian Goose), Arizona the Cactus Wren, New Mexico the Road Runner, Minnesota the Common Loon, Louisiana the Brown Pelican, South Carolina the Carolina Wren. Third, if there is no special historical or geographical reason to pick a bird, legislators will demonstrate the political courage that is so commonly associated with their profession and pick a bird that everybody else has picked.

Of the fifty states, only twenty, including the above, have chosen unique State Birds. Several other birds are shared by two or three states: the Black-capped Chickadee, the Goldfinch, the Robin, and the Bluebird (though Missouri and New York took the Eastern Bluebird, while Idaho and Nevada picked the Mountain Bluebird). But then come the real copycats.

The Eastern Meadowlark apparently did not impress anyone enough to make it as a State Bird, but as soon as European settlers had reached the Great Plains, they were obviously ready to put themselves down as backers of the *Western* Meadowlark. Kansas, Nebraska, North Dakota, Wyoming, Montana, and Oregon saw fit to include the western species in their state pantheons. I can see how plains dwellers would want a grassland bird as their symbol, but honestly, couldn't someone have used the Dickcissel, or the Prairie Chicken, or *something* original?

135

THE VERB *TO BIRD*

Meanwhile, certain Deep South legislators apparently appreciated irony in a big way. To represent their individualistic natures, so violently demonstrated between 1861 and 1865, the representatives of the people of Texas, Arkansas, Tennessee, Mississippi, and Florida all copied one another, and did so by selecting the Mockingbird—a bird whose most notable feature is its relentless copying of other birds.* It seems nigh-unbelievable that these five, formerly among the most states-rights-oriented members of the Confederacy (leaving out South Carolina and Virginia), would all express themselves in such—dare I say it?—union.

And then comes the group for which I have to feel the deepest shame: the Cardinal group. According to Peterson, in the South, the Cardinal ". . . vies with the Mockingbird for first place in the affections of garden lovers." It certainly seems to have vied successfully for those of politicians, and not just in the South. No fewer than seven states (and two teams in two professional sports) have tapped the Cardinal as their representative: Illinois, Indiana, Ohio, Kentucky, West Virginia, Virginia, and North Carolina. This is a massive chunk of territory, stretching from the Great Lakes to the Atlantic and encompassing almost all of the Ohio Valley, yet within it there was not a single legislature with the creativity to pick a bird different from its neighbors' bird.

North Carolina and Virginia couldn't even come up with different State Flowers, both ending up with the dogwood. No matter which way you're going when you cross their border, you see a welcoming sign with a Cardinal sit-

*Worse, though the *Encyclopedia of Southern Culture* notes that "the bird has been, indeed, particularly tied to the imagery of the South"—it's the only bird with its own entry in the *Encyclopedia*, at least—it's technically called the *Northern* Mockingbird.

ting on a dogwood branch. Some visitors claim the only way to be sure which state you're entering is to look for a second sign warning you that radar detectors are illegal—that one's Virginia.

Make no mistake—I love my adopted state. I'm happy as a clam here and do not intend to depart for North Carolina or anywhere else. The Old Dominion has a lot of wonderful traits, but it also has had some problems making a name for itself—fitting for a state where both the governor and the senior Senator are currently named Warner. This identity crisis is compounded by the fact that Virginia and West Virginia were one state until 1863. You might think that the split necessitated the creation of a whole new package of state symbols, with the people of each state keeping their favorites, but in fact Virginia didn't adopt a state bird until 1950. I suspect that the General Assembly was acting less out of devotion to the Cardinal than out of a McCarthyist fear of nonconformity with its neighbors, and its choice certainly hasn't helped Virginia achieve greater distinction.

Most of these problems are the fault of Virginians long since retired or dead, but it's not as if today's people are helping to make a unique name for themselves. So I ask you, fellow Virginians, can't we do something to establish ourselves in the public mind? Can't we link our home to something unique, something startling, something distinctive? Can't we, for instance, choose a new State Bird?

Granted, on its own merits, the male Cardinal is a spectacular songbird: brilliant red, with a heavy orange-red bill, a conspicuous crest, and a black face to contrast all of the above, but we have so many cool native species, and so many are as yet unused by a single state. We could associate ourselves forever with the startling swiftness of the Peregrine Falcon or the hardiness of the Northern Raven.

We could claim for ourselves the imposing dignity of the Great Blue Heron or the mystery and wisdom of the Great Horned Owl. Or if we're more practically minded, we could bring in tourist dollars aplenty by following the ways of Madison Avenue; after all, no state yet has taken advantage of the allure and suggestiveness of the Tufted Titmouse.

10
The Cardinal Sin

Don't think: Look!
    –Ludwig Wittgenstein, Philosophical Investigations

There is a lesson to all this, I promise.

I learned this lesson from the Cardinal, a lovely bird that seems to have lost some of its pizzazz, probably because it is so familiar. If they were rare, Cardinals would be pursued by birders the way Whooping Cranes are today, but they are far too well adapted to human intrusion to be endangered by us, and far too bold to hide from us. They are suburbanites, birds of towns and parks and playgrounds and feeders, where eyes are always watching, and they are vivid enough to attract the attention of all but the totally colorblind. As a result, they are seen in great numbers, both in real life and in artistic representation: their images are co-opted for sports teams, Christmas ornaments, corporate symbols, cocktail napkins, greeting cards, you name it. I once flipped through a catalogue from the Coldwater Creek company—it was the "Fall Migration" issue, which alone discouraged me from ordering anything—and noted, in its forty-odd pages of animal-festooned clothing, throw rugs, jewelry, and gifts, more festoonery of the Cardinal than any other songbird. Cardinals are bright and beautiful, yet (east of the Rockies, at least) they are unchallenging and familiar—the kind of combination which invariably makes something an icon of Establishment taste.

This is not necessarily bad, mind you; the tuxedo, the Pastoral Symphony, and the vodka and tonic are all examples of Establishment taste, and the world is a better place for their presence. Of course, we must consider that Establishment taste also banishes to the woodshed much that is great and good about the world. Among other things, old *Swamp Thing* comics, cheap beer, overstuffed burritos, and Robyn Hitchcock songs will never be embraced by the Establishment. But if we embrace the Cardinal, what are we embracing?

The history of the bird offers a good deal of insight into this question. Back in 1917, L. Nelson Nichols, in T. Gilbert Pearson's *Birds of America*, had no doubts about what the Cardinal represented, and how it was linked with the history of the region where it is most plentiful:

> All through the Southern plantation country this is the bird that typifies everything that is elegant and chivalric not only to the colored cotton pickers and plantation laborers, but to the country gentlemen. Novels have been written in which the Virginia Cardinal and the Kentucky Cardinal and the Carolina Cardinal have given a tone of aristocratic elegance to the plots. The bird is indeed a fine specimen of bird character, whether found on a Southern plantation, or at its northeastern limit in Central Park, New York city [sic], or at its western limit in the dingy chaparral of southern Arizona. . . . Some have called him an FFV (member of one of the First Families of Virginia). Better yet, he is an FF of America.

I'm curious, I must admit, about *which* novels use the Cardinals of Virginia, Kentucky, and Carolina to add "a tone of aristocratic elegance"—I didn't notice this in *The Handmaid's Tale, Middle Passage,* or *Cryptonomicon,* among others—not to mention puzzled by exactly how the Cardinal can be seen to be "a fine specimen of bird character." Does he carefully follow the Naval Academy honor system, neither lying, cheating, stealing, nor tolerating those who do? Does he cleave to his mate, forsaking all others, until death do them part? Does he have references? Is he willing to relocate?

Clearly, though, I'm not the only birder to link the Cardinal with deeper sociological ideas. The phrases "elegant and chivalric" and "country gentlemen" (not to mention the nowadays offensive "colored cotton pickers and plantation laborers") could come from any work discussing the mindset of the upper-class Southerner prior to the Civil War. (Indeed, this passage seems to suggest little if any awareness on Nichols's part that the war had already been fought, the cotton pickers freed from slavery, and a good many of the plantations burned.) There is no denying that for over two centuries the South has been at least partly hypnotized by the powerful image of the cavalier, developing an attachment to panache and style equaled only by Rostand's Cyrano, who would have fit right in with a lot of the young men who ended up wearing gray during the Civil War, or, in some cases, let less wealthy men who didn't own slaves wear gray for them instead.

There can be little doubt that a handsome and conspicuous bird like the Cardinal would appeal to such members of the Southern cavalier class. Even its name suggests the widespread sympathy many genteel Southerners felt for the traditional European system of hierarchy and nobility, as well as suggesting a certain lack of fealty to the Puritan

Protestant ideals favored by the settlers of the Northeast; can you imagine William Bradford or Cotton Mather naming a bird after an official of the Vatican? Not unless you can imagine a Catholic naturalist calling a new species the Lutherbird.

The Cardinal's name is a bit puzzling; the word "cardinal" has nothing to do with the color red, or didn't originally, at least. *Cardinalis* comes from the Latin root *cardo,* which means "hinge." Those church officials on whom hinged such vital tasks as selecting the pope became known as cardinals, and their high rank was noted by their bright red vestments. The naming of the bird would thus make sense, but as I thought about it, I still found it curious that a bird of the southern United States, where Catholicism was relatively rare in colonial times, should be named after a high-ranking priest.

Carolus Linnaeus, the Swede who in the mid-1700s formalized the process of assigning scientific names, clearly had some reason for giving the bird the binomen *Loxia cardinalis*; *loxia* comes from the Greek for "slanted" or "crooked," referring to the bird's heavy, triangular bill. (The name *Loxia* is applied today, to my mind much more appropriately, to the Cardinal's cousins the crossbills, the halves of whose bills actually twist out of line like a liar's crossed fingers.) *Cardinalis,* on the other hand, seems as unlikely a choice for the Lutheran Linnaeus as it would for an Anglican colonist.

Why *is* the Cardinal called the Cardinal? This was the question I began to ponder, and the more I read about the history of the bird, the less sense it made; people usually don't name beautiful creatures after officials of other churches, particularly not when their own faiths have had more than a little conflict with that of the officials so honored. The Cardinal's name, I felt sure, was worth investigating.

Investigating the name, however, required a decision on which name to investigate. The current scientific name was evidently chosen by an ornithologist so stupefied by the bird that he was unable to get more than one name out of his mouth: thus the species is known as *Cardinalis cardinalis,* a repetition that will get your spell-checker asking after your intentions every time. But the bird has also gone by a host of *other* scientific names: *Cardinalis virginianus,* or *Richmondena cardinalis,* or *Richmondena cardinalis cardinalis,* or even *Cardinalis cardinalis cardinalis,* depending on which text you examine. The taxonomic ideal of using Latin to permanently establish official names for international scientific discussion has, in the Cardinal's case, gone unachieved; the bird has had almost as many scientific names as vernacular names, and the latter are plentiful. In English, it is technically referred to as the Northern Cardinal, another dagger of irony for a bird so associated with the South, but it has also been referred to in a great many other ways: by family (Cardinal Grosbeak), by anatomy (Crested Redbird), by geography (Virginia Redbird, Virginia Nightingale, Virginia Cardinal, or Kentucky Cardinal), by paradox (Red Blue Jay), and by just plain obvious fact (Redbird, Red-bird, or even Red Bird).

This last was the name given to the bird by Mark Catesby, an English artist and naturalist whose major contribution to ornithology was his 1731 work *The Natural History of Carolina, Florida and the Bahamas.* Catesby died a generation before Audubon was born, making some innovations that Audubon, a more talented painter, would employ himself, especially the practice of posing birds in botanical backgrounds, rather than against a field of white. Catesby also died before Linnaeus's *Systema Naturae* fixed the method of scientifically naming species, so both the English *and* Latin names he gave his birds were often different from those eventually settled on by the scientific establishment. The American Robin was, to him, the "Fieldfare of Carolina," while he graced the Baltimore Oriole with the inexplicable name "Bastard Baltimore," which if nothing else would have considerably livened up the play-by-play announcing for American League games: "Ripken homers, giving the Bastards a two-run cushion."

Catesby referred to the Cardinal, on the painting itself, as "*Coccathraustes ruber:* The red Bird." He obviously found the bird extremely impressive, painting the male sitting alert and upright in the leaves of a hickory, and noting the following concerning its name:

> They are frequently brought from Virginia and other parts of North America for their beauty and agreeable singing, they having some notes not unlike our nightingale, which in England seems to have caused its name of the Virginia-nightingale, though in those countries they call it the red-bird.

Peter Limburg takes issue with the name "Virginia Nightingale" in his *What's-in-a-Names of Birds* (a work whose own nomenclature is not without room for criticism), calling it "odd because the Nightingale is famous for its beautiful melodies and the Cardinal's song is a monotonous 'Cheer! Cheer! Cheer!'" I must dissent, sir! The song of the Cardinal may be many things, but calling it monotonous is not only inaccurate but insulting. To whom? Well, to—um—well, the bird itself, certainly, and to birders, and Southerners, and Stanford grads, and maybe to the Vatican, for that matter. I can't offer a legitimate comparison to the Nightingale, having never heard one, but I can say that the Cardinal's voice is far more varied than Limburg claims: in spring, it's easy to hear the whistles of the bird, rendered variously as *whoit whoit whoit, birdy birdy birdy, hip-ip-ip-ip-ip-ip-ip,* and even "a rich and rounded *cue-cue* that penetrates the grove" (T. Gilbert Pearson).

Indeed, though Catesby claimed that as a rule American birds have poorer voices than their European counterparts, he made two specific exceptions. The first was the Mockingbird, which the *Encyclopedia of Southern Culture* gives him credit for having "discovered," and which Catesby claimed was called by the Native Americans "*Cencontlatolly,* or four hundred tongues." The second American songbird so excepted was "the red bird known as the Virginian Nightingale," whose singing he was admittedly less enthusiastic about than that of the "Mock-Bird of Carolina." John K. Terres describes the male Cardinal's "rich whistled songs" flowing forth "with innumerable variations," though the number of songs is apparently numerable at between twenty-four and twenty-eight, depending on whom you ask. One frequent call sounds to me like a clear and distinct *woojit woojit*. Whatever Limburg says, even my wife appreciates birdsong enough to call the Cardinal by the name of "the Woojit Bird," though she's also under the impression that the "Mock-Bird" is a cheap bird substitute made from lemon juice and Ritz crackers.

This profusion of names for a single songbird suggests a certain amount of mystery even in the most familiar birds. Given the Cardinal's fondness for human beings, and vice-versa, you might expect that its history is known in as much detail as that of the Battle of Gettysburg. Such, to put it mildly, is not the case. In investigating the phenomenon of state bird selection, I had grown curious about the reactions of early Americans to the Redbird, but

I just couldn't seem to find much information about the subject. Thomas Harriot's *Briefe and True Report of the New Found Land of Virginia* was published in 1590, only five years after England's first attempt to colonize Virginia, but though he discussed in great detail the native people, plants, and animals of Roanoke Island (in what is now North Carolina), he said not a word about the Cardinal. Harriot's one-paragraph discussion of American fowl is admittedly skewed toward game birds; he was, after all, trying to recruit colonists, and would therefore have included birds on the basis of abundance and flavor, rather than color or song, as you can see from the list below:

> Turkie cockes and Turkie hennes: Stockdoves: Partridges: Cranes: Hernes: & in winter great store of Swannes & Geese. Of al sortes of foule I have the names in the countrie language of four escore and sixe of which number besides those that be named. . . . There are also Parats, Faulcons, & Marlin haukes. . . .

It's primarily a gastronomic list; Harriot's mention of the Stock Dove, a European species, was probably made in reference to the equally edible and then abundant Passenger Pigeon, or perhaps the Mourning Dove. I have no idea why prospective colonists would be encouraged by the prospect of eating either "Hernes" (a creative spelling of *herons*) or "Marlin haukes" (nowadays *merlin hawks,* the small falcons sometimes called Pigeon Hawks or just Merlins). Whatever the spelling, there is no mention of the Cardinal, unless it is numbered somewhere among the four score and six unnamed birds. I find that remarkable; how could you not notice a flaming red bird with a pointed head? If you did notice it, surely you'd mention it.

It seems astonishing, but I'm inclined to believe that Harriot, overwhelmed with the strangeness of everything in the New World, must have missed the Cardinal.

Catesby, on the other hand, missed very little, but his purpose was science, not advertising. His work dated from a trip made in 1722, well over a century after the British began colonizing North America, and was, frustratingly, the earliest ornithological commentary I could find on the Cardinal. Later writers, such as Thomas Jefferson and the scores of twentieth-century authors I consulted, were largely concerned with the bird's contemporary status and habits. The early history of the Cardinal, and specifically the peculiarity of its name, seemed as yet unwritten. I decided it was time to start at square one.

In American ornithology, square one is occupied by a single work: Audubon's *Birds of America*. It is not possible to overstate the importance of this book to American birding; if Peterson's *Field Guide to the Birds* is the birder's Bible, *Birds of America* is the Ark of the Covenant. John James Audubon's time (1785–1851) neatly overlaps that of the major exploration and conquest of North America's interior, and his art brought to life for his countrymen the myriad creatures of that vast area. Though he worked a century after Catesby, Audubon effectively eclipsed him. The period from 1813 to 1838 was a particularly busy one for him, as he determined not merely to see every American bird (an obsession whose breadth, while stunning to me, is at least within my comprehension) but to *paint* every American bird.

This was not a simple project.

First of all, there were the technological limits of the era to overcome. All you need to know about the transportation system is that the law allowed the stumps of cleared trees to be left in the roadway so long as they were no more than six inches high. There was of course no photographic equipment, meaning Audubon had to paint from life, or, as he preferred, from death—being able to blast a finch out of the sky was, in those days, as necessary to a birder's success as a knowledge of field marks is today. In order to keep those models from decomposing, a birder also needed a working knowledge of taxidermy.

Then there was the difficulty inherent in the act of painting itself, a difficulty compounded by Audubon's determination to make each bird's portrait *actual size;* to contain the larger species, the original work had to be printed in a size known as the Double Elephant folio.

The 435 plates of the first folio of *Birds of America* were 39½ inches by 29½ inches. The book was thus a full meter in height and wider than the rover sent scurrying about the surface of Mars by *Pathfinder.* It should come as no surprise that one volume of the original series weighed in at fifty-six pounds, because we are talking about a book the size of a bath towel—closed. If you opened it, it would be wider than a double bed. Coffee tables must have cowered in terror at the mere mention of Audubon's name.

Finally, there was the not inconsiderable problem of putting enough food on the table to feed himself and his wife, who, being married to a birder, was of course long-suffering, but in her case even more so than most. That Audubon was able to stay married is quite remarkable; that he was able to do so *and* complete his series of paintings is no less than astonishing.

If you doubt this last, imagine yourself as Audubon, going after *one* bird—a fairly common bird, preferably easy to spot and to shoot, like the Great Blue Heron: Unless you live near the heron's waterside habitat, you must travel untold miles over stump-filled roads by horse, buggy, or some combination thereof, grinding your coccyx into a fine powder as you go. On the day after your journeying (you'll doubtless need a good night's sleep to recover), you wake up, grab a quick breakfast, and head out toward the river carrying your handmade shotgun, whose accuracy is questionable but whose odds of exploding in your face are pretty good. You spot a likely looking thicket on the shore and squat there for several hours, peering at birds and taking occasional shots, which usually miss and promptly scare off every winged creature in earshot for some time. Eventually, after squinting patiently down your gun barrel, you put an unhealthy load of birdshot into a GBH, who like as not falls into the water, necessitating a quick swim on your part. You remove the enormous carcass from the river and sling the bird over your shoulder, noting that its wingspan is greater than your height, and you return home, banging your knees against its vertebrae the whole way.

Upon reaching your studio, you have a choice: (a) set up your easel, mix your pigments, and hope there's enough daylight left to work by, since you need to get the basics of this bird down on canvas before it gets much deader and your best artificial light source is a lamp full of whale oil; or (b) stuff the thing properly, *right now*. If you pick (b), you get to remove from the carcass all those nasty slithery bits that tend to start smelling almost immediately, especially since they're still mostly full of half-digested fish. Then you must take additional hours to build a framework that will support the dead heron in a plausibly lifelike posi-tion, keeping in mind all the while that said position must take up a rectangle no larger than 39 inches by 29 inches. We'll ignore the lifetime of study and practice necessary to make the painting a *good* one, noting only that, once you have completed your portrait of *Ardea herodias,* you have 434 species to go.

That is why, when birders are mentioned, the name of Audubon carries such weight. His status is like that of Johann Sebastian Bach; it's not just due to his being famous, or even his being talented, but to his being absolutely relentless. As much as I admire Roger Tory Peterson—a man who saw every species of bird in America, whose life list was in the thousands, who was one of only two men to have logged all seventeen extant species of penguin, and who painted birds enough to fill the field guides of millions of people—I must stand in utter awe of John James Audubon.

And so I turn, as to a Zen master, to my battered copy of *Birds of America,* the 1950 Macmillan edition which contains only 288 of the original's plates and measures roughly six inches by eight, but which, surely, must contain the historical perspective on the Cardinal that I seek. I find the page and turn to it; there, glowing in red, is the bird. And what information, what wisdom, do I find? I record it below, in its entirety:

265. Cardinal
Resident in thickets, tangles and gardens in the southern and south-western states north in smaller numbers through the central states to Ontario. Lacking in New England. Length 6–9 inches.

Imagine opening up a volume of Shelby Foote's classic *The Civil War: A Narrative* to observe his thoughts about Lincoln, and seeing only "He was an unusually tall man. I'm also fairly sure he had a beard." That would be the equivalent experience. Upon reading the above, I felt not so much betrayed as aghast: *This* was all the master had to say about the Cardinal? It wasn't even accurate! Cardinals *are* seen in New England—though not as commonly as they are in the South—and I've certainly never seen an adult under eight inches long. What the heck was this book trying to pass off as ornithology?

I soon realized, however, that the fault was not Audubon's, nor even that of Ludlow Griscom, the writer of the introduction and captions in my so-called "popular edition" of the book; this version was intended as an introduction to Audubon's paintings, not to the birds themselves. Besides, the National Geographic guide asserts that "this species has expanded its range northward during the 20th century," and I can't really fault a forty-five-year-old book for not having up-to-date information on ranges anyway. To track down the true history of the Cardinal, I'd have to look elsewhere.

My next step was tracking down a different copy of *Birds of America*—a much larger copy. The National Audubon Society has reprinted its namesake's masterwork several times over the years, usually in miniature, but some miniatures are more miniature than others. The reduction in this case was to *Baby* Elephant Folio, which approximates the size of an unabridged dictionary, though it has fewer pages. It measures a mere twelve by fifteen inches, but in it are all 435 plates of Audubon's birds, and the greater size, compared to my own book's, was instructive. Colors are clearer, details sharper, and several odd hues which appeared in my tiny version—the alarming blue of the legs and bill in the Baltimore Oriole plate, for instance—are clearly seen to be Audubon's own choices, rather than mistakes in the printing of my copy, and in the larger form they work far better. That the larger edition was edited by Roger Tory Peterson and his wife, Virginia Marie, was also a bonus. That it includes a comment by Audubon on the Cardinal was serendipity itself. That the entire comment in question was

> In richness of plumage, elegance of motion, and strength of song, this species surpasses all its kindred in the United States.

was, however, a bit disappointing. I went back to the search.

This time I made it as far as the Orange County Public Library. There I discovered no sign of Edward Howe Forbush's 1925 masterwork, *Birds of Massachusetts and Other New England States,* another book in which I had placed great hope, but I was able to find a 1939 condensation of the work, titled *A Natural History of American Birds of Eastern and Central North America,* with additional material by John Birchard May, who had assisted Forbush on the original three-volume edition. Again I found myself disappointed. Since the Cardinal is a relatively recent arrival in New England—the extreme northern range given in this text is "the southern Hudson Valley"—Forbush, focusing on New England, said nothing about the bird. May discussed its "loud but melodious whistles" and "unusual brilliancy," but said nothing about its history.

I detoured in my search, passing through E.B. White's "Mr. Forbush's Friends," the essay in which I had learned of Forbush and his contributions to birding. It is a detour worth taking, if only for White's tersely witty accounts of birders like "Mr. Harold Cooke, of Kingston. Found puffin in garage, offered it spaghetti. Spaghetti was accepted. February 1, 1922." Sadly, it does not contain any mention of Cardinals, which presumably had not yet entered the area where Forbush and his friends were concentrating their efforts.

Clearly, it was time to take off the kid gloves. I loaded up the car—well, I put my backpack and a couple of XTC tapes in it—and I headed for the Library of Congress.

It should be understood at the outset that what happened was not my fault. I had planned the outing carefully. Rather than brave the dangers of D.C. traffic, I stopped in Vienna, Virginia, and boarded the Metro; from there I would be whisked to the Capitol South stop, stroll to the LOC, and there plow through stacks of otherwise unobtainable historical documents about the Cardinal. I had done my homework. I knew that the Library of Congress has closed stacks: You must first decide what book you want from its description in the catalogue; then you must ask a staff member to find the book for you; then you must read it in the reading room. Nothing leaves the library, and no one gets to wander through the stacks misfiling critically important books. In terms of security, it's a reasonable system.

It's also a deeply frustrating one. I myself tend to treat books with a reverence most people find extreme. I reread them—the good ones, at least—and do my best to keep them in good shape. For one thing, I don't write in them. Even if I'm reading a novel with one of my classes, I almost never take notes in it; I'll jot them down on post-it notes and slip them into the book, but I can't bring myself to actually write on the pages. (Highlighting textbooks, on the other hand, I find acceptable.) I never fold back one side of a paperback, or even a comic book. And I can't bear to throw books away, even when they're worn, coverless, or stained with the bodily humors of small children. To casually damage or discard a book, or worst of all, to deliberately burn one, is to me an act of utter barbarism.

And there I was, in the grandest library on earth, my nation's central temple to knowledge, the Vatican of the printed word, and *I couldn't get to the books.* I had to spend an hour hunting through the computerized catalogue, getting call numbers and brief, incomplete descriptions, and then was permitted to fill out requests for no more than five items, which would be brought to the holding area in an hour's time. I sat, waiting, wondering what would come, and when, and if it would be what I had hoped for.

My wife compared the experience to that of Martin Luther, and I'm not sure she was completely off the mark; certainly I felt as though the direct connection between me and the Word was stretched, bent, and clogged, if not completely severed, by the complex bureaucratic process that lay between us. The chance to wander through stacks, skimming through old books for potentially useful ideas, skipping swiftly from idea to idea like a dragonfly from leaf to leaf—all this was gone. Instead I sat in a marvelous rotunda, staring at stained glass and wondering whether salvation would be granted me.

As it turned out, I was right to wonder. I gave six requests to the LOC staff that day, but only four of the books which arrived were the ones I'd actually asked for. If I'd made the mistakes myself, I could have said "Oops!" and put the books back on the shelves, but with the closed-stack system, I'd lost an hour waiting and would have to lose another hour while the correct book was found and brought to me.

While I waited, I strolled out of the Jefferson Building and looked at the massive LOC complex; the Jefferson, the main building, is the most impressive, but the Adams and Madison buildings, which stand on two sides of it, are also nice. The bronze doors of the Adams Building are cast with the images of the various gods of knowledge on them: the Norse Odin, the Celtic Oghma, the Egyptian (and ibis-headed) Thoth, and others from the pantheons of the world guard the entranceway.

Of birds themselves, however, there was little sign. Our nation's capital is, like most major cities, sadly lacking in bird life, and what little there is comes almost exclusively from other lands. In most cities, this wouldn't be so annoying, but here, on the lawn of our nation's treasury of books, in the very shadow of the Capitol dome, I found it downright offensive that the only birds visible were European imports: the ubiquitous European Starling and House Sparrow. (Though I didn't see any, there was probably a pigeon or two around, but even they are descendants of escaped Rock Doves, also of Old World origin.)

Upon my return to the Adams Building, I had new reason to feel annoyed and offended. Two of the books I'd requested turned out to be the same book, one a facsimile of a colonial work, the other a modern "translation" of part of it, a fact which had not been made clear in the catalogue. That gave me a grand total of three useful books out of the six I'd requested. Recognizing the way things were going, I moved to the reading room swiftly and hoped to plow through the three books before anything else went wrong. As it happened, something already had: I had left all my pens in the Jefferson Building. Gritting my teeth, I scoured the Adams reading room and discovered a stubby, eraserless golf pencil. I was eventually able to bring it to something resembling a point, but after half a page of notes on Linnaean nomenclature that looked like a scorecard from the PGA Dadaist Open, I gave up and went to the photocopiers. Typically, the one I used was malfunctioning, or so it seemed; actually it was just stuck on two-side copying and wouldn't give me my copy until I paid for the other side to be done, but it was yet another reason to feel like the system was out of control and I was trapped in it.

Breathing harder now, I went back across the street to the Jefferson Building, where I discovered that it was now past 3:30, and no more requests for books could be made. I had already handed in all the books I'd gotten from the Adams Building stacks, and I couldn't get any more here. The day's efforts had resulted in exactly twelve photocopies. What now?

Luckily, I had brought a book of my own: Jane Mendelsohn's splendid *I Was Amelia Earhart.* And the Metro trip back to Vienna was almost the perfect length for reading it.

Now I was thoroughly frustrated. I had hauled myself and my notes all over north and central Virginia and had nothing to show for it but a pencil stub and an attitude problem. All I could be sure of was that Catesby had called what he saw "Red Bird" in 1731, and that Audubon had called the same bird "Cardinal" in 1838. I could infer that the first person to use the name *cardinalis* was Linnaeus, in 1758, but where was the proof? Couldn't anyone tell me about the Cardinal?

Well, yes, as it happens; the Coldwater Creek catalog (Fall Migration, 1996 issue) was happy to give me some valuable ornithological data:

> One of the truly welcome sights of winter is the warm red plummage [*sic*] of a Northern Cardinal highlighted against

the snow. Only the male Cardinal is that unmistakable bright crimson. But both male and female have beautiful voices and raise them often in rich and varied song. Brighten someone's day with this toasty, long-sleeved 100% preshrunk cotton tee with a trio of Cardinals screenprinted on the front.

Now, I knew, I could rest.

Did I tell you there was a lesson to this story? I could have sworn I did. Anyway, here's how I learned it.

I was back in the Orange Public Library one afternoon, punching keys on the computer catalogue and getting diddly-squat for my trouble. I tried subject searches on *taxonomy* and *Cardinals;* author searches on great taxonomists like Catesby, Linnaeus, and Louis Agassiz were equally fruitless. There was nothing in the library by or about Roanoke naturalist John White, no biographies of Linnaeus, or even Peterson; I was stuck.

In frustration, I went to the reference shelf, the first and often the only stop for ninth-graders with research assignments. (Actually, I'm dating myself; nowadays they go to the computer, run a web search for "bird," get 165,000 hits, stall in bewilderment, and give up, complaining that there isn't any information out there.) There were certainly encyclopedias with information on birds, but large reference books tend to have a general approach; they don't have room for the minutiae about each species, let alone the minutiae about the *name* of each species. I poked and prodded along the shelf, flipping open huge, heavy books and hoping, praying, for some bolt from the blue, something about the Cardinal's name that would supply the answer for which I'd fought rush hour traffic and the vagaries of the Metro system; for which I'd beaten my skull against the thick, cottony, but impenetrable bureaucracy of the Library of Congress; for which I'd suffered the indignity of being denied the chance to look for my own books. I had been hunting for months, and I was tired of the chase.

And that, in a nutshell, was the problem: I had been hunting. I should have been birding.

Birding involves being open to the moment; you cannot plan on seeing what you want to see. It's okay to look for a particular bird that you don't see, certainly, but the essence of birding is to look attentively at the bird that you *do* see.

At the Library of Congress, I had been hunting, pursuing a particular idea, and I couldn't catch it; because of the closed stacks, I couldn't even be sure of what I was pursuing. In the Orange Public Library, however, I could bird. I could stop looking for my invisible quarry and see what was actually there.

What was actually there? A book, sitting about two shelves up and to the left of the nature encyclopedias. What were its field marks? A red and white spine that read *A DICTIONARY OF AMERICANISMS On Historical Principles.* In other words, it was a book about the contributions to the English language made by Americans. Like names for things invented and discovered in America. Like New World birds.

I had been hunting for information about the Cardinal in order to learn about its name; I should have been looking at names in order to see that of the Cardinal.

With that insight, I opened the book and found an entry for *Cardinal.* As I read it, I realized just how much hunting I'd been doing, and how little birding. The reason for the Cardinal's name suddenly became as easy to see as the bird itself.

What I knew when I began my hunt was true enough. It is certainly the case that the early settlers of the southern United States were largely English, that Catesby was an Englishman, and that Linnaeus was a Swede; it is equally true that none of these people would be especially likely to name a bird "Cardinal." Given that initial knowledge, I had pursued their writings in hopes of finding out why they had done something so unlikely; I had been thinking, not looking; hunting, not birding. If I'd been birding, I would have seen what was there: the obvious fact that these people *didn't* name a bird "Cardinal."

The entry under *Cardinal* contained three particularly interesting items. One was a quotation from Benjamin Franklin, who in 1786 commented, "It is rare that we see the Cardinal Bird so far north as Pennsylvania." This told me that, of our Founding Fathers, Franklin at least knew of the bird's canonical name. Thomas Jefferson, on the other hand, in his 1787 *Notes on the State of Virginia,* referred to it as both "Red bird" and "Virginia nightingale," though he did include Catesby's and Linnaeus' scientific designations for the sake of completeness.

The second item of interest was a fragmentary note from *Willughby's Ornithology,* a 1678 work authored by "Ray," which read: "The Virginian Nightingale . . . Mercurialis affirms, that by the Portugues it is commonly called, The Cardinal bird, because it is of a scarlet [purpurei] colour, and seems to wear on its Head a red hat." This put a new twist on things. It made perfect sense for the people of a Catholic nation to call a bird "Cardinal," but where in the world would the Portuguese be seeing it?

This was answered by the third item, a translation from the journal of one Henri Joutel, who wrote: "There is a sort of Bird, all red, which for that Reason is call'd the Cardinal." The translation was published in London in 1714, but the journal was apparently written in 1687; its full title is *A Journal of the Last Voyage Perform'd by Monsr. de La Sale, to the Gulph of Mexico.*

And suddenly, at the sight of the name we now spell La Salle, I knew who had named the Cardinal: the explorers from France, Spain, Italy, and Portugal who had been tramping all over the American wilderness since before Thomas Harriot ever got a good look at Roanoke Island. La Salle, de Soto, Cartier, Ponce de Leon, Vespucci, Verrazano, and their crewmen may not have been colonists, but all were from Catholic kingdoms. (Even English explorer John Cabot had been born Giovanni Caboto in Italy.) For these men, the similarity between *Cardinalis cardinalis* and the College of Cardinals would be immediately apparent. I had been hunting again: looking in the colonists' writings because colonies came before states. I had neglected to consider where colonies come from: from prospects detailed by scouts and sailors, and occasional outright liars like Erik the Red, who gave Greenland its name in hopes of generating colonists. By the time Mark Catesby painted his "Red bird," the ports of the European continent and the West Indies were probably already familiar with the tales of the brilliant bird the sailors called "Cardinal." From there to the desk of Carolus Linnaeus was just a short flight.

I had been guilty of the sins of pride and prejudice: I had foolishly believed that the bird's name could be given only by someone like me, a birder, or someone who lived in the Cardinal's home territory. By opening myself up to chance, by abandoning my preconceptions, by ignoring the hoped-for in favor of the seen, I had learned much more than the origin of a single name. I had learned that the nature of birding is far more universal, far closer to the path of wisdom, than I had ever dreamed.

So, now you have your lesson.

Chinese Zen master Huang Po said, "The foolish reject what they see, not what they think; the wise reject what they think, not what they see." He saw what Wittgenstein saw, and what I saw now in the Orange Public Library:

Don't hunt: Bird!

Part Three

Birded

11
Too Much Nature

The New York Dawn has
four columns of slime
and a hurricane of black doves
that paddle in putrescent waters.
  —*Federico Garcia Lorca, "The Dawn"*

I never had any trouble understanding either Garcia Lorca's feelings or those of Eddie Albert's character in *Green Acres*, perhaps because I've dragged my own wife from her home in a city of several hundred thousand to an area so rural that a large chunk of it is still known as the Wilderness; the only reason I wasn't singing "Keep Manhattan, just give me that countryside" in the moving van was that we were moving from Fayetteville. Nevertheless, one of the most productive birding sessions I've ever had was in a part of the world many birders would consider utterly beyond the pale: Long Island. Because of its natives' complicity in the release of the House Sparrow, European Starling, and House Finch, I long bore a suspicion that these were in fact the only birds within the Empire State.

165

Many a friend from Upstate pointed out that New York City is a fairly small part of the state, and that there was plenty of territory for birds to inhabit, but I couldn't bring myself around. Even seeing reports of Peregrine Falcons sailing about the towers of Rochester couldn't make me think of New York as a mecca for birds.

I can now testify, however, to those wildlife viewers not from the immediate area, that Long Island attracts a pretty fair variety of waterfowl, and I never even visited any of its numerous wildlife preserves. How did I discover this life-altering fact? By driving north early one March and visiting my wife's old college roommate, Elaine, in Huntington.

Elaine is brilliant, savvy, and musically gifted, and though she's not a birder, she does have a pretty strong affinity for the outdoors. I used to consider this last unusual for someone raised in Queens, but I wasn't alone. Back in our college days, in fact, several of her visiting Long Island chums were apparently amazed that any sane New Yorker would go away to school in a little place like Chapel Hill, where the tallest building wasn't even fifteen stories high and there wasn't a single Indonesian restaurant. I figured they were just generally upset by the large amount of Nature in the area. This may have been due to our plan for offering them recreation, which was perhaps a little misguided, but well intended: we took them on a canoe trip.

We wanted to offer our scenery-deprived guests a chance to sample a little of what passes for the great outdoors around Chapel Hill. My hometown is not exactly the boondocks; we are talking about the home of a major university, after all, and professors want indoor plumbing as well as tenure. The town isn't the Big Apple, though— even with all twenty-thousand-plus students, it's well shy of having one percent of NYC's population—and it has a number of rural areas within easy reach. One of these is the watershed around University Lake, the main water supply for the town, which has been kept relatively free from development. Since I'm comfortable in a canoe, at least on still waters, I took the job of giving Elaine's friends a little paddle around University Lake while Kelly and Elaine stayed at the dock. To a large degree, it was a good plan. The lakeside scenery was pleasant, but some of it had unexpected effects on my passengers, whom we'll call Hildegard, Bronwyn, and Siegfried.

Canoes are light, portable, and safe, but they're not very stable. In canoes, sudden moves are frowned upon. Nonetheless, about five minutes into our trip, Hildegard set up some pretty serious vibrations when she saw something moving in the water. It wasn't just any thing moving in the water, admittedly; it was a snake. But since I had pointed it out to her in the first place, I didn't think she had much reason to start jumping around.

"Hey, y'all," I said cheerily, gesturing with my paddle toward an S-shaped ripple some twenty feet off the port gunwale. "There's a snake over there."

"WHERE?" said Hildegard, pivoting a full ninety degrees in the bottom of the canoe and just about pitching me into the drink.

"Right there," I said, regaining my balance.

"Don't go near it!" cried Bronwyn.

"It's just a water snake," I replied. "They're not poisonous."

"Don't go near it!" she repeated.

"How do you KNOW it's not poisonous?" said Hildegard.

I blinked. It had never occurred to me that there might be any question of which snakes were and weren't poisonous. North Carolina has four types of poisonous snakes: rattlesnakes, copperheads, cottonmouths, and coral snakes. This was a water snake. Of course it wasn't poisonous. To me, this was like looking at a Buick and saying "How do you KNOW it's not edible?"

"Don't worry, y'all, he won't bother us if we don't bother him," I lied, hoping to restore calm. Water snakes are certainly not venomous, but they are among the most hostile snakes I know. They will bite if they can, and not just in self-defense. (Some years later, while paddling with friends down Little Rockfish Creek near Fayetteville, I watched a water snake drop from a tree hanging over the watercourse straight into the canoe in front of mine, sending both occupants over the sides in a flash.) I saw no particular reason to get any closer to this snake, and the idea of keeping a solid aluminum canoe hull between us and him seemed a good one to me. Unfortunately, the girls were wriggling fiercely in the bottom of the canoe, which was making it much more likely that we'd get an up-close-and-personal encounter with the snake, in its chosen habitat, even. The less panicked the girls felt, I reasoned, the less likely we were to capsize and get ourselves fanged, but I suddenly thought of another reason for me to panic: *What, exactly, are the odds of city-dwellers knowing how to swim?* I was spared the chance to use my lifesaving training, however, when the snake swam off toward the shore and allowed me to reestablish our equilibrium and paddle onward.

As we cut smoothly over the deep green water, I pointed out a few of the beauties of the area: the cypresses stretching out of the shallows near the lake's southeastern end, the Wood Duck houses nailed to some of their trunks, the cattails rasping against each other in the spring breeze, the surrounding forest glowing green in the sun. I noticed that one pine tree's bark had been largely stripped away near its base.

"Hmm," I mused aloud. "Looks like a porcupine's been over there."

"Where?" said Siegfried.

I pointed to the stand of trees along the shore. The pale wood of the stricken tree stood in sharp contrast to the shady mat of pine straw and the gray-brown trunks. "Might be a beaver, but I don't think they'd be living in a man-made lake. . . . Probably a porcupine."

My passengers swiveled their heads around and continued to look blank.

"They gnaw on the bark. Rodents have to gnaw on stuff to keep their incisors from growing too long. Plus they can eat any grubs or insects they find under the bark."

Three heads turned to look at me, and their bewildered expressions asked: *Are you Daniel Fuckin' Boone, or what?*

I wanted to protest. I'm from *town*, dammit! I complain when I can't get coffee in the morning, and I've camped only a few dozen times in my life. I can't make a fire by rubbing two sticks together or capture a rabbit by making a snare out of a sapling. I was never a Boy Scout and I am *not* prepared!

But to someone who grew up in Queens, I reasoned, my knowledge of animals other than pigeons might seem vast.

Largely as a result of this experience, I had formed a prejudice of my own: *Nature ends at the New York border.* Imagine my surprise, then, some years later, when Elaine invited us to visit her in Huntington, and it turned out to be not only the birthplace of Walt Whitman, but also a nice little town. It sits roughly halfway out the length of Long Island, nestled in hills and dotted with small shops. I had expected an endless series of apartments, punctuated by the occasional deli, but I found a near-Chapel-Hillian profusion of coffeehouses and used-book stores; trees were plentiful and healthy, though snow was still on the ground and no leaves were visible on the branches.

Elaine spent the week of our visit guiding Kelly, the boys, and me in and out of the city by rail, helping us experience the wonder that is the Museum of Natural History, and babysitting so Kel and I could go out for coffee one night; in short, she was the perfect hostess. Moreover, knowing how I get the urban heebie-jeebies after a while, on Saturday, she took the family on a trip to the New York State Fish Hatchery in Cold Spring Harbor.

All I knew of the place was that *Cold Spring Harbor* was the title of Billy Joel's not-so-successful first album, the one where the record execs sped up the tape slightly because they felt his voice was too deep to have any commercial potential. That it was a town was a surprise to me; heck, that it was a harbor was a surprise to me. The harbor itself sits directly across the road from the hatchery, giving visitors a broad view of the water, though I didn't spend much time looking that day because of the cold and drizzly weather. There was also something odd about the lay of the land behind the hatchery, but until the rain let up, I was content to head into the hatchery's main building. Inside the buildings were terrariums full of salamanders and frogs, and the kids were in hog heaven for a solid hour. Once the weather turned, we went back out to examine the pools full of trout and let the kids pay twenty-five cents a pop for handfuls of food pellets to throw in. In a different pool was a huge mass of greenish algae and goo, which turned out to be the outer covering of a seventy-five pound snapping turtle; needless to say, no other animal life lived in that one. All in all, Elaine had done a far better job of finding suitable entertainment for us than we had for Hildegard, Bronwyn, and Siegfried.

After leaving the hatchery's interior, I realized what was odd about its grounds: the hillside behind it was in fact an earthen dam. I obviously sensed something, for it wasn't long before I went into full Birding Compulsion Disorder mode, ignoring my family and friend and jogging up to the dam. A stairway climbed along it, and mounting it, I gazed out onto a man-made lake strewn about with waterfowl. One duck was fairly close by, a gray bird with a patch of green on its head and a shining white forehead. I had never seen one like it before.

This, I knew, was trouble.

Because I don't hunt, and am therefore not often in places where ducks and geese abound, I knew that I would have a good shot at spotting some lifers here—ducks and geese were darned sure abounding on this lake. I also knew that, with my wife, kids, and hostess waiting for me in the car, I'd be lucky to have three minutes to look at anything out there. Finally, I knew that, without my binoculars, I'd be lucky to identify anything out there other than the Mallards. There were some large ducks near the far shore, and their sloping profiles looked a lot like that of the Canvasback, a long-sought lifer, but rather than peering intently into the cold March wind, I did something I almost never do in the presence of birds.

I turned away.

I did what even grownups have trouble doing: I delayed gratification. I ran back to the car, leaped in, and headed back to Huntington. Upon reaching Elaine's, I dug out my Peterson and checked my white-pated duck. Sure enough, it was a lifer, my first American Wigeon (aka the Baldpate). Now I knew what I had to do: get back to that hatchery. The place was a veritable smorgasbord of new waterfowl species. Triumphantly, I informed Kelly and Elaine that I was getting up early on Sunday to drive back with my equipment.

Had I been expecting cries of rejoicing, I would have been disappointed.

Sunday morning dawned, and I layered myself in wool and nylon, since a stiff March breeze was blowing off Long Island Sound. Having gloves on is always a bit awkward when I'm birding, but I felt they were necessary that day, with a wind-chill factor of what must have been some hideously negative number. Rarely have my choices in cold-weather gear been rewarded as they were that morning. The sky was crystalline blue and the sunlight bright, but the cold penetrated deeply into my body. All in all, what little nature there was on Long Island was doing a marvelous job of reminding me of its presence, and I hadn't even gotten to my car yet.

I drove back to the hatchery and parked, discovering as I did so that its parking lot was shared with a small church up the hill; the stairs that climbed the dam did so largely to allow churchgoers to reach the doors from the lot. I felt little guilt about taking a parking space—I was, after all, performing my own variety of religious ritual—but it took me a good while to find one, and I was getting impatient to see what avian bounty lay before me on the waters. I'd been patient long enough, and was reaching the *gimme gimme gimme* stage.

I clambered out of the car, up the stairs, onto the shore, and into the full blast of the wind; I would swear it was coming from across the lake *and* from across the har-

"*I clambered out of the car, up the stairs, onto the shore, and into the full blast of the wind.*"

bor, and possibly a couple of other directions as well, as Gogol insisted the winds in Saint Petersburg often did. Nonetheless, I didn't flinch, but raised my field glasses to my eyes and gazed out upon a flotilla of birds.

The angle of the sun was still very shallow, so the play of light and shadow on the water was exaggerated; birds drifted in silhouette against patches of brilliant ice-white light, and in other places glowed with color in the shadow of trees along the shore. Seagulls had set up a raucous feeding frenzy off to my right, where a small shelf of ice still clung to the surface of the lake. Some gulls and a few ducks stood stupidly on the ice, as if expecting to be able to swim on it; their eyes radiated a dull disappointment even at this distance.

There were scores of Mallards, which I ordinarily might have failed to notice, but this particular group was unusual; whether due to the oblique angle of the winter sun, or to the plumage itself, the males had particularly glossy heads, and the reflections were much less green and much more purple than I had ever seen before. Was this a race of violet-headed ducks? I had no way of knowing, nor did I ponder the question long. There was too much else to see on the water—Coots, for instance, clucking noisily in the shallows near me. I was after more exotic prey, however, and I peered into the distance; in silhouette I saw the sloped foreheads of what I'd thought might be Canvasbacks, and I began what seemed like one of the longest vigils of my life: waiting for the ducks to move out of the glare and into the shadows so I could spot a field mark or two. The frigid wind didn't help time pass any more quickly, but at last a pair of the birds sailed into dark water and turned from flat black shapes into three-dimensional multicolored figures. Sure enough, they were Canvasbacks.

For a bird I'd never seen up until that moment, I had long held some strong ideas about the Canvasback. I knew them well from paintings, of course, not just those of Audubon and Peterson, but from the countless paintings of game birds that dress up the walls of hotels and offices. Look at the walls and observe the species—it's probably a duck. If it's not a duck, it'll be a quail—the faculty lounge at my school is rife with quail paintings. Apparently the Establishment pays no attention to birds unless they're seen at the end of a shotgun.

I noticed something about Canvasbacks that I'd never noticed in the paintings, though: their faces appear almost doglike. Maybe it's the coloration, their bills wet, black, and leathery, and their heads rufous-brown, or maybe it's the expectant expression they have—they seem to be waiting for you to throw them something, or shoot something for them to retrieve. You almost expect them to have chew-toys in their mouths. It's not a goofy dogginess—they don't slobber and caper, certainly—but it's somewhat un-ducklike, in any case.

Most ducks have a serenity when they swim, and the Canvasbacks were no exception, but there was something moving strangely out on the water. Eventually I spotted a small, brown swimmer with a very narrow bill and a ragged crest paddling about jerkily right at the edge of my vision. The outline suggested a merganser, a relative of the ducks and geese distinguished by a spikelike, saw-edged bill; the dusky brown color suggested a female. There was only one species of American merganser that I'd ever seen, and I found myself hoping fervently that this was another one. A quick flip to pages 62 and 63 of my Peterson guide confirmed that this was, in fact, another lifer: a female Hooded Merganser. I eventually decided that it was swimming so strangely because the water was so cold, and it couldn't quite make up its mind whether to continue swimming or try flying, which would expose its wet belly to the blast of the Arctic wind. It wasn't a choice I would have liked making, either.

I stood on the shore of the lake for an indeterminate length of time, and I moved only because my eyeballs were beginning to freeze solid in the wind. Moving off the dam, I was at least somewhat protected from the worst gusts, and a few minutes of walking back down to my car served to reestablish the circulation to my extremities. I was about to climb into the driver's seat when I looked across the highway at Cold Spring Harbor. It was right there, only a few yards away. There were bound to be birds on and around it. The wife and kids were still asleep at Elaine's. What could a quick look hurt?

Traffic was light at this hour, still well before brunch, so I was in no real danger as I crossed two lanes of blacktop and strode down the far side of the road. There was a bit of marshland, I now could see, between the road and the harbor itself, but I didn't have much time to examine it, because I immediately startled a pair of ducks out of the marsh. They rose to eye level swiftly, but ducked back down behind the reeds in only a few instants. At once, I dropped to my knees and thanked the heavens for my gloves.

That may sound odd, but there was a reason. Gloves make turning pages in one's field guide very difficult. As a result, I had been struggling with the book up on the dam, unable to move from one page of ducks to another with much swiftness, and had been forced to spend more time gazing at the wrong pages than I'd have liked. In this case, however, what I'd been forced to look at had been the painting and description of the Gadwall, a gray duck with no noteworthy field marks except its speculum. "Speculum," from the Latin for "mirror," is the name for the iridescent patch on the trailing edge of a duck's wing; in Mallards, for example, this patch is bright metallic blue. In Gadwalls, Peterson noted, it is pure white.

About the only thing I had been able to observe about the escaping ducks were their white speculums. They were Gadwalls. Thanks to my gloves, I had another lifer.

I eventually wound up on a public dock over the waters of Cold Spring Harbor itself, absorbing the full brunt of the north wind for a good twenty minutes as I gazed out into the bright sunshine. I made one more addition to my life list when a pair of Red-breasted Mergansers swept by, but the bay was covered with birds. I noted a half-dozen Mute Swans, a large contingent of Double-crested Cormorants, some Canada Geese, some Mallards, a mob of Ring-billed Gulls, and no fewer than eight Great Blue Herons, all of which were trying hard not to look cold, but none of which were succeeding. I sympathized. I had logged a full morning's worth of birds—four lifers, plus the Wigeon the day before—and I was chilled to the bone. If nothing else, I could now say with complete confidence that Cold Spring Harbor, unlike so many other places, was both vividly and accurately named.

No, I could say something else, too: that contrary to popular belief (popular at least in the South) the state line of New York is not the borderline between Nature and the Void. If anything there was too much nature on Long Island for me to handle, at least as long as part of that nature was a stiff March wind. I had now seen that the small towns of Long Island were much like the more familiar small towns of the South, both in terms of their bird life and in terms of the hospitality you might be shown by the natives; not a soul had complained about my wandering around their churchyard, their parking lot, or their dock, and I'd gotten a good look at birds both unfamiliar and beautiful.

I'd also have to say that I'm still tempted—powerfully at times—to turn a water snake loose in Yankee Stadium; at least now I can't say I'm proud of myself.

12
The Mother of All Geese

The devil damn thee black, thou cream-faced loon.
Where got'st thou that goose look?
     –William Shakespeare, Macbeth, V, iii

I'm a longtime fan of Shakespeare's work, and that may be why I have something of a love-hate relationship with waterfowl, most notably with Canada Geese. Despite their name, Canadas are no strangers here in central Virginia; they sometimes appear in flocks whose size boggles the mind. Indeed, my mind was once boggled by the size of an individual goose. I was driving to work in the first rays of the morning and chanced to look up into the heavens, and in doing so I saw a Canada goose that was approximately twenty-five feet long.

For once, the old cliché about nearly putting the car into the ditch was quite literally true, because I was unable to drive in the throes of my sudden fear that this immense goose would descend upon my car and crush it. The sensible little voice in my head was saying *There's got to be a logical explanation for this–are you sure of the scale?* even as a much less sensible and much louder voice in my head was shrieking *BIG GIANT BIRD! AIEEEEEEEEE!*

Before my car sought the safety of the low ground beside the road, however, I noticed that this enormous waterfowl was equipped with tires, a feature I didn't recall Darwin mentioning as a successful reproductive strategy, and that its wings were suspiciously fixed in position. The sensible little voice seized on these facts: *Aha! Manmade! Toldja toldja toldja!* (The other voice was temporarily silenced, probably to catch its breath, which it hadn't stopped screaming to take for some time now.) I kept driving, taking frequent glances upwards, and finally achieved calmness and recognition at the same time: despite the fact that it seemed to bear the elongated black neck, black bill, and white chinstrap marking of a Canada Goose, this thing was an ultralight airplane.

Upon arriving on campus, I discovered that this cruel hoax had a purpose: the ultralight was doctored up to look like a gigantic *Branta canadensis* in order to lead a flock of real birds. It had come down from Canada, as one might expect, along with several dozen geese who had never before made the migration south; they wouldn't follow a plane, but they were more than willing to follow a twenty-five foot internal-combustion-powered "goose." The ultralight I had seen was actually one of three flown by Operation Migration, a Canadian-American research project that is attempting to develop methods of teaching migration to captivity-raised endangered birds newly released into the wild. The group chose Canada Geese as the initial research subjects so that the teaching techniques could be fully tested on a well-established bird before they're attempted on a rare bird like the California Condor. Passing over our campus and noting its fields and ponds, pilot Bill Lishman had landed the evening before, along with his caravan, and obtained permission to spend the night in Woodberry's relative safety and privacy. When I saw him, he was making his initial takeoff in preparation to lead the flock further south; I imagined them as a squadron of happy wanderers, cheerfully winging their way toward warm weather and honking "Valdereeeeee, valderaaaaaaa" at the top of their lungs, right up until the point when their giant leader threatens to pull the car over *right this minute* unless they shut up.

Luckily for Tom Parker and me, the pond off Woodberry Forest School's fairway number two is far too small to handle a goose of that size, but our first moments of birding together did involve geese and took place at the top of the hill overlooking that pond. We weren't doing much looking at first, though; instead, we stood several hundred yards away and listened to an astonishing and seemingly endless stream of honks. It was not, however, the *basso mega-profundo* that a gargantuan goose would produce, and as we paused near the top of the hill and looked down, we could see that whatever birds were there were of ordinary size. In fact, the two birds floating toward the right-hand side of the pond looked a little hunched-up for Canadas, who enjoy extending their towering necks the way pianists enjoy wiggling their fingers.

"I don't know," I said. "Sure sounds like Canadas."

"Let's get a little closer," suggested Tom.

Whatever they were, I could see that at least one was black and white, and as we got to the 150-yard marker (for the golf course, not the pond), I made a tentative identification.

"Hooded Merganser?" I said, peering through my binocs. The head and back of the bird were both black, but the chest was white, and there was a large patch of white at the back of its head. "I suppose it might be a Bufflehead . . ."

"No," said Tom instantly. "Buffleheads are *really* small ducks." I didn't know much about Tom's birding expertise at the time, but I did realize that a man whose home is filled with tiny models of waterfowl might know from Buffleheads.

We continued to tramp over the wet grass, occasionally raising our binocs, until all was revealed to us: on the left of the pond, in the shadow of a scrubby cedar tree, were four full-grown Canada Geese, two of whom were honking like Dexedrine-crazed cabbies; on the right, hugging the opposite shore in fear or embarrassment, sat two Hooded Mergansers, a male and a female. The male Hoodie has a black head and bill, but also bears an erectile crest that, when raised, gives him the profile of a Trojan warrior. The crest's white feathers, tipped with black, make it visible even when lowered, but it's downright alarming when fully fanned out. The female, typically, was drably following behind her mate, waiting for him to make the first move toward panicking. Eventually, he made his move and the pair flew off toward the Rapidan, giving Tom and me a good look at their field marks in the process. The Canadas just sat and honked, as unimpressed with us as we were with them.

Given this checkered history with geese, you might wonder why I was ever eager to see a Snow Goose. Perhaps it's the same yearning for a Romantic image of freedom that led the young Sigurd Olson, who later served as president of the National Parks Association, to wish for the chance to shoot one down; I'd like to think I'm well-adjusted enough that I don't need to kill, stuff, and mount a wild thing to feel connected to it, but the desire to see it may not be all that far removed from the carnivore's natural desire to catch and eat it. The image of geese presented in T.H. White's masterful *The Once and Future King* is one of unlimited freedom, wild wandering, and simplicity, and when the young Wart is transformed into a goose by Merlin, the desire to join the flock, take to the skies, and escape the complications and demands of human relations is one that tugs mightily at him (and the reader), even if the geese under discussion are White-fronted Geese (*Anser albifrons*) instead of Snow Geese (*Chen caerulescens*). I could therefore imagine no sight more perfect than, on a day of wind and rain, the sight of wildness incarnate, white-feathered and whirring away on its great migration. A skein of long-necked birds high overhead, their black wings standing out against their pure white breasts, honks trumpeting out bravely against the weather . . . this would be a sight worth seeing.

At least, I *think* it would be a sight worth seeing, but it's unfortunately not anything like my first look at a Snow Goose. That look came from the passenger seat of Tom's car as it pulled around from Raymond Pool to Shearness Pool at Delaware's Bombay Hook National Wildlife Refuge. The wind and rain were both present, but that was about it for the scene I had imagined. For one thing, there was just the one bird, not an entire flock. For another, it wasn't flying. It was barely moving. It was in plain sight beside the dirt road, standing all of six feet away from the car, and it was no more impressed with us than the Canadas on the number two hazard had been. Its pink legs and beak seemed a bit off-color, maybe a little muddy, and its white plumage seemed merely pale, leached of color rather than actively white. As I looked more closely at its bill, I thought the blackish "lips" that outline the bird's mouth made it look as if it were faintly sneering at us. All in all, it was as grim a lifer as I've ever seen.

—

Sometimes what matters most, however, is not what you see, but the context in which you see it. Canada Geese are common as dirt and getting commoner in the mid-Atlantic region, but I'll never forget the first Canadas I saw in the vicinity of Woodberry. Only a day or two after moving to Virginia, I saw a gaggle when I took a walk down the old road from our house to the campus.

I say "old" not because the road itself is all that old, but because it is no longer a road to the campus. This is not because the campus has moved, or even because we have moved out of our old house, but because of the heavy rains of June 1995, which caused the Rapidan River to leap out of its banks and rise to a level some six feet higher than the road. This in itself wouldn't have mattered, except that the road crossed the Rapidan on a single-lane bridge. And yes, that use of the past tense is deliberate.

The flood that rose in northwestern Virginia on June 27 was not just a bad flood, or a severe flood. Some called it the "flood of the century," but this is inaccurate—it was more like the flood of the millennium. It's hard to be sure; the United States Geological Survey had a stream gauge on the Rapidan in Greene County, upstream from us, but it was destroyed by the raging waters. National Weather Service estimates placed the flood crest at over thirty-one feet at the gauge point—a five-hundred-year flood. Much of Madison County, where Woodberry is located, took in over ten inches of rain between June 21 and 28; close to a third of the county got more than twelve inches; a significant chunk got more than twenty. On June 27, ten inches

"Canada Geese are common as dirt . . ."

fell in only four hours in the little town of Etlan. Some eighty people across the region were rescued, many by helicopter, but overall, the storm and flood killed three people, in addition to destroying millions of dollars' worth of homes, fences, livestock, and crops, and washing out several bridges.

One of the washouts was the single-lane bridge linking Woodberry's campus to its southern entrance road. Its loss would have been sad in any case, since it had been a campus fixture for nearly a century, but there was a twist that made the loss even worse: the bridge had been closed for the better part of a year while it was being renovated, repaired, and repainted, at a cost of three hundred thousand dollars. It washed away three days before its scheduled reopening.

I approached the river for the first time, strolling down from atop the hill, six weeks after the flood. I was aware that the bridge was out. What I was unaware of was the height of the bridge; the road was perhaps twenty-five feet above the surface of the water that August morning, leaving the broken butt-ends of the bridge as cliffs from which to peer out over the river.

The southern cliff, where I stood that day, is a marvelous place to see birds; once you walk out to the edge, you're exposed to the whole river for hundreds of yards in either direction. Whatever sees you immediately takes off in a panic, but if you hang back a bit, you can spot any number of species: Belted Kingfishers, Wood Ducks, Green Herons, Great Blue Herons, Eastern Phoebes, Baltimore Orioles, and Cardinals are among the birds I've logged from the wreckage of the old bridge. That first day, though, I was so aghast at the twisted steel and shattered pavement below me that I almost didn't notice what was drifting down the stream from my left: some forty-two Canada Geese, all sitting serenely on the water, as oblivious to the remnants of the flood as ravens loosed from the Ark.

It was a lovely moment, and one I'll never forget. It was also fleeting. As I turned and strode to the edge of the gap, I stepped out into plain sight, and thereby caused my first official panic on the Rapidan. The whole body of geese began honking furiously, spun around in the shallows, and furiously paddled upstream. That they did not immediately take wing I viewed as a compliment, but perhaps it was simply that they felt they were more than a match for me if I decided to fight them. Or maybe they had a twenty-five-foot friend waiting for them upriver.

13
The Stoneless Land

I can bring the ocean through what was land:
Wise man don't build no house upon the sand.
—Jim Wann & Bland Simpson, "I'm the Breeze,"
from King Mackerel and The Blues Are Running

I must agree with my learned Tarheel colleagues, Messrs. Simpson and Wann, even as I recognize that when your house has to go either on the sand or in the water, you choose the sand. Their all-too-valid point, however, is that sand shifts; what is built on an Atlantic sea island may not be there in a few years, especially if a hurricane blows through. In coastal Carolina, the very landscape is fluid.

The area's infrastructure, as you might imagine, is therefore rather fragile. South Carolina's Cat Island, for instance, is tenuously connected, by a single narrow causeway, to Cane Island, which has another narrow causeway linking it to Gibbs Island, which lies a short causeway's distance from Lady's Island, itself connected by two bridges to Beaufort and Port Royal. Most people consider these towns as part of the mainland, but they are actually on an island; you have to cross the Whale Branch River to get to them from the north, and the Broad River separates them from the mainland on the southwestern side. In this part of the world knowing the tides is at least as important as knowing the traffic patterns is in Los Angeles, or the subway routes in Manhattan, or the dates on which Fort Bragg's soldiers are paid in Fayetteville. When the tide is up, more boats start moving, and the drawbridges, which must open for them, have less clearance underneath. Traffic on the bridges, like the tide itself, ebbs and flows accordingly.

The coastal areas of the Carolinas are fluid in many other ways: rivers flow slowly into the sounds and salt marshes; tides move in and out twice a day, spring tides and neap tides each twice a month; beaches slowly erode, while inlets are choked with sand; storms punch holes through barrier islands and throw shoals up in unexpected places; piers, houses, and roads disappear into the Atlantic in a matter of decades, sometimes in only a few years. The lighthouse on Hunting Island is now separated from the Atlantic by less than a quarter-mile of palmetto forest and beach. My mother can remember when there were also two rows of houses and a blacktop road between the light and the ocean; my grandfather, born in 1910, told her that the beach used to be two miles from the lighthouse. Granted, he was prone to exaggerate, but visitors to Hunting Island State Park are reminded of what used to be there whenever they stumble on the occasional cracked and eroded piece of asphalt in the surf.

There is a tide in the affairs of men, too. People flow in every summer and flow out again by Halloween; the main streets of Myrtle Beach and Hilton Head fill with cars, drifting one way, then the other, their speakers crashing like surf as the night rolls on. My parents' tidal rhythms followed a somewhat longer cycle. My mom grew up in Beaufort, while my dad's stint in the Marine Corps brought him to nearby Parris Island, where they met in 1962, departing for North Carolina as husband and wife shortly thereafter. In 1995, they returned, completing a circle that even a seventeen-year locust would have to respect, and moved into a house perched above the seawall by Cat Island Creek. The creek is really just a small side channel of the Beaufort River, and if my dad stands on his dock, he can hear, less than a mile away across the waters, the sound of Parris Island's drill instructors, counting off steps with a beat as inexorable as the tide's own, if a tad quicker.

You might expect that the area's birds would show a similar, almost paramilitary rhythm in their routines. Certainly I am one who believes that, like the lever Archimedes said could move the world, a properly placed Marine D.I. could make all of nature stand at attention. In many ways, however, the birds are completely cut off from time; the mild climate keeps migration to a minimum, so that most of the birds you can see in the summer will also be there during Christmas break. The exceptions are usually seen on winter days: migrating waterfowl such as the Ruddy Duck, the Bufflehead, and the Common Merganser, all of which I first saw drifting with the tides on Cat Island Creek.

Regardless of the season, I have found Cat Island a wonderful place for birding for a variety of reasons: there's the river and the marshland, which attract all sorts of waders, gulls, and waterfowl; there's the golf course, which brings in its own wonders; there's the location, near the southernmost tip of South Carolina, which puts a birder in range of many American species that don't go far from the tropics; there's the weather, which is inclined to be balmy, except during the occasional hurricane; and there's the fact that my dad has a much better pair of binoculars than I do and won't know if I borrow them for a few hours early in the morning.

Unfortunately, there are several million other things that make Cat Island a tough place for birding: bugs. Insectivorous birds (a category which includes almost every species to some degree) flock to the sea islands because there are bugs aplenty there: cicadas, butterflies, mantises, moths, you name it. You might expect that a birder in these parts would be grateful to Mother Nature for providing this bounty of bird food, but in truth we tend to be a little annoyed with the old gal, because the most bountiful insects are those types which enjoy gnawing on human flesh. Mosquitoes, chiggers, sand gnats, ticks, and pretty much anything with a taste for blood will try to taste yours; the only parasites you won't encounter are vampire bats. And of course, some insects may not have any particular use for your bodily fluids but are more than willing to bite you, sting you, or even lay their eggs in you.

The worst of the bugs are without question the mosquitoes, which are to the Beaufort area what fog is to London. They aren't so bad if the wind is up, or if the midday heat is extreme, but in the morning or evening, when the weather is calm, their desire for breakfast and dinner is as strong as yours or mine. These times become their hunting season, and consequently, the times when the birds that eat mosquitoes also appear; swallows, martins, kingbirds, and wrens can usually be spotted going about their business during the peak mosquito hours, though you have to put yourself out as bait in order to spot them.

Another alarming member of the insect fauna, and one far more useless to the birder, has appeared more recently: the fire ant. I have suffered mosquito bites since childhood, and I have learned to live with them as most Southerners have learned to live with humidity; we complain, we itch, or we sweat, and we sometimes snap and vacation in some other climate for a while, but in the end, we shrug and say, "So it goes." I have not become so stoic about fire ants, however, since I went more than thirty years before encountering them. These bugs offend me; they seem as unnatural as the hole in the ozone layer, a disruption of the nature I'm used to. Worse, they take an already unpleasant situation and ratchet up the nastiness quotient a few more notches. Believe me, the only thing the South needs less than an increase in heat and UV radiation is the introduction of another biting insect.

To add insult to injury—literally—the bites aren't merely painful, but ugly. My first fire ant bites, a pair that appeared overnight on my left calf, looked like pimples. Big red ones full of whitish ooze, the kind that sometimes crop up on the back of your neck, the kind that fourteen-year-old boys can summon up on their own noses just by making a date. They also made clear the logic behind the name "fire ant." Burning, itching, tingling, the kind of feelings the makers of hemorrhoid medicines would like you to have during their commercials—these were the sensations to which I was now exposed. What I'd missed, however, was any sight of my assailants.

I got a good look at them a week later, when I realized that a pair of them were biting my right foot. I also realized why I'd missed them the first time: they're surprisingly drab looking. Most animals with venom advertise their presence; some do so with bright colors, like the brilliant stripes of the coral snake or the scarlet hourglass of the black widow; others develop bizarre anatomical additions, like rattlesnake rattles or cobra hoods. Fire ants, on the other hand, are just small brown ants, without any particularly striking field marks to warn away larger animals. Not only does this seem deeply sneaky and unfair, it seems Darwinistically suspect. If predators can easily see and identify a venomous animal, they'll probably leave it alone; with the fire ant, however, the animal who stumbles into the nest or starts munching down ants will do most of its damage long before the bites begin to sting and drive it away. Wouldn't it make more sense if the ants were, say, Day-Glo orange, so that every forest creature would give them a wide berth? All I can say is that, if there were poisonous birds, you can be darned sure they'd have plumage that would make the Painted Bunting's look like something from a Bergman film.

Despite my ant bites (the last that pair of ants ever made, I might add), I was determined to get in at least one serious session of birding while I was in Beaufort. Most of my birding there is opportunistic in the extreme: a strange duck floats past the dock, so I reach for the Peterson guide, or something small wings its way across the creek, so I go grab the binoculars. But every once in a while, I want to get up with the sun and devote a few hours to birding and nothing but birding—especially not to anting.

There is a pink that exists only inside conch shells and on the undersides of clouds. It is not in the least a pastel. It is not "cute." Pepto-Bismol bottles covet it deeply. Flamingoes only *wish* they could achieve such a hue. Even a dedicated sky-watcher won't see it too often, but such is occasionally the color richly displayed in the east as I wander forth on a Cat Island birding trip. Even the sight of a lone Snowy Egret overhead can't distract me from the pinkness of the clouds on such mornings; no, it usually takes the sight of dozens of white waders to do that. Happily, on Cat Island such a sight is easy to come by.

Waders is a term used to refer to a host of birds. Ornithologically, it usually means shorebirds such as sandpipers, but most birders (and most dictionaries) use the word to refer to herons, egrets, cranes, storks, and ibises, all of which tend to be larger birds, as well as the smaller plovers and sandpipers. The essential factor they all share is long legs (relative to their body sizes, at least), which allow them to wade into the shallows after their prey and not get their feathers wet. Many waders also possess long daggerlike bills, with which they can spear fish or frogs, though most will also take insects, crabs, snails, crayfish, or in some cases even small mammals. Because of these basic similarities, however, it can take a bit of work to tell certain waders apart.

To give you some appreciation of just how much work can be involved, consider our smallest waders, the sandpipers known to most experienced birders as "peeps." This is not so much an affectionate nickname as it is a cry of frustration. Peeps are tiny birds with tightly wound mainsprings and no field marks to speak of—the distinguishing features (if I may use the term) of the smallest species of American sandpipers are so few and unclear that they make the various members of the notorious *Empidonax* flycatcher group look about as similar as Shaquille O'Neal and Elizabeth II. As a result, the name "peep" is given to any unidentifiable member of this group, which includes the Least, Baird's, Western, and Semipalmated Sandpipers.* Page 135 of my Peterson guide, on which images of these four are reproduced, is a mind-numbing array of identical brownish-gray streaks, stubby black bills, and pointed wings.

Even in his descriptions, Peterson is at a bit of a loss for these species. The various plumages, habitats, bill shapes, and leg colors of the Western are described in minute

*Some birders, including Jack Connor, also extend peephood to the White-rumped Sandpiper and the Sanderling, but these are a good deal easier to identify than the other four peep species listed.

detail, but in the end, he is forced into resignedly stating, "Short-billed winter males are almost impossible to separate from Semipalmateds except by voice." He is even occasionally reduced to describing a bird's "look," a vague indicator of the sort that my students would find marked with red, with the legend "Be specific, please!" in the margin:

> Least Sandpiper: ". . . known by its smaller size, *browner* look . . ." Baird's Sandpiper: "Larger than Semipalmated or Western, with a more *pointy* look. . . . Back of immature has a rather *scaled* look."

If nothing else, though, this description disabused me of the notion that Steve Martin's epic poem "The Pointy Birds" was a work of fiction.

Jack Connor, in *The Complete Birder,* summarizes the peep problem quite succinctly: "Warblers and hawks can be exasperating; shorebirds can be ego-crushing." He then takes thirty-odd pages offering birders detailed advice on how to identify forty-seven different plovers, turnstones, curlews, godwits, sandpipers, and related species—but nearly a fifth of those pages are devoted exclusively to the peeps.

Luckily, peeps are birds of the beach, or sometimes the mudflats; they don't go where there's heavy vegetation, and you'll certainly never see one in a tree. If you visit the Low Country woods, however, you can find plenty of other waders perched in the branches above you—sometimes dozens of them, clear and bold and big.

One of the easiest to spot is the Great Blue Heron. Indeed, because it is comparatively easy to see, the Great Blue doesn't seem to have that much cachet among experienced birders, a situation I find deplorable for several reasons. First, as I've said before, rarity shouldn't be the only yardstick by which we measure the excitement of watching a bird. Second, the GBH is stately, graceful, and striking in its build and plumage; the long black plumes on the white head of the breeding adult give it an appealing look, bemused yet dignified. Third, despite its relative commonness among herons, it has made it onto the cover of both the Stokes and National Geographic field guides, though it shares space on the latter with the flashier Bald Eagle, Blue Goose, and Painted Bunting. And fourth, I think I can concisely explain why it's so easy to see: it's *huge*.

I came to appreciate this last fact in South Carolina some years back, as I watched a GBH fly out of the rising sun and pass right over my head. Intellectually, I was well aware of the bird's size, but emotionally, I was stunned by the enormous expanse of bird soaring directly above me in the light of dawn. A full-grown Great Blue can reach four feet in height, with a wingspan of six feet. The average height for an American male is five-foot ten, and for a woman, five-five. Most of you, then, could step on one wingtip of a Great Blue Heron and still get rapped on top of the head with the other, for which I could hardly blame the bird.

Or look at it this way: How many other birds on the continent of North America can beat that wingspan? A whopping great total of six: the Golden Eagle, the Bald Eagle, the California Condor, the Whooping Crane, the Brown Pelican, and the White Pelican. (If you go out to sea, you may find an albatross or two to beat it, but I'm talking about between coasts.) There are eight hundred or so birds native to the United States, so when we look at the GBH's size, we're talking 99th percentile; in other words, statistically, this bird scores 800s on both the math and verbal SATs.

And then you should consider that, of the big birds listed above, the Whooper and the Condor are on the edge of extinction, and both the Brown Pelican and the Bald Eagle have until recently been officially listed as endangered or threatened. Only fifty-eight California Condors exist in the wild at this writing, and even the captive population is only a little over twice that. The scary thing is, these figures are actually a great improvement—only twenty-two of the birds were alive in 1982—but it was still a chilling thing to discover that the bird flat-out doesn't appear in the 1996 Stokes field guide. Things are a bit brighter for the Whooping Crane, but not much; there are fewer than 250 Whoopers left in the wild, plus another hundred in captivity.

Fortunately, the pelicans and eagles have come a long way from the days of DDT's ravages. Today there are over ten thousand breeding Bald Eagles in the United States, and well over ten thousand breeding *pairs* of Brown Pelicans, but that doesn't mean either bird can be found just anywhere. Since most of the Eagles are in Alaska, for example, the Bald was still listed as endangered or threatened in the lower forty-eight states until 1999, while for decades the Louisiana population of Brown Pelicans had to be supplemented with imports from Florida. The White Pelican was removed from "Blue-List" (or generally threatened) status by the National Audubon Society in 1982, but local populations may still be threatened due to drought and/or loss of habitat. The Golden Eagle has received federal protection since 1962 as part of the Bald Eagle Protection Act; immature Goldens and young Balds are close to identical, so the act was expanded to keep our national bird from being killed by mistake. Nonetheless, the Golden is still "uncommon to rare in the east; fairly common in the west," according to the National Geographic field guide.

In short, despite the existence of these other massive species, the Great Blue Heron is probably the biggest wild bird most Americans will ever see.

Even the GBH has been the subject of local concern for the National Audubon Society since 1986, "though over-all numbers are improving," as reported in Paul Ehrlich and company's 1992 catalogue of endangered and threat-ened species, *Birds in Jeopardy.* Thinking about the shadow of the Great Blue passing over me in the glare of an Au-gust dawn, I find myself fervently hoping that numbers don't lie.

To the layman, however, a treeful of common waders, which is something you can often see in the early morning near the coast of South Carolina, would probably look like nothing more than lots and lots of big white pointy birds. A slightly more studied person might call them cranes or storks. A novice birder or well-informed layman might call the whole bunch of them egrets, which is exactly what I did until I decided to study up on the matter. As it happens, egrets, herons, and bitterns are members of the same family, the Ardeidae, so calling all white waders "egrets" isn't *that* inaccurate, but it's hardly precise. And even if the tree has nothing but egrets in it, how can you tell them apart when every one is white?

Easy. Learn the field marks and try hard to ignore all but the most basic names. White waders are large and vivid, and their field marks are clear, so even a novice can identify them with a little bit of attention to detail.

The **Great Egret** is also known as the *American Egret* or *Common Egret,* and early in the century it was best-known as simply *the Egret,* though it has also been called the *White Heron, White Egret, Greater Egret, Great White Egret,* and *Long White.* Whatever it's called, it is easily the largest of the white Ardeidae species, reaching a meter in height, and is also distinguished by its yellow bill and black legs.* Earlier in this century it narrowly survived a brush with extinction that was caused almost entirely by headgear; apparently no fashionable woman could do without Egret plumes on her hat, and prices on Egret skins went from ninety cents apiece in 1886 to over ten dollars by the start of the Depression. According to T. Gilbert Pearson's 1936 edition of *Birds of America:*

> In the far West a few Egrets still are found, but very rarely . . . the National Association of Audubon Societies has been employing guards to protect the few remaining breeding colonies as far as they are known. These nesting places are distributed from the coastal region of North Carolina southward to the Florida Keys, but it is debatable whether the species can be saved. . . .

To see this written about a species now as abundant as the Great Egret, a bird mentioned not a single time in *Birds in Jeopardy,* causes a momentary feeling of pure weirdness. We are used to thinking of ourselves—modern-day Americans, that is—as the great despoilers of the wilderness. It is a bit surprising to realize that, at least in some ways, we're actually kinder and gentler to our environment than our great-grandparents were. Neither the Labrador Duck, the Great Auk nor the Passenger Pigeon survived to see Prohibition passed, let alone repealed, but a quick look at a modern map of the Great Egret's range will show it nowadays breeding as far north as Cape Cod and Minnesota, with no mention of any rarity. That a conscious effort was made to save these birds is also worth

---

*Those of you who own Faith No More's *Angel Dust* album can see the Long White on the cover.

noting, and its success gives us hope for such species as the Whooping Crane and the California Condor. Unfortunately, I can't help but think that, as well meaning as the Audubon Society's efforts were, the Great Egret was in truth saved by the whims of fashion, which finally drove its expensive plumes out of style.

The plumage of the smaller **Snowy Egret** is the purest white among the egrets—I think it's probably the whitest bird there is—and it is shaggy enough on the head to present a distinctive silhouette; the bird also has a black bill, black legs, and bright yellow feet, commonly referred to as its "golden slippers." Since it is a heron, it has, like Aragorn son of Arathorn, many names: *Little Egret, Lesser Egret, Snowy Heron, Little Snowy, Little White Egret, Little White Heron,* the morbid-but-memorable *Bonnet Martyr* (far and away my favorite), and, just to be as confusing as possible, *Common Egret.*

The **Cattle Egret** is smaller and chunkier than the Snowy, with a stubbier, yellow bill, and it is often seen in pastures, chasing after the insects stirred up by passing herd animals. Patches of butterscotch-colored plumage appear on its head and back during breeding season, but it's usually all white. It is the only white heron without an alias, and it is also the only Old World bird I know that immigrated to the United States of its own volition, rather than having been introduced, though it has since been taken from the mainland to Hawaii. For some reason, around 1880, flocks of them began spreading out from Africa and Eurasia, flying to South America and Australia without any known human assistance. My 1936 *Birds of America* makes no mention of them at all, but by the 1950s, the northward-moving birds had established themselves in Florida, and today their summertime range includes the entire continental United States. I think Mother

Nature did this just to show people like Eugene Schieffelin that, when it comes to introducing new species, there's a right way and a wrong way.

The *Little Blue Heron*, oddly, is white when it's little and big when it's blue. ("Big" in this case is relative—an adult is about half the size of a Great Blue.) The immature bird is pure white, developing patches of darker feathers as it grows, until it becomes a slate-blue adult with a maroon head. Luckily, the juveniles often hang around with the adults, aiding identification, and both stages have a distinctive bill: pale gray-blue at the base, with a black tip. The adults are stately, the immatures striking, but the piebald feathers of the adolescent have got to be among the most awkward signs of puberty anywhere.

There are other white waders in South Carolina, but they are not members of Ardeidae,* and an observer can spot them almost immediately simply by the way they fly—neck extended. (In flight, herons and egrets pull their necks back into an S.) One is the *White Ibis*, also called the *Spanish Curlew, Stone Curlew*, or *White Curlew*. It is not, as you might expect, a curlew. Slim and graceful, Ibises are easily told from egrets by their long, downcurving red bills, though they seem to have at least a nodding social relationship with the Cattle Egrets, with whom they can often be seen flocking. The feathers of immature Ibises are a muddy brown, except for the white bellies and rumps, which can, like everything else related to white waders, cause confusion.

*There are actually two more white Ardeidae in America, but they are rare forms (usually called "morphs") of darker species, and moreover, are confined to Florida, so they cause relatively few headaches among birders elsewhere. The **Great White Heron**, also called the Florida Heron, is really a rare form of Great Blue Heron, while on occasion a **Reddish Egret** may be white, rather than reddish. Most of the headaches they cause occur among birders who think too hard about their names.

Lastly, there is the **Wood Stork** (or *Wood Ibis,* though it is much, much larger than any ibis). It is huge, white, long-legged and long-necked, but is easy to distinguish from the herons by virtue of its naked, wrinkly black head. Seen soaring high above on a thermal, Wood Storks are simply gorgeous; seen closer up, they aren't. They're still striking and graceful, but under close observation, those heads make their beauty a good deal less ethereal. It's best to appreciate these birds as you would the toes of a veteran ballerina. If you've ever looked at a dancer's toes—I mean *really* looked at them, close up, after they've been through years of pounding and flexing and gnarling and blistering —you'll know exactly how to appreciate a Wood Stork: from a healthy distance.

One of Cat Island's best spots for watching waders is a small piece of high ground between the seventh green and eighth tee of South Carolina National Golf Course. It overlooks Chowan Creek (which may also be spelled "Cowan" or "Cowen," depending on your map) and a large pond so choked with reeds that I think it probably qualifies as land. If you look eastward in the early morning, not a lot of birds will be visible, thanks mainly to the huge ball of fusing hydrogen shining into your eyes, but if you're lucky, you may spot the telltale tail of a Caspian Tern over the water. Unlike other large terns, the Caspian's tail is not very forked, while the comparably sized Royal Tern has a tail with sharp points that look like they came off Freddy Krueger's gloves. Herons and egrets are also easy to see from this vantage point.

Gazing back toward the seventh tee, you'll have the sun out of your face, but this may not solve all your problems. I'm thinking specifically of one morning when my gaze came to rest on a bird atop a small live oak near the pond.

It had an overly large triangular bill, a feature that screams "seed-eater" to even a fairly new birder, and it seemed to have brown wing bars, which suggested the handsome Blue Grosbeak. Trouble was, this bird wasn't blue.

Not to worry, I reminded myself, the female Blue Grosbeak is a warm brown.

No, go ahead and worry, came my inner answer, because this bird wasn't brown, either. It had a dark head, glossy black or dark blue-gray, and a pale breast with a faint wash of brown. *Kingbird?* I asked myself, rejecting the possibility almost at once; the Eastern Kingbird is indeed marked by a dark head and white underparts, but one look at this enigma's bill put that thought into the circular file—this was definitely not a bird that ate insects as its staple.

Then there were those wing bars. The term "wing bars" refers to any small horizontal lines of a contrasting color on a bird's wing. They're usually most visible when the bird is at rest, and they're not usually very large, but they play an exaggerated role in making field identifications. Some species are visually distinguished almost entirely by the presence (or absence) of wing bars, and a quick glance through the songbird pages in any field guide will give you a good look at this vital field mark. In addition, wing bars are frequently paired, like the bars of a captain's insignia, and are usually white, so any deviation from this norm is noteworthy—and the Blue Grosbeak is just about the only bird I know with wing bars that are chestnut brown.

Eventually the bird gave a loud *chink* and turned, revealing definite blue patches on its back; these facts allowed me to conclude that it was a Blue Grosbeak, but apparently not an adult male.

And here, for once, I must give credit to two non-Peterson field guides (neither of which I was using at the time, alas) for being right on top of the Blue Grosbeak situation when Roger Tory himself provided less-than-complete information. Where Peterson says the "immature male is a mixture of brown and blue," and leaves it at that, forgoing an illustration, both the National Geographic and Stokes guides show this mixed plumage prominently in their illustrations and clearly label it as belonging to the male in its first spring. Fair is fair. After all Peterson and I have been through, however, you can't expect me to abandon him on the basis of one minor imperfection.

The young Blue had my attention, but something flashed by on my left, landing in the thick leaves of the same tree. I had only caught a glimpse, but that glimpse was in itself a near-certain indicator: a bright red underside. Other birds have red throats or red breasts, or are red almost all over, but only one bird is red below and not above: the Painted Bunting.

If I'd been really cocky, I'd have let the ID stand on that fact alone, but I'm a little too insecure for that. Instead I stooped and shuffled and bent and squinted until I could see a bird—a small, green, and utterly nondescript finch that nonetheless filled me with glee, because I knew it had to be a female Painted.

After my declamation on how bright colors equal popularity, you may be wondering why a bird whose green is barely more vivid than that of your average Milk of Magnesia bottle would be such a source of pleasure to me. One reason is that, despite my previous experience with the male Painted, I'd never seen a female; it may not match the Vegas coloration of its counterpart, but it's the only pale green finch in the country, and that's got to be worth something. In addition, one of birding's pleasures is the sense of closing on your quarry. I'd had a glimpse to put me on the trail of the Painted male. Now here was its mate, increasing by circumstantial evidence the chances that my initial identification had been correct. All I needed was the confirming appearance of the male to ice the cake. A few more stoops and squints went by, and suddenly there it was: the male Painted Bunting, just as red and blue and green as the dots on your TV. Part of me was trying to be blasé about it: *You've seen it before–don't fawn over it, just log it and go about your business.* Another part of me shot back *Yeah, suuure–once a man has seen one naked woman, he loses all interest in them.* The first part of me shut its trap, and I continued to ogle the pair for a good five minutes before reality intruded.

Reality, in this case, came in the guise of a dump truck. A house was being built in the woods beyond the seventh hole, and with daylight now burning brightly, there was a truck arriving on the site to clear out some of the debris. The powerful grunts and grinds of its diesel engine were more than enough to send the Buntings, as well as the Grosbeak, in search of deeper cover. As I watched them, I briefly spotted the telltale white eyebrow stripe of a Carolina Wren, a skulker who, true to form, ducked almost immediately into the brush and vanished. Then, also true to form, he let loose what has to be the bird world's loudest call relative to the size of the bird.

At under six inches, the Carolina Wren will never be considered spectacular in the same way as a Whooping Crane, but its *teakettle teakettle teakettle* cry is astonishing in its volume, the knob of which, as Spinal Tap's Nigel Tufnel would say, clearly goes up to eleven. I am also puzzled as to why a bird whose habits are so reclusive and whose brown and buff plumage is so clearly adapted for camouflage would have such a skull-crunchingly loud voice. (I very seriously doubt that chameleons announce themselves with a loud *AOOOOOOOOOOGA!*) This dichotomy between the Puritan and the brazen is, I suppose, fitting for the state bird of South Carolina, where Christian conservatism is the main political doctrine, but where the state university's athletic teams are called the Cocks.

Eventually, almost every one of my birding sessions in the Low Country is called on account of bugs. The skies may be full of swallows and flycatchers, slurping insects into their gullets at a furious rate, but they make not a dent in the cloud of mosquitoes that hover over me. One nice thing about birding, though, is that even after you've quit, you can still make progress. Sometimes I'll spot one more species in a neighbor's yard as I head home, and it may even rekindle my fire, despite soggy sneakers and a liberal coating of insects. More frequently I'll simply wander out on the dock for a quick look around. Sometimes I might see a pair of Brown Pelicans, or the big head and ragged crest of a Belted Kingfisher, a species noteworthy for bucking a major trend among birds: most male birds are far more brightly colored than females, but the male Belted is two-tone, blue-gray and white, while the female is additionally graced with a rust-colored breastband. It's not a radical reversal of the norm, the way, say, equal pay for equal work would be among humans, but it's unusual.

But sometimes, all I want is a sign, some indication that there's nothing interesting left to see that morning. The Kingfisher vanishes, and suddenly there are no birds anywhere. The morning hours are over, the heat of the day is coming on, and everything is seeking shade. Everything. Under the canvas roof covering the cabin of his boat, my father has hung a large plastic Great Horned Owl, intended to deter birds from roosting and leaving guano all over. Nonetheless, in its shadow I once saw three Boat-tailed Grackles. Feeling the heat of the sun growing worse and worse, they were unimpressed by the plastic owl, or just too hot to care.

That day I felt the same way. Coated in wet grass and smeared with swatted insects, I returned to the house. The heat was rising and a new day dawning in the wetlands; the tide was changing, and the birds were all in hiding. Whether they'll come back out is the question now.

My brother once complained about the look of a brick house that was going up near our parents' place. "I don't like the bricks," he said. "They don't go with the other houses around here. I think they should have used wood, or maybe stone."

"Stone?!?" said my mom. "There are no stones in Beaufort!"

It was one of those times where someone states plainly a fact you've always known but never brought up to consciousness: there are places without rock. Like the soil of ancient Sumeria, the soil of Beaufort County is sand or mud, and the only local substances for building with are wood or shells. What little permanence there is in Beaufort is the permanence of water—"permanence in motion," as author Stephen R. Donaldson has called it—and not the "permanence at rest" that is stone. The granite upon which the New Englander rests his understanding of the world is unknown to the Sea Islander, whose only constants are the cycles of the sun, the seasons, and the waters.

The dawns and dusks and ebbs and flows have gone on for centuries, but recently the commercialization of the Sea Islands has been advancing like a hurricane surge. A second bridge from Beaufort to Lady's Island was constructed in the 1980s, opening the islands for development in a big way. A McDonald's, a Food Lion, a movie theater, and a tanning salon are among the businesses that have opened on Lady's Island since that time, and property values on the islands beyond have shot up as much as twenty times over. The shrimpers and farmers who were long the islands' main inhabitants have now been joined by movie producers (*Forrest Gump* was shot in Beaufort, as were *The Big Chill, The Prince of Tides, The Great Santini,* and part of *G.I. Jane*) and wealthy summer escapees from Charlotte and Atlanta. Some natives, like some birds, are driven out by such changes, but I'm given hope for them all when I see that others adapt: Bubba's Bait Shop, on Saint Helena Island, has its sign out front, handpainted in the lopsided letters that usually spell out "CANTeLOPe" or "SWeeT CoRN" in front of a vegetable stand. Under the name, in the same letters, is the address of Bubba's website.

14
Crossing Delaware

. . . as one small candle may light a thousand, so the light here kin-
dled hath shone unto many, yea in some sort to our whole nation.
—William Bradford, History of Plymouth Plantation

I welcome all of Tom Parker's nuggets of birding wisdom, but in retrospect, perhaps the most welcome was the
statement he made one day when a group of us were trying to decide whether to make an early June birding ex-
cursion to the mountains or to the coast. Tom pursed his
lips and said, "Well, if we go to the mountains, we'll have
trouble seeing the birds in all the leaves. If we go to the
coast, we may not be able to identify them, but we'll at
least see them."

He was right—if you want to see birds, the shoreline is
the place to do it. But be forewarned: he was also right
about the problems of identification. Such was one of the
lessons of Delaware.

Delaware gets comparatively little attention as states
go. It's small, containing only three counties, and it's not
populous, leading to humorist Ian Shoales's pondering

"Why is it that I've never met anyone from Delaware?" It's also crammed into a jumble of convoluted Eastern Seaboard states whose borders must seem incomprehensible to natives of boldly squared-off frontier states. It can't even claim its own peninsula, being forced to share it with Maryland and Virginia—the "Mar" and "Va" in "Delmarva."

It does, however, have three things of which it can clearly and legitimately be proud: the nickname "First State" (since it ratified the Constitution before any other state did); the Delaware River (of "Washington Crossing the" fame); and the coolest mascot for a state university's athletic teams that I know: the Blue Hens.

It also has something of which I was completely ignorant until Tom proposed that we visit it: the Bombay Hook National Wildlife Refuge in Kent County, just outside Dover. (Yes, most of the state is just outside Dover, but Bombay Hook is less than ten miles from the city limits.) From Woodberry Forest, though, it would be a pre-dawn drive of over three hours, across the Rappahannock, the Potomac, and the Chesapeake, to the shore of the Delaware River; it is a measure of either my collegial respect or my uncontrollable desire to bird that I agreed to go.

That respect and/or uncontrollable desire was sorely tested on the morning of our trip, a Tuesday in early June that dawned in as cold and gray a fashion as any Thursday in November. My wife felt the wintry air in the room when I got out of bed; she opened one eye, mumbled "Happy Thanksgiving," and rolled back into the bedcovers I had recently warmed. I went into the early morning darkness in search of my hiking boots and some extra pairs of socks; the floor was freezing cold, especially for the beginning of summer vacation. The patter of rain on the windows led me to believe that I would also want a waterproof jacket and a hat with a bill to keep the rain off my glasses. In short, though I had every excuse to climb back into bed, I dressed, tucked binoculars and Peterson guide into my jacket, set my Oakland A's cap firmly on my head, and headed out to meet Tom and our colleague Wallace Hornady.

The trip itself had been Wallace's idea, but it was Tom who gave us both a destination (Bombay Hook) and a means of getting there (a gold Taurus wagon). I decided my role was to provide distraction from the unpromising weather, which I did almost immediately, by mentioning that I'd heard Randy Travis's cover version of Roger Miller's "King of the Road" on the radio that morning. Since Wallace directs our choir, I knew my comment might be enough to get him piping "Trailer for sale or rent . . ." to the exclusion of anything else. I just had to hope Tom would concentrate on getting us to Bombay Hook. I had been poring over maps of the Delaware coast since I first heard him speak the name of our destination, and I still hadn't found anything on the shoreline that even remotely resembled a hook. Indeed, the smooth banks of the Delaware River and Delaware Bay seemed to me aggressively unhooked, except for the odd protuberance of Cape May on the New Jersey side. Then again, there wasn't anything especially Bombay-like about the refuge, either, at least not on that morning; one doesn't ordinarily associate Bombay with forty-degree temperatures, high winds, spattering rain, and thick mists. Had the refuge been called Seattle Hook, or maybe Brigadoon Hook, I would have understood perfectly.

The headquarters of the refuge was a small gray structure which looked something like the central building of a rest stop on the interstate, and inside there were birds everywhere. Stuffed and mounted, mind you, but everywhere. Geese and ducks hung from the walls, and several large glass cases contained everything from a Great Blue Heron to a Red-tailed Hawk. An enormous Mute Swan spread its wings atop one wall, dwarfing the Snow Goose below it. A clipboard by the restroom door listed interesting species seen recently by visitors: "Black-throated Blue Warbler; male, singing atop Sweet Gum; Bear Swamp Trail." "Common Egret; in breeding plumage; Raymond Pool." The racks on the walls contained posters, mobiles, and field guides, all featuring birds (and amphibians and mammals, to be fair). I was pleased to note the headquarters was fully stocked with the Peterson guide, as well as the Stokes guide and those of the Audubon and National Geographic societies. The refuge's own pamphlets bore waterfowl and shorebirds prominently on the fronts, and one read simply *Birds*.

Clearly, we were not pioneers here.

I wandered the lobby, staring at the maps and photographs, while the more practical Tom went to the ranger's window and began quizzing the woman behind it on the birding prospects for the day ahead. The refuge covered about ten square miles, which included several miles of coastline, but the trails over which we could drive or walk did not reach the shore, extending no more than half a mile east beyond the headquarters building. The trails did, however, stretch several miles north and west of our position, and curled around a variety of ponds, marshes, and inlets, in which all sorts of interesting things might lurk.

Tom was nodding excitedly at the window, so I joined him. "Avocets!" he announced. "They've had Avocets here, and Black-necked Stilts! I've never seen either one of those."

Wallace and I hadn't either, so the idea of searching for them appealed to us both. The question of *where* to search was thornier.

The ranger was equivocal. "The thing is, I've heard people say they'll see Avocets here one day, and the next the birds'll be gone. I don't know where they're going, but they're not always in the same place."

"Avocets!" we chorused.

"If you don't see them in the refuge, you may want to drive south and check out the coast around Port Mahon or Pickering Beach."

"Avocets!" How the trip had suddenly become a search for the American Avocet I don't know, but the thought of seeing this bird had fired our imaginations. Why? Well, if nothing else, the Avocet is striking, an extraordinarily slender wader, standing almost two feet high, with its back and wings boldly pied black and white; in breeding plumage, its gray head turns a rich, warm, almost rosy shade of tan. More peculiar, however, is its long, black, slender bill, which curves gracefully and noticeably upwards, something like Nixon's nose in the political cartoons of my youth. It doesn't look much like any other kind of bird, and the prospect of viewing such uniqueness filled our hearts with a greedy glee which obscured the fact that we didn't know what the hell we were doing.

We thanked the ranger and piled back into Tom's car. The rain had temporarily stopped, but the wind continued to howl out of the northeast. As long as we were in the car, this posed no problem for us, but the shotgun seat of a Taurus wagon is limiting to a birder. We were therefore faced, no more than a quarter-mile down the road, with a choice: brave the elements, or waste three hours' drive.

We were birders; there was no choice.

Alongside the road, in a tangled thicket just behind the spot where Tom pulled over, we saw inordinate amounts of yellow. Some of it turned out to be Goldfinches, twittering and piping musically as they darted back and forth from the trees and vines on our left to the grass and marsh on our right. Another small chunk of yellow was visible on a small warbler that had ducked into the lower branches of a small locust tree; it remained carefully screened by foliage for several minutes, eliciting from me the first blasphemy of the morning, but luckily, its partner turned up atop a shrub moments later, proving it to be a Yellow Warbler, clear and bold in the morning light—well, the morning lack-of-darkness, anyway.

The rest of the yellow visible in the thicket turned out to be honeysuckle, which delighted Tom and Wallace; they rhapsodized about the haze of sweet aroma in which we moved, and kept looking askance at me, wondering why I wasn't joining in. Actually, the reason was quite simple: I have a very weak sense of smell.

When I admit this, I'm often treated to a variety of expressions of pity, but I can't say that I feel especially handicapped; perhaps I just don't know what I'm missing. Certainly my condition has some effects on my life, but they don't seem especially problematic. Everyone worries about my sense of taste, but I can taste things just fine, thanks, though my weak nose might explain why I'm so particular about food textures. Anything gelatinous is just plain out for me—Jell-O, custard, banana pudding, aspic, Watergate salad, and such hold no more appeal for me than does a big slab of raw, quivering lard. I don't think my palate is especially delicate, either; I tend to enjoy strong flavors, which meant that, for me, the first taste of Honey Mustard and Onion Sourdough Pretzel Pieces was pretty much an epiphany.

I didn't bother telling my birding partners all this, simply saying, "My sense of smell is very bad." Tom and Wallace knitted their brows in concern, then went back to happily snorting honeysuckle, but I didn't mind; I knew my condition would be vindicated. Someday.

Eager to spot some shorebirds, we pulled the car to a small parking area just beyond the thicket; there we began to appreciate how unusual Bombay Hook really was. A look around the compass should demonstrate what I mean.

On the south side of the east-west running road were fields, with small marshy areas serving as hedgerows. There was a line of trees about sixty yards away, but it appeared to be little more than a finger of green sticking into the golden-brown marsh. Over this were dozens of Common Grackles and Red-winged Blackbirds, issuing *checks* and *screeps* and *qweerts* as they flew, and a few Goldfinches darted about, white rumps and golden bodies contrasting cleanly with their black wings. Somewhere we heard the distinctive call of the Bobwhite.

To the northeast was a meadow of tall grasses and wiry weeds, all about chest high; it looked as if it had been burned off some months ago, but the cover was now fairly thick. Beyond that was another stand of trees, this one heavily populated with evergreens. Atop one spiky brown plant I spotted a male Yellowthroat, his black mask easily visible; in the trees were more Goldfinches.

Due north were deciduous woods: maples, sweet gums, and oaks, with a covered observation tower roughly thirty feet high. I could see from the map that the forest land jutted out into Raymond Pool, and that the tower stood somewhere near the end of the peninsula, but there was no sign of the water from where we stood. Catbirds were calling in the greenery.

To the northwest we had a glimpse of an inlet circling down from Raymond Pool; tall reeds and cattails nearly obscured the stretch of muddy water. Above it was the whir of dozens of Tree Swallows, while Red-winged Blackbirds cackled liquidly from among the stalks.

In other words, here in the middle of the second smallest state in the Union, we stood at the juncture of four different countries.

—

We pressed on down the path toward the observation tower, spotting still more Catbirds and Goldfinches, but we were brought up short by a startling silhouette above us: a large wader, dark and spindly, with neck extended and a pronounced downward curve to its bill. To me, it was one of *those* moments. You've probably had them, too —the sort of moment where your preconceptions crash against reality hard enough to leave you temporarily dazed. *Those* moments don't come often, so you remember them when they do.

For example, one summer my family accompanied my father to Boston on a business trip, and I had the good fortune to spend several hours prowling Harvard's museums, where I had one of *those* moments. I was about twelve years old, and I had the certainty so common in the young that I already knew all there was to know about the animals on display in the dioramas. In short, as I reached the gallery at the far end of the museum, my preconceptions were puffed up like the Hindenburg and primed to be brought to earth with the same swiftness.

If I remember correctly, the gallery was three stories high, and the overwhelming impression was one of dark brown wood, which seemed to frame everything: rails, columns, ceilings, windows, doorways. As I looked up, though,

I saw hanging from the ceiling a skeleton of absolutely enormous proportions. No surprises there; my generation was raised on dinosaurs, so a sixty-foot string of vertebrae was nothing new to me. I started at the tip of the tail and scanned the animal all the way up to its gigantic skull, which was liberally covered in thick brown hair.

Hair.

Not standard equipment for a dinosaur.

I blinked, and the skull stayed just as hairy. There were other skeletons above the first, and they too had heads festooned with long brown hair. Not a one was under forty feet in length from nose to tail.

What the hell was I looking at? No animal that size had ever had hair; even a woolly mammoth wouldn't be that big! My god, I'd been lied to! Sometime in the distant past, beasts the size of basketball courts had walked the earth, and some conspiracy had silenced all my textbooks!

I must have stood there for thirty seconds, with this new information giving a Hamilton Beach treatment to my cerebrum, grappling with an emotion that I can only describe as fear: fear that everything I knew was wrong. If this creature were real, then everything from the number seven to the speed of light to the color of the sky had to be called into question; the universe had been yanked out from under me.

And then I noticed that the head of the enormous animal above me was fully a third the length of its body.

And then I noticed that the hair of the enormous animal above me was growing inside its mouth.

And then I noticed that the hind legs of the enormous animal above me were conspicuously absent.

With a twang that was almost audible, the universe snapped back into place.

I was looking at a whale.

The "hair" was baleen, also known as whalebone, the screenlike substance with which the largest whales filter plankton from seawater. Whether due to poor lighting or my own ignorance, I had taken it for hair and subjected myself to one of *those* moments.

The sight of this bird above us was one of *those* moments, too. The preconception was "Those birds don't live here." The reality was that no other bird matched the silhouette.

It had disappeared behind the trees before I could get a word out, but when I did, several came out in a rush.

"I'll be damned! That was a Glossy Ibis!"

I may never know why I had decided the Glossy Ibis was a bird of the tropics, seen by Americans only in the hottest swamps of Florida and the Gulf Coast, but that's the belief I was lugging around with me through the salt marsh of Delaware that day. I was so certain of its tropical nature that I was already doubting my identification when Wallace raised an eyebrow and spoke: "Could it have been a curlew?"

Tom, however, was already shaking his head; his timing in these matters is impeccable. "No. Curlews are much smaller. That was an ibis."

It had gone down beyond the trees ahead of us and to our left, so we moved swiftly along the path, hoping to catch sight of it from the tower, or at least from some cleared space up ahead. Clambering up the wooden steps of the battleship-gray tower, we eventually reached a platform some twenty-odd feet above ground level and immediately made several discoveries:

First, the Glossy Ibis was nowhere to be seen.

Second, the muddy shallows of Raymond Pool were graced with a number of Black-necked Stilts. A close relative of the Avocet, the Stilt is one of those birds whose name is absolutely apropos; not only is the back of its neck black, but its reed-thin legs seem somehow to be longer than the bird itself. It stands no more than two feet tall, but the red legs, described by Peterson as *"grotesquely long"* (italics his), appear to make up at least three feet of height. The plumage is bold black and white, making it easily visible against a background of gray-brown mud, and the bird's needlelike bill is perfectly suited to probing into that mud in search of food. Wading just below the tower were two Stilts, and we could see three or four other pairs stalking patiently around the edges of the pool. When they took off, their legs trailed behind them like Isadora Duncan's scarf.

Third, it was cold as the bejeezus up there. We had not realized just how well the trees screened the fields below from the wind blasting out of the northeast, but now that we were out of their lee, we absorbed the brunt of the chill factor. Only twice in my life have I been colder in the month of June. On one occasion I was skinny-dipping in a Vermont mountain stream which I feel sure flowed with liquid helium. On the other occasion I was hiking through a rain cloud near Shining Rock in the Smoky Mountains and became so delirious with cold and hunger that, after three hours of soggy walking, an hour of setting up camp, and forty-five minutes of trying to get wet birch bark to catch fire, I became convinced that no finer meal existed in any five-star restaurant on earth than the steaming hot cup of Lipton's Instant Beef Stroganoff I finally bolted down.

This June chill was not so extreme, but it was still pretty alarming for three teachers who had thought they were on summer vacation. The sight of the Stilts more than made up for the initial discomfort, but we eventually noted that the pool's mudflats were thick with other birds. Tiny "peep" sandpipers were the most numerous, along with a few Semipalmated Plovers, Mallards, and the usual Red-winged Blackbirds. Some of the young Blackbirds, usually just a heavily-streaked brown and white, had a rosy tinge, almost yellowish at times, which gave us fits for some moments as we peered through our binoculars, trying to assign the birds to a more exotic species. In this, we failed miserably, and within a few moments, we decided it would be better to get out of the wind than to pursue this ibis sighting any further.

Any lingering doubt about the ibis, however, was dispelled when we approached the next large expanse of water, Shearness Pool, and found a large white sign displaying some of the more common bird species at Bombay Hook. These included, among others, the Glossy Ibis, which inhabits coastal areas of the Gulf and the Atlantic from Mobile to Canada, as a quick check in my Peterson guide revealed. Also pictured were some birds we'd already seen: the Black-necked Stilt, the Semipalmated Plover, and the Least Sandpiper—I didn't bother changing my mental list from "peep," though—as well as the Snow Goose, which appeared only moments later by the side of the road. As we looked around Shearness Pool, we also saw Forster's Terns, Canada Geese, Black Ducks (another lifer for me), more Stilts, more peeps, a Lesser Yellowlegs, and a Great Blue Heron, as well as two Bald Eagles soaring around each other above the trees across the water.

In the course of our journey through Bombay Hook, we saw some fifty species of birds, but a quick reference to Finagle's Law ("The perversity of the universe tends toward a maximum."—Larry Niven) will tell you which bird was not on the list: the American Avocet. We saw Mute Swans and Red-tailed Hawks, a Blue Grosbeak and a Black-crowned Night Heron, but nothing long and pointy with its bill turned upwards. By 3:00 P.M., we were ready to eat and then head to the beach for a final crack at the Avocet.

Leaving the confines of the refuge and getting back to civilization (where we devoured meatball subs and almost became warm again) was surprisingly easy. A healthy biker would have no trouble riding from Dover to Bombay Hook and back, especially since hills are all but nonexistent in Delaware; the state's highest point is a mere 448 feet above sea level and is almost in Pennsylvania anyway. As we turned down the road to Port Mahon, though, I began to feel a distinct difference in the nature of the wilderness on either side of the road. In Bombay Hook, nature had been treasured and carefully set aside; near Port Mahon, nature had been invaded, found unprofitable, and left to its own devices. The marsh grass was high enough to mask a lot of the area, but the road itself tangibly displayed neglect by whacking us on the backside every few seconds. Potholes were plentiful enough to make the de facto level of the road a good six inches lower than it pretended to be. Tom eventually piloted us to the end of the marsh road and brought us to the edge of the Delaware River itself, where we were treated to the sight of human endeavor being all but abandoned. Broken pilings jutted from the water at irregular intervals. Near the beach stood unpainted and mysterious wooden buildings which listed dangerously toward the waves, while across the road a few off-kilter telephone poles struggled pointlessly to hold aloft their lines. I rolled down the car window to take in this scene of decay and laughed heartily.

I was laughing because the side of the road was decorated by a large pile of seafood: greenish crabs, blackish eels, and bait fish which might have been menhaden but looked a bit scalier. They had obviously been lying there for some hours, and the area's flies were having a high old time with them. Tom and Wallace tried gamely to avert their noses, but I, proudly anosmatic, simply peered out the window, over the pile of carrion, and toward the shoreline, where a large flock of Herring Gulls was sharing the sand with a teeming mass of peeps and Willets. I might not appreciate the joys of honeysuckle, but no mere heap of dead fish was going to keep me from birding.

Tom eventually moved upwind and joined me in an examination of the beach, which was narrow, rocky, and brushed by waves whose heavy foam was about the same appealing color as the tailpipe of a '71 Volkswagen Beetle. In places there was a corrugated iron seawall, but in others it was either seriously bent or entirely absent. What beach there was, however, gave us a lesson in appreciating nature's handiwork, even when that handiwork seems silly at first.

The instrument of this lesson was the Ruddy Turnstone, a squat little shorebird which combines features of the plover and sandpiper families, and which is one of the most bizarre-looking things on the beach. Start with a pair of bright orange legs. Top them with a teardrop-shaped body of rusty red, with a black-and-white rump and tail. Make the belly white and the breast black, and over the head, just spatter the black and white wherever you want, Pollock style. Remove the neck entirely, and give the black bill just a slight upward tilt at the tip. The result is a mass of bold colors and baroque lines that would be entirely appropriate on an album cover from 1968. It does not, however, look like a bird with much chance for survival in the real world.

Astonishingly, though, on this rocky beach, the Turnstones were almost invisible. The gray sand was covered with any number of pale and rusty pebbles, and the outlines of the birds seemed to vanish among the tiny curves and shadings of the stones, while the russet, black, and white actually blended in with the colors of the shore. Unless the birds were moving, you could barely find them. It was amazing.

Still more amazing was the discovery, when we looked a little closer, that the patches of beach not covered by Ruddy Turnstones were in fact largely made up of peeps. The gray-brown streaks that make them indistinguishable from one another also make them indistinguishable from dirt; frankly, I think it's miraculous that these birds manage to find each other to mate. Almost every available square inch of beach had a bird on it, but to casual observation, the only birds around were the enormous Herring Gulls, standing a few dozen yards downriver and calling vulgar gull-words into the wind.

That three dedicated (or at least obsessive) birders would have trouble noticing birds may beggar the imagination, but we were working under two severe handicaps: the astounding natural camouflage mentioned above, and the presence of another animal, in quantities that actually did beggar the imagination—horseshoe crabs.

Well, not horseshoe crabs as such, but rather their earthly vessels, big, brown, chitinous, multi-legged, and dead. I'm not exaggerating when I say that there was at least one horseshoe crab corpse per square yard of beachfront up to the high-tide mark. Most were belly-up, their stiffened legs moving fractionally in the wind off the bay, but some were plunked down in the sand in their natural position, and except for the complete lack of movement, looked just as they had in life. The rocky area between the narrow beach and the road itself held the thickest distribution of crabs, but wind and tide had managed to spread them onto and even across the road, leaving some marsh

"What beach there was . . . gave us a lesson in appreciating nature's handiwork . . ."

grass on the far side festooned with what looked like smooth, enormous birds' nests. We drove north along the shore for perhaps a mile, turned around, and headed back toward Dover, trying hard to keep our eyes on the bird life, but constantly feeling them drawn toward the crustacean charnel house that lay around us. Never in my life have I been so happy to have a weak sense of smell.

Every spring, horseshoe crabs rise out of the shallows of the mid-Atlantic coast and surge onto the beaches of Delaware, Maryland, and Virginia, intent on laying enough eggs to propagate the species for another year. Given an annual mortality rate like the one we saw on the shores of Port Mahon, they have to lay one hell of a lot of eggs, but this prodigious egg-laying is itself the cause of no little carnage, because every spring, when the crabs come out of the sea to spawn, the shorebirds come down to the sea to feast. We were probably a good week late for the height of the crab roe festival, but we soon decided that there might still be egg-craving birds on Pickering Beach, where we would make one last stab at fulfilling our quest for the Avocet.

Surprisingly, at least to me, the road to the beach was all but deserted. The reasons for the lack of fast-food joints and beachwear establishments became clearer when we reached the intersection with the beach's main drag. "Main" is perhaps a misnomer, since there was only the one drag, and it extended only a few hundred yards to our right and even less to our left. The beach houses numbered two dozen or so, and there wasn't a soul in sight: no cruising teens, no surly locals, no beer-sedated GI's, no buses full of delinquent high-school bands en route to Disney World. It was as if all rules regarding beach populations in June had been rescinded due to the weather.

But that was certainly reason enough: the afternoon remained as unlike a day in June as any night in February, except that the sun hadn't set yet. As Tom parked the car, I looked at my watch and saw that it wasn't quite four; we'd been birding for six hours. With a final burst of energy, we staggered down a public path through the dunes, emerging into a north wind which, though warmer now than it had been that morning at Bombay Hook, was blowing a good deal harder. Wallace's ruddy cheeks were beginning to glow from windburn, and my A's cap attempted liftoff more than once. For no particular reason, we turned north and began marching along the sand.

The waters of the Delaware Bay were churning furiously, and I recalled that these were the waters Washington and his men had dared on Christmas Eve two centuries ago. The crossing had taken place some miles above us, across from Trenton, where the bay narrows into the Delaware River, but the chop we could see on the surface was enough to send any sensible small-craft user back to port, and the Jersey shore was flat-out invisible.

I thought briefly about putting my hand into these waters, crossed by greatness all those years ago, but a second look at them brought that idea to a screeching halt. If anything, the water looked worse here than it had at Port Mahon. Have you ever sampled a cup of strong coffee, tried to cut it with about four ounces of skim milk, and still found it undrinkable? Well, if you took that cup of coffee and left it on the nightstand for a couple of days, it *might* achieve the same shade of cold, oily, brownish-gray as the waves that were lapping at the sand. I cannot call what was being cast onto the shore "foam," any more than I can look at a Turkey Vulture, recently emerged from the chest cavity of a dead elk, and call the big greasy feathers surrounding its neck "down." I suppose it might be technically accurate, but I associate a certain degree of fluffiness with those terms, and this stuff was no fluffier than is steel wool. And when I considered the number of beachgoers who enjoy a good frolic in steel wool, the reason for Pickering Beach's lack of development became clear.

Keeping near the high-tide mark, and catching the occasional wind-driven grain of sand in our eyes and teeth, we trudged on, encouraged by the sight of gulls on the beach a few hundred yards away, and also by the numerous horseshoe crab corpses littering the beach, a sure sign that shorebirds ought to be around here somewhere. A few crabs still had some life in them. Since some of these were upside-down and unable to right themselves, Tom obligingly turned them over, freeing them to head back into the bay (where the pounding surf would no doubt flip them onto their backs again, but I refrained from pointing this out). The wind stayed in our faces, preventing us from speaking to one another, and ensuring that nothing in front of us would smell us coming. Nonetheless, our approach was noted by a good number of the birds, and they took off down the beach en masse. We were stopped in our tracks.

Sometimes I try to count birds, but it was obvious that there was no point in my doing so here. The numbers were simply too large. It would have been like trying to count the particles of soot coming from a smokestack, or the seeds blown off a field of dandelion tufts. Birds rose up in waves, black against the sky, as first one, then another, then another and another and anotherandanotherandanother panicked, raised its wings, and leaped up into the wind; watching the fear running down the beach was like watching the head of a match scraping down a strip of sand in slow motion, first smoking, then sparking, then bursting into flame. As they whirled above the waves and took off down the wind, they dropped down low over the water to our right, where I could see among them any number of peeps, as well as thousands of Ruddy Turnstones, their pied heads and backs showing clear against the gray even as they streaked along. There seemed to be larger sandpipers among them, maybe somewhat reddish, but focusing on a single bird in hopes of getting a field mark was like trying to read the license plates of oncoming traffic from across the median on the interstate. They passed us, eventually, and the sky was noticeably lighter when they were gone. There was nothing to say. We continued up the beach.

We were soon well north of the strip of beach houses. Marshland lay on our left, and a shallow stream was running parallel to the shore. Ahead of us we saw the stream take a hard right and flow down to the bay, leaving a small stand of tall grasses between its course and the spot where we stood. Across the stream, we could now see, there were birds on the beach. Cautiously we worked our way up to the dunes and approached the stream from behind the stand of grass, walking carefully to avoid stepping onto mummified crabs. The sand across the stream was liberally covered with peeps and Ruddy Turnstones, all diligently probing for crab eggs, but Tom had noticed something else.

"Red Knots!" he said.

At Port Mahon, Tom had proven to us the value of looking carefully at large swarms of peeps; in one such group he had spotted a single Dunlin, its black belly clearly visible, but only if you ignored the thousands of non-black bellies around it. Here, once again, his wisdom was proven: scattered throughout the mass of peeps and Turnstones were other chunky sandpipers with brown backs and a reddish wash on their bellies that looked exactly like the

color I'd seen whirring by in a cloud of birds a few moments before. They were Red Knots, the day's sixth lifer
for me. I made a mental note to follow Tom's advice in all
future shorebird viewings.

The thousands of ticktock feeding motions became
hypnotic after a while, and the wind continued to howl,
but no other species appeared, no matter how hard we
looked. There were no Avocets on the beach, and it was
getting on toward dark. It was disappointing, but there
wasn't much more to be seen here. We turned our backs
to the wind and walked down along the hard sand, now
cast with millions of spindly footprints and overturned
pebbles; the Turnstones, true to their name, had flipped
them over in search of horseshoe crab roe and other
delights. As we departed, an occasional flock of birds
whizzed past us, always a mixture of peeps, Turnstones,
and Knots, with the occasional gull soloing by at a higher
altitude. It was almost five o'clock.

We were driving back through the marshland from
Pickering Beach when Tom slowed the car and asked,
"You guys want to pull off here and look around real
quick?" There was a small, unpaved access road on the
left.

"Yeah, sure," said Wallace and I, and Tom turned in
without another word. The road didn't go far before it
curved back around to the east and split in two; we took
the left fork and almost immediately came to a large mud
flat. It might, at high tide, have been full of water, but right
then it was about eighty percent mud, and it extended for
what must have been half a mile to the east and about the
same to our south. The flat was oddly geometric, almost
rectangular in shape, leading me to believe its formation

was not entirely natural. Oil drums and bits of scrap metal poked out of it near the shore. I was reminded of what I'd once seen when I leaned over the edge of a bridge across the river Ouse in England: below me, half awash in the shallows, had been a supermarket shopping cart. I didn't see one in this mud, though it would have fit right in, but birds were all over: we could easily see terns and Willets, and a number of Black-necked Stilts appeared as well. Most startling, though, were the Black Skimmers.

The Skimmer, a large and striking relative of the terns, is one of my favorite birds. All black, white, and red, it moves like a classic roadster, making maximal speed appear minimally difficult as it skims along the surface of sea or river, just barely keeping its wingtips dry. Then it drops its outsized lower bill, which is noticeably longer than the upper, and dips it into the water, slicing out its prey as an airborne scalpel would. Cool just drips from these birds. I've long been fascinated by Skimmers, but here I was treated to a new sight. Not only were a pair of them slicing neatly along the remaining pools of water, but there appeared to be a whole flock of them squatting on a mud-bar far from the shore, looking for all the world like a party of surly black terns. As we peered out at them, they took off, and I was treated to the sight of what must have been thirty or forty slim, scissorlike black birds wheeling around in the deepening gray; they looked like feathered knives tossed aloft by a master juggler. All by itself, this sight had made turning off the main road worthwhile.

Nonetheless, there was more to see. The pool's regularity was useful to us, because there was a long and more or less straight stretch of water, uninterrupted by mud, extending from our shore to the east, and gazing along it at the Skimmers, Tom had gone suddenly rigid.

". . . the fifty-seventh species of the day, the seventh new addition to my life list: an Avocet."

"Look out there!" he cried.

I was pretty sure I knew what he was looking at, and as I trained my binoculars on the edges of the water, I saw it as well. The head was surprisingly dark, but its rich rosy tan was unmistakable, and when the bird turned in profile, I could easily see the upward curve of the bill.

The long day was over; it was an Avocet. Graceful, bizarre, striking, and completely unexpected, seen by chance after the search for it had been all but abandoned, the fifty-seventh species of the day, the seventh new addition to my life list: an Avocet. We watched it lower its attenuated feet carefully into the shallows, prodding and slicing at the mud with its bill. We saw the boldly pied plumage of the back; we saw that there was another Avocet across the straight channel from the first; and we saw that night would soon be upon us.

The drive home was rainy and uneventful, but as I climbed into bed, I realized that my cold and miserable June day had come to a sort of perfect closure. It had a completeness that few endeavors ever provide and which tied up the day's lessons clearly. I knew now the importance of looking closely at what seems dirty, unnatural, or repetitive, and that there is much to be appreciated in even the tiniest states. Most clearly of all, however, I knew that it was going to take a chisel to get "King of the Road" out of my head.

15
Laughing at
Broken Hammers

I never liked Woody Woodpecker much—maybe because of that damned laugh—but I've always loved real woodpeckers. They're bold, conspicuous, colorful, loud, and yet there is a bit of tragedy in them—they seem haunted by their very strangeness, their fragile overspecialization. They are beautiful, though; the Picidae family includes what may be the most beautiful bird in the world.

Whether you like bright colors, stark contrasts, or easily discernible field marks, you've got to like the Red-headed Woodpecker. This is no misnomer: its head is blatantly, completely, inarguably red. From nape to crown and back over to the point of the throat, we are talking red. And not just any red: not the rusty wash of the American Robin's breast, or the patchy orange-red of the House Finch, or the rufous-burgundy backside of the Red-tailed Hawk, or even the scarlet of the Northern Cardinal. No, this head is crimson, deep and bright, like a prize tulip. And setting off this head, in a style both classic and timeless, are the back, wingtips, and tail, all in jet black, and the underside, rump, and secondary wing feathers in pure white. Other birds may use the same color scheme to good effect—certainly the Black Skimmer, the Rose-breasted Grosbeak, and the Pileated Woodpecker are high on the list of chic birds—but the cut, for lack of a better word, of the RHW's outfit makes it the James Bond of avian fashion.

Unlike Bond, however, woodpeckers know nothing of secrecy. They are admirably sincere. A bird that slams its head against solid wood with a drumming sound audible for miles is not trying to sneak anything past anyone.

That head-slamming has worried me on occasion, though, because it doesn't seem as though it could do the birds much good, neurologically speaking, and I've seen some very peculiar behavior from woodpeckers. On one of our excursions around the school grounds, Tom Parker and I found them dropping out of character all morning.

First came the treetop appearance of a gray-brown bird, which we saw perching on a tiny limb near the crown of an almost bare maple at the edge of a field. We'd been scoping out the minute treetop flits of Yellow-rumped Warblers, so this bird's larger size made an immediate impression on us. We pegged it as an American Kestrel, or Sparrow Hawk, a common bird in our neighborhood. It was sitting oddly, though, and rather uncomfortably, and it didn't assume the upright position common to the Kestrel, but instead hunkered horizontally. Moreover, its tail was ragged at the end, not trim and neat, and I saw that its beak was not at all hooked, but was as long and straight as a chisel.

It was a Yellow-shafted Flicker.

This was the ornithological equivalent of Pat Boone performing heavy metal songs in leather, studs, and tattoos; it really happened, but who'd have expected it? Flickers are not, in the strict sense, perching birds; the term "perching" technically refers to members of the order Passeriformes, which includes flycatchers, larks, swallows, jays, titmice, nuthatches, wrens, mimic thrushes, thrushes, kinglets, waxwings, shrikes, starlings, vireos, warblers, blackbirds, tanagers, and finches, among others, but not Flickers, who like all woodpeckers belong to the order Piciformes. Woodpeckers don't perch, as a rule, because they have a number of anatomical differences from perching, or "passerine," birds; these differences explain why you usually see a woodpecker braced vertically against a tree trunk or along a branch, rather than squatting across a twig near the treetops. Most have zygodactyl feet, meaning two toes face the front and two face the rear, which keeps the birds from pitching over backward when they're clinging to a vertical surface. Their tails are stiff and spiny, which also helps prop them up against the trunks and gives them a bit more leverage for their preferred feeding method, which, as mentioned, involves repeatedly slamming their heads against solid wood. Woodpeckers' bills are straight and strong and sharp, and their tongues are, as Peterson notes, "remarkably long," both useful traits if you're trying to punch a hole in a tree and suck out the insects from deep within. All in all, then, there's really no reason ever to see a woodpecker perching; they get along just fine without it.

But here was a Yellow-shafted Flicker, blithely gripping a branch too small for him and doing his darnedest not to tip over in a spirited spring wind. As if he realized the improbability of the situation, he suddenly gave up and made a bounding flight down the treetops, leaving Tom and me to wonder at his behavior.

We were still wondering as we passed back into the patchwork of field and forest that surrounds the school and noted yet another member of the Picidae family in an improbable spot. How improbable? Think like a wood-pecker for a moment: Your entire anatomy has been de-signed by nature to allow you to yank food out of the in-nards of trees; you were born in a tree, and have spent most of your life in trees, probably because they generally have fewer bird-eating predators on them than does, say, the ground; you are moreover possessed of wings that al-low you to fly to any height on any tree you care to. Given all this, where are you going to spend your time?

If you said "In a tree," you're thinking more like a wood-pecker than was this particular bird, which was squatting in the middle of a barren cornfield without so much as a tall stalk nearby. It was a Downy Woodpecker, a small, handsome bird familiar to residents of town and country. It will cheerfully eat suet if you put it out, but it will also happily visit a yard just to bang holes in trees and eat bugs and larvae. What I had never, ever seen one do until then, though, was set foot on the ground. Only two species of woodpecker have ever touched the earth in my presence: the spectacular Great Green Woodpecker of Britain and the Yellow-shafted Flicker. Each is an ant-hunting bird that will waddle up to an anthill and pounce on it like Godzilla on Tokyo, gorging on the denizens to its heart's content.

Both the Flicker and the Great Green, however, can be excused for this behavior, because both are, despite the red patches on their heads, roughly the same color as the ground on which they sit. The Flicker's barred brown back and gray head give it a dirtlike camouflage, at least to the casual observer, while England's green and pleasant land is a good match for the plumage of the Great Green. They are also both sizable birds, bigger than some birds of prey, and would doubtless put up a reasonable show of resistance to anything that tried to nab them during their ant-picnicking. The Downy, on the other hand, is the smallest American woodpecker, at just over six inches, and has a boldly pied black-and-white plumage that wouldn't camouflage it against anything except a Rorschach test.

So, psychologically speaking, we see here a Flicker that is trying to act like a perching bird and a Downy Woodpecker that is trying to act like a Flicker. Neither is comfortable with the niche in which it finds itself, and each is attempting, by acting out its extra-species fantasies, to find itself a new niche.

This is absurd behavior, but woodpeckers are on many levels absurd. Their absurdities, however, are the primary reasons for their success. By virtue of their chiseled bills, their peculiar feet, their bizarre tongues, and their ability to bang their heads repeatedly against solid objects, they are superbly suited to their particular environments. Unfortunately, woodpeckers are not adaptable. Their strength is their specialization. They're really, *really* well suited for living in trees, and wherever there are forests, you'll find woodpeckers; they are, however, totally unsuited for life without trees. Woodpeckers are not found in unforested deserts, or on ice shelves, or soaring on thermals out over the Gulf Stream.

You don't have to be a tree-hugger to see the potential hazards of this strategy in modern America. In the past few centuries, human beings have done their best to clear the continent's forests from the maps, and not a few animals living in those forests have been cleared as well. One of these is the most endangered American woodpecker in existence: the Red-cockaded Woodpecker, more commonly abbreviated the RCW. A native of the scrubby pine forests of the southeast, the RCW is almost wholly unsuited for living near people. People need houses, and if there are houses around, there will be fewer pine trees. In addition, houses mean fewer fires in the forest that remains, since fires tend to freak out homeowners. The pines, however, need occasional fires to help their seeds germinate. If there are not enough fires, there are even fewer trees. And if there aren't enough pine trees, there won't be any place for the RCW to nest. It's a striking bird, a black-and-white woodpecker slightly larger than a Downy (with a tiny spot of red on the male's head), but it's almost wholly dependent on the complex life cycle of pine trees.

This is the tragedy of the woodpecker: to be supremely good at something that is no longer doable. That tragedy is still being played out, but we already know how the first act ended, and who the victim was: the Ivory-billed Woodpecker.

The demise of the Ivory-billed Woodpecker has been one of the longest, slowest, and least definitive deaths on record. I have been birding for over thirty years, and from the first, almost every field guide I have owned has mentioned the Ivory-bill and its extinction—all the while including a painting of the bird and mentioning that it is only *probably* extinct.

Indeed, its decline began long before I began birding —but oddly, it doesn't seem to have finished declining even yet.

In 1936, T. Gilbert Pearson wrote in *Birds of America* that the Ivory-bill "must be numbered among those species of which we are accustomed to speak as being 'nearly extinct.' . . . So far as the vision of the average man is concerned, the bird has already gone to join the Dodo and the

Great Auk." This pessimistic view is backed up by the fact that the Ivory-bill is one of the few birds of which no photograph is included in the book.

In 1950, the Macmillan edition of *Audubon's Birds of America* called the Ivory-bill "a magnificent woodpecker of primeval timber of the southern states, now practically extinct chiefly from lumbering."

In 1963, Roger Tory Peterson said in *The Birds*, "The unadaptable ivory-billed woodpecker . . . has not been recorded with certainty for some 10 years." The book's editors went on to say, "If indeed it is still extant, the ivory-billed woodpecker numbers no more than six individuals."

In 1992, Norman Boucher, in *A Bird Lover's Life List and Journal*, said that the bird "will likely soon be declared officially extinct."

Call birders what you will, but you cannot call them hasty. Pearson wrote his gloomy assessment before my father's birth, while Boucher made his prediction the year after my first son was born. The Ivory-billed Woodpecker, whose last confirmed sighting was in 1944, has remained on the edge of extinction through four generations of Cashwells.

There is good reason for this lack of haste. The Ivory-bill's habitat, virgin forestland, is by its very nature a place few people ever go. It would be entirely possible for a bird to survive in such a place without a birder's laying eyes on it. The ornithologist's fondest dream, that of a small colony of Ivory-bills existing somewhere in the deep woods, has been as hard to kill as the bird itself, and possibly harder.

Reports of Ivory-bill sightings are made every so often. I can recall reports from Texas, where an area known as Big Thicket was rumored to hide several of the birds, as well as other tales from Florida, Louisiana, South Carolina, and even Cuba, but none has ever achieved any kind of official status, and no objective evidence of the bird's continued existence has been reported. In a world where Bigfoot sightings are still reported from time to time, this should come as no real surprise, but I keep hoping for some kind of closure where the Ivory-bill is concerned: Is it extinct or not?

I'm probably not going to get a firm answer. For one, the very inaccessibility of the sighting locations works against their being verified. It's easy to get hundreds of birders into Central Park to check on an unusual warbler, but you're not going to get many Audubon Society members to haul their spotting scopes into the mountain forests of Cuba to check on a possible Ivory-bill sighting. Too, Ivory-bill "sightings" are also made by mistake—frequently. The Ivory-bill's cousin, the Pileated Woodpecker, is both large and spectacular, and seeing one is enough to thrill any birder with a pulse. Unfortunately, it is similar enough to the Ivory-bill that a casual birder may simply notice the points of similarity without recognizing the marks of distinction. Both birds are huge for woodpeckers, almost crow-sized, with red crests, long bills, and bold black-and-white plumage, especially under the wings. The Pileated has a dark bill, black-and-white stripes on its face, and white patches on the leading edges of its underwing; the Ivory-bill, on the other hand, has a white bill, no striping on its face, and white patches on the leading *and* trailing edges of the wings, while the female's crest is black, not red. They are distinct, but in the excitement of spotting a Pileated, one could easily confuse it with an Ivory-bill.

Nonetheless, like Bigfoot, the Ivory-billed Woodpecker's continued existence cannot be conclusively disproven. On April 1, 1999, a Louisiana State University forestry student named David Kulivan reported that he had seen a pair of woodpeckers in a wildlife refuge on the Pearl

River north of New Orleans. He reported that the female's crest was black, that the birds' bills were ivory-
white, and that both the call and the feeding behaviors
of the birds were unlike those of the Pileated. Though ornithologists were skeptical, especially given the date, Kulivan provided enough detail to encourage several expedi-
tions to the Pearl River. After more than a year's searching,
including an expedition of veteran ornithologists spon-
sored by the Zeiss company, no indisputable evidence was
obtained. Several trees were found with the bark stripped
off in a manner that suggested an Ivory-bill's feeding style,
and at one point the researchers recorded a series of ar-
restingly loud raps like those the bird was said to make,
but later analysis suggested that the sounds were distant
gunshots. No birds were seen, no calls were heard.

So what do I think about the Ivory-bill? I think it's good
to have something out there about which we can't be certain—something which is, on the face of it, so absurd that it
can't be true, and yet may be. If nothing else, it keeps us
from assigning certainty where it doesn't belong.

A few years ago, I was scrambling up the rocky Ridge
Trail of Old Rag Mountain in Shenandoah National Park
and reached above me for a handhold. I was most surprised to find myself gripping not rock, but a painful
handful of fibrous spikes. I was even more surprised when
I saw what had wounded me, because I thought it was extinct.

I had grabbed the spiny husk of a chestnut.

The American chestnut tree was once the dominant
tree in the forests of the Blue Ridge, but in the early part
of the twentieth century it was all but wiped out by a fungus accidentally imported from Asia. I had never seen an
American chestnut, let alone touched one, and at the time
I would have sworn that the blood pooling in my palm had
been drawn from beyond the veil of extinction. It was ab-

surd, but it was true. I pulled a spine out of my hand and laughed. But even then, I knew I was laughing at the sad remnants of a lost beauty. As I learned later, the blight fungus is still present in eastern woodlands, and though a handful of American chestnuts may be sprouting at any given time, the saplings rarely survive long enough to produce nuts. Scientists are working gamely to breed a blight-resistant American chestnut, but the forest is unlikely ever to again resemble the one that covered Old Rag a century ago, despite the hardy young tree that stood, against all odds, on the exposed ridge of the mountain.

And I think about the drive I made on I-95 back around 1988. I was passing through the swampy forest-land south of Florence, South Carolina, and I saw a large black woodpecker fly over the road. I assumed it was a Pileated and thought nothing more of it—I didn't even note the date—until I reached my destination and had a moment to look through my Peterson guide. The 1980 edition has the Pileated in the middle of page 189. At the bottom is the Ivory-bill, with the question of its extinction raised clearly ("Very close to extinction, if, indeed, it still exists"). Both birds are shown in flight, with wing patches clearly visible.

And then I recalled that my bird had had white patches on both the leading *and* trailing edges of its under-wings . . .

Mistaken memory? Odd color morph of a Pileated? Sunlight gleaming through the trailing wing feathers? Was I fooling myself, or just being a fool?

I didn't know then—I don't know now. Carl Sandburg wrote of an anvil that "laughs at many broken hammers." I don't know whether I saw such a hammer; nobody knows whether the anvil of the modern world has broken the Ivory-bill or not. And I don't know whether to laugh or cry.

16
The Dickcissel Apocalypse

The use of traveling is to regulate imagination by reality, and instead of thinking how things may be, to see them as they are.
—Samuel Johnson, quoted in Life of Samuel Johnson

Stupid, sure, I'll grant that. But was it actually *insane* to get up at six o'clock on a Sunday morning to catch a ride with a total stranger and go driving all over east Iowa looking for birds?

That was the question I was asking myself as I stood outside Slater Residence Hall, a twelve-story slab of brick rising up from the bluffs west of the Iowa River in the heart of the University of Iowa campus. In Iowa City. Iowa City, Iowa, that is.

Despite friendly people, a top-notch summer institute in debate (which was my official reason for being there), and what may be one of the most gorgeous college campuses that no one in the United States knows of, Iowa City has a flaw that should by now be pretty obvious: nomenclature. Plainly put, the word *Iowa* is used in Iowa City the way *like* is used in most junior high cafeterias. ("She was

244

like 'No way' and I was like 'Yes way' and then she was like 'As if . . .'") Perhaps it's due to the trouble many non-Iowans have in locating the Hawkeye State on the map, or to their confusing Iowa with similarly named states; either way, some of the natives apparently see the humor in this Iowan overkill, which is how I came to spot one T-shirt emblazoned with the Hawkeye logo and bearing the legend *UNIVERSITY OF IOWA–Idaho City, Ohio.* Luckily, birds are not named the way every feature in the Iowa City area is, or we'd have some major problems. Had taxonomy included the Bird, the Small Bird, the Small Bird with Wing Bars, the Large Bird with Wing Bars, the Not-Quite-So-Large-as-the-Large-Bird-with-Wing-Bars Bird with Wing Bars, and so on, no one would even know who Audubon was, let alone the name of anything he ever painted.

This may be just the prejudice of a man cursed to fill out forms for the rest of his life with "High School: Chapel Hill High School, High School Road, Chapel Hill, North Carolina; College: University of North Carolina at Chapel Hill, Chapel Hill, North Carolina," but I for one am glad the powers that be gave us the bird names they did. Woodpecker. Thrush. Nuthatch. Killdeer. Loon. You can tell by the name that there is some kind of entertainment value in watching something called a Killdeer, if only to find out whether or not it can kill a deer, and if so, whether it will eat it, and if so, how. And you've got to love something called a Loon, if only because it's so much fun to say to a friend, "I saw a LOOOOOOOOOOON today."

This is, coincidentally, exactly what most people would have said if they had seen me standing in front of Slater Hall at 6:00 A.M. waiting for a total stranger to take me off into the wilderness—and no doubt to pull a hunting knife on me, truss me like a hog, carve satanic symbols into my skin, and bury me in a shallow grave in the Iowa City

245

Landfill, Iowa City Landfill Road, Iowa City, Iowa. I didn't actually expect that to happen, however, because I had already gotten in touch with this stranger, whose name was Jim, by leaving a message at the Iowa Ornithologists Union hotline, and the hotline's answering machine message made it plain that the only kind of insanity Jim was likely to suffer from was the kind that made people like me get up at 6:00 A.M. on Sunday to go look at birds that would be there all day.

("Iowa Ornithologists hotline?" one friend cackled when I mentioned it. "What do you do, call it if there's some sort of bird emergency? 'Help, my wife's being attacked by a bird! Send help!' Is that it?"

"That is a complete misunderstanding of the way birders' minds work!" I retorted, bristling. "Of course you wouldn't call a birders' hotline to say that! You'd call to say, 'Help, my wife's being attacked by a bird and I'm not sure if it's a Northern Shrike or a Loggerhead Shrike—what's the difference?'")

When I had dialed the IOU hotline, the tape-recorded message had said nothing insane, threatening, or even surprising, though it had been delivered in the flat Midwestern tones I still found vaguely exotic. "Thank you for calling the Iowa Ornithologists Union hotline," said the voice. "Unusual birds recorded through June 26th for the Iowa City area include: Prairie Warbler at Lake McBride State Park, Blue-winged Warbler at the Hawkeye Wildlife Area . . ." and so on. After the list of unusual birds, I was allowed to leave a message, which I did. I said I was an out-of-towner who was hoping to bird on Sunday morning if any Iowa City natives thought having a North Carolinian along might be fun. And then I said "IOWAIOWAIOWA" and hung up.

When I got a call from Jim a few nights later, he was painstakingly nice, asking if I'd like him to pick me up at Slater, allowing me to set the time, and even deigning to ignore the tape-recorded insult to his home state. He asked if I had plans to add any specific birds to my life list.

"Well," I said, "I've never been in this part of the country before, so anything I wouldn't be likely to see in the Southeast would be great."

Instantly Jim reeled off the names of a half-dozen species that live in Iowa but rarely, if ever, turn up in my neck of the woods, starting with the Dickcissel, a small finch of the central United States grasslands that visits small towns in the Southeast about as often as Prince Philip does, and possesses an equally keen grasp of working-class social mores. Jim was of the opinion that we could spot a Dickcissel almost instantaneously upon leaving the city limits. He seemed so certain that I imagined them lined up at the border like cultists at an airport, waiting to press upon us literature about the coming Dickcissel Apocalypse. He was almost as upbeat about our chances of spotting other Midwestern species.

I considered my options: I could allow myself to be chauffeured about the area by a man who clearly knew it well and knew which birds were in which parts. Alternatively, I could borrow a car of unknown reliability from one of my fellow debate coaches, take a potentially inaccurate map with me, and meander aimlessly about an unfamiliar wilderness, seeing nothing but weeds. Or I could walk, which, given my stamina and on-campus location, would lead to a whole lot of sightings of House Sparrows.

I told Jim to pick me up at six.

When Jim arrived in front of Slater, I was certain I'd made the right decision. He was fiftyish, gray-haired and hale, a part-time professor at the Dental School of the U of I who obviously knew his birds big-time. He was modest and collegial; in my experience, many expert birders tend to be that way, having a keen appreciation of just how far their birding expertise will get them in the outside world. And, true to his word, once I'd shaken his hand, thanked him for his kindness, and clambered into the passenger seat of his Toyota, he carried me swiftly through some stunningly beautiful riverside scenery to the outskirts of

". . . the coming Dickcissel Apocalypse."

town, where, hearing something through his open window, he brought the car to a rapid halt on a dirt road between two pastures. There, sure enough, squatting on a power line with a pamphlet on redemption under one chestnut wing, was a Dickcissel.

He was not a large bird, and in other circumstances I might have mistaken him for a particularly handsome House Sparrow or, had I been closer, a miniature meadowlark. His yellow breast was crossed by a black bib, and his gray head was thrown back to let loose his song, a clear, true-to-the-name "DICK SISS SISS SISS!" that once again made me thankful Audubon was not an Iowan. I peered carefully through my binoculars, vaguely aware that we were in fact stopped in the middle of a dirt road that might be used by large farm vehicles with razor-sharp blades underneath, and confirmed the field marks in Peterson, whose *Field Guide to the Birds of Eastern North America* covers all of Iowa and most of Nebraska and South Dakota, its western neighbors. This bird was definitely a Dickcissel. Idly, I checked my watch; it was twelve minutes after six, and Jim had already found me a lifer.

From that point on, my trust in Jim's ability to identify birdcalls from a moving automobile grew steadily until it reached near-total confidence, and my feelings of inadequacy grew proportionately. He stopped on a dime in the Hawkeye Wildlife Area when he heard a Warbling Vireo going nuts in the top of a cottonwood tree—sure enough, another first for my life list. He cocked his head and suddenly pulled over by a hedgerow near Amana and we were able to spot a pair of Bell's Vireos—my first—in the shrubbery. Vireos are notorious for being both hard to see and easy to hear; they're small, usually dull green, and inclined to stay hidden in the leaves, but they're also loud and talkative. Red-eyed Vireos can vamp on their monotonous

Here I am—where are you? song for hours at a time, and once you know what it sounds like, you'll hear it in every corner of the forest. Even briefly spotting a vireo, however, takes time and effort, and knowing their songs is also a big help, as Jim was all too clearly demonstrating.

My crumbling self-image was somewhat restored when I was brought up short at the same instant as Jim by a call that is utterly unmistakable, but apparently quite unusual in Johnson County, Iowa: the two-syllabled eponymous call of the Bobwhite. (I thank the fates that I didn't have to say "Another lifer!" to Jim that time.) As far as Jim knew, no such bird had ever been reported in that county, but we'd both heard it clearly and there was no doubt in either of our minds. I will go to my grave certain that I am the co-reporter of Johnson County's very first Common Bobwhite. And people say birding has no rewards.

The morning was not purely a hunt for new birds for my life list. I was blessed with a good look at a number of birds that I had seen before, but not in the same proportions. Cardinals, Mockingbirds, and Blue Jays abound in Virginia and the Carolinas, but not in Iowa in early July. Iowa was instead liberally peppered with lone Indigo Buntings, perched boldly at the tops of roadside trees and singing their deep blue tails off. Baltimore Orioles, a study in sharp color contrasts, flame-orange and jet, ruled the treetops, as often as not ganging up to chase a crow or hawk away from their nests. Red-headed Woodpeckers, the most formal birds in America, their perfect black-and-white ensembles setting off heads of deepest velvet-cake crimson, appeared with a frequency I hadn't seen since early childhood. And Red-winged Blackbirds were actually teeming, their liquid warbles rattling from every field and their scarlet epaulets peeping out from dark plumage everywhere you looked.

Nor was I entirely a piece of luggage on this trip. I did Jim the favor of spotting a Barred Owl on a branch in the shadows of early morning, and had its species nailed down by the dark eyes before he could even bring his binoculars to bear. I can take full credit for the Belted Kingfisher we spied over a pond near Lake McBride. Of course, I can also take full credit for making Jim turn the car around to check out three briefly glimpsed silhouettes on a wire which, when more closely inspected, turned out to belong to three Brown-headed Cowbirds, of which we had seen some thirty-five thousand already. And since they reproduce by mitosis, like amoebas, there were six on the wire by the time we got back on our way.

Jim took this with gentle tolerance, as he took most of the other abuses I heaped on him, such as my continual harping on Iowa's remarkable number of utterly straight roads that intersect at perfect right angles, a feature of the landscape that I was unable to stop mentioning. Those from the rural Midwest, who know that a "Kansas Yield Sign" is a red octagon with the letters S-T-O-P on it, probably don't understand the fascination this Euclidean precision holds for those of us from back East. It's because we hail from states where straight lines are all but accidental; where I come from, the state road construction crews travel with large loads of curves and merges in the backs of their trucks, and are required by law to insert them at regular intervals or face a hefty fine. The idea of being able to test your tire alignment by simply letting go of the wheel and seeing if you drift onto the shoulder is totally foreign to us.

Hell, we Carolinians spent years working out ways to *survey* in a straight line. If you study the history of the place, you'll learn that the dividing line between North and South Carolina was originally drawn by a survey crew that couldn't even figure out basic latitude. The border was supposed to proceed from the Atlantic coast in a northwesterly direction until it reached the thirty-fifth parallel. I'll grant that the surveyors did manage to go northwest from the shore, but when they decided to turn due west, they were short of the thirty-fifth parallel by a good fifteen miles. Undeterred (or more likely unaware), they marched west until they encountered a piece of Native American land surrounding the Catawba River, land that the South Carolina government wanted on its side of the border. The survey crew, who were no doubt offered a percentage of whatever natural resources the Indians were about to be bilked out of, obligingly made a detour northward around this territory, fiddled around near the Catawba, and eventually ended up well *above* thirty-five degrees. From there, they could have returned to their original westward line, or even searched for the elusive thirty-fifth parallel, but instead, they simply turned left and tromped seventy miles straight to the ridgeline that culminates in Sassafras Mountain, the highest point in South Carolina; in fact, their line from the Catawba to Sassafras ran a bit north of true west, but neither this nor their original mistake was ever corrected. Legend has it that later government officials in South Carolina were prepared to go to war with their northern neighbors to get the territory they were entitled to. Luckily, they were persuaded that the Palmetto State was now several square miles larger than it would have been with competent surveyors at work, and the saber rattling ceased almost immediately.

Carolinians are thus, as you might imagine, unused to lines as features of the landscape, but what does a Carolinian see when he stares down a country road in Iowa? A line. It may go over a bridge, or through some trees, or up a hill, but it is a line. It does not turn randomly toward a swamp, a house, a gas station, or a gigantic South of the Border billboard bearing a neon-yellow fiberglass giraffe just to the left of the legend "STRETCH YOUR DOLLAR WEETH PEDRO! 458 MILES." Where the Carolina road is a never-ending compromise with the terrain around it, the Iowa road is a bold symbol of man's unwillingness to bow down before mere geography, a pointedly unnatural and forthright construction of human ingenuity and elbow grease. And passing a slow-moving gravel truck on one is a damned sight easier, too.

In any case, Jim's patience with me was nigh-beatific. He didn't even ridicule me when I told him I didn't have the all-but-ubiquitous House Wren on my life list. This may have been because he was standing in very wet grass near a boatyard at Lake McBride State Park, surrounded by what must have been a House Wren gathering on the order of the Million Man March, and any sudden paroxysm of laughter would have caused him a nasty fall, but I prefer to think it was just common courtesy. I tried to offer him the same when he asked me to confirm a few unexpectedly weird sightings, such as the sudden appearance of a lone Double-crested Cormorant out of a clear blue sky, or the brief glimpse of black, white, and red that we were able to prove, by collective process of elimination, had been a Rose-breasted Grosbeak.

The most bizarre sighting of the morning took place in the most bizarre landscape of the entire trip. After rolling over hill and dale, through field and forest, past lake and strip mall, we took a dirt road out of the heavily wooded heart of the Hawkeye Wildlife Area and came eventually to a scene that looked to me extraterrestrial.

The first, overwhelming impression was of flatness. I grew up in hilly country, and am used to a horizon shaped like Kate Winslet. Not so this place; the sky seemed to take up a full one hundred eighty degrees of arc. Even the sky-line of the lowlands where my parents live has some variation of level; granted, it's not much, but when you're standing in the surf, staring at the endless blue plane of the Atlantic, behind you is a dune higher than your head.

This Iowan landscape, though, was the kind of flat most people never see except on pool tables. What made it even odder, to me, was the sudden and near-total lack of plant life. Trees were visible, certainly, but so were clouds, and I'm not sure the clouds weren't closer. Aside from a few nearby clumps of trees, the only suggestion of woods was a line of dark green-gray on the horizon. We stood upon a hemisphere of dirt.

Other than dirt, the only thing there was water. Great pools of it. Some of these appeared to be mere puddles, just shallow washes full of excess rain, but other parts looked vast and deep, stretching toward the woods on the horizon, which had to be miles away. In the larger stretches of water stood the remnants of trees, their trunks jutting up without leaf, branch, or even color, but nearby there were only muddy pools lying waveless on bare ground. I thought about James Blish's classic science fiction story "Surface Tension," and wondered if any of these puddles contained intelligent microscopic life forms struggling to discover other puddles. For their sake, I hoped not, because none of them looked very inviting.

"This is the Iowa River," said Jim, who was rather blasé about the whole scene. "This area gets flooded pretty often—you shoulda seen it two years ago during the big summer floods."

I almost wished I had seen the floods right then—huge amounts of water I'm used to, but this limitless wet-and-dry landscape was downright disturbing. Nevertheless, I put my binocs to my eyes and scanned the area. I noted a crowd of Great Blue Herons dining contentedly in the myriad pools, but then I spotted something on the wing far away, something just barely paler than the trees.

"I think there's a couple more herons in flight over there," I said, spying two large birds beating their wings in a stately fashion, their great blue-gray bills before them.

Jim was silent a moment. "How many you see?" he said, his own glasses trained on the same area.

"Two," I replied, watching them sail gracefully between the bare trunks of the distant graveyard of trees.

"Those are pelicans," said Jim. "There's a bunch of 'em."

"What?" I answered in disbelief. I'd seen pelicans, after all. Pelicans are (a) dark brown and gray, (b) coastal, and (c) as Southeastern as I am. "Brown Pelicans? Here?"

"White Pelicans," Jim corrected me. "There's about nine or ten of 'em."

I peered into my lenses. Just the two light-gray birds appeared, no matter how hard I squinted. They were pale, and might be whiter close up, and there did seem to be black on their wings, but still, why would a Gulf Coast bird like the White Pelican be in Iowa in midsummer?

I kept looking. "I don't see—oh."

There they were, a little behind the two I had spotted: a line of great birds in perfect formation, sailing motionless through the tops of the trees. With only two, there was room for doubt, but seeing the full complement of eleven meant certainty: pelicans. Nothing else flies like that, serene, untroubled, almost daring the air to throw them an updraft so that they can make a subtle, nearly invisible adjustment to their flight feathers and continue un-perturbed. If pelicans were drivers, they'd own huge, rec-tangular American luxury cars with plush interiors; they would get into the interstate's passing lane at the first op-portunity and would set the cruise control at eighty, then lean back against the headrest, drape one wrist over the top of the steering wheel, and look out at the traffic under heavy-lidded eyes, waiting for their destination to roll up over the horizon.

"The first-years don't breed, so a lot of 'em stay here instead of going all the way north," said Jim, snapping me back to reality, or what passed for it around here. "It's a shame we can't get any closer to them."

A shame, yes, but I think I'll remember my first look at a White Pelican all the better for the circumstances in which I saw it, and almost could not see it: at the very edge of vision, where the sky and horizon blend, while I stood in the morning light on the surface of another world.

If the first White Pelican sighting of my life was science fiction, my first look at an Upland Sandpiper was pure air-port novelette: cheap, a bit tawdry, and no real challenge. It started out, however, as something very different; we were near Amana, rolling down a dirt road between a pas-ture and a cornfield, when Jim heard a Western Meadow-lark and stopped the car. When he said "Western" rather than "Eastern" Meadowlark, I jumped out with binocs a-flashin', because I knew I would likely never again be in the presence of a man who could tell the difference be-tween the two.

I'm not immune to subtle distinctions of all kinds. I know, for example, the telltale signs that a particular War-ner Brothers cartoon was directed by Chuck Jones, and not Friz Freleng or Tex Avery; I am not, however, a man who can discriminate between meadowlarks. Sure, I know Peterson says the Western's yellow throat feathers actually extend slightly onto the cheeks, and that the bird is paler overall than the Eastern, but the only real difference is in the call. And I don't know the call.

This may be the real distinction between birders. The truly obsessed birder knows the calls. The less acutely obsessed birder does not. I can identify only a few birds by call alone. The Bobwhite is pretty obvious, as are the Killdeer, Chickadee, and Grackle, all of which helpfully announce themselves when they see you, saying "bob-WHITE," "kill-DEERRR, kill-DEERRR, kill-DEERRR," "CHICK-a-dee-dee-dee," and "rusty-hinge-breaking-off-gate," respectively.

Meadowlarks are beyond me, but there I was, standing in one of the few areas where both the Eastern and Western species abound, with one of the few people who knew both calls, and I had my equipment ready. As soon as I heard the sound Jim had identified as a Western, I brought the binocs to bear and spotted black-V-on-yellow: the telltale mark of the meadowlark's breast. This one was sitting primly atop a barbed-wire fence in the pasture, about thirty yards off. A few seconds later, she opened her mouth and let forth a—well, I don't know exactly what she let forth, to be honest, but she was certainly the one doing it, and Jim said it was a Western's call, and that's good enough for me. Besides, six cheek feathers were clearly yellow.

We had barely begun moving toward the car when a small, stubby bird flashed across our path in a streak of brown and settled in the tall grass of the roadside. It could have been almost anything, but I optimistically decided it must be a Sedge Wren, which I'd never seen before, and made ready to pursue it. At that moment, however, with all the subtlety of Rush Limbaugh objecting to a plank in the Democratic Party platform, there was a loud "KIP-IP-IP-IP" from above, and down fluttered an Upland Sandpiper.

There was no mistaking it; it may as well have sent out a press release. There in plain view was every field mark Peterson had considered worth mentioning: the "mellow whistled *kip-ip-ip-ip,*" the small head, the "shoe-button" eye, the thin neck, the brown feathering, the thin white line along the trailing edge of the wing.

"Well," Jim allowed in measured tones, "There's an Upland Sandpiper."

I nodded and obligingly recorded it in my field guide's life list.

But the Upland Sandpiper was not satisfied yet. In obvious torment over the possibility that we had failed to identify it, the bird fluttered down to a fencepost and perched lightly atop it, holding its wings elevated for a moment as it did so. I looked at Peterson's description on page 130 and discovered that the bird was, in fact, plagiarizing from him: "Often perches on fenceposts and poles; holds wings elevated upon alighting."

"Thanks," I called to the bird. "We've got it."

"KIP-IP-IP-IP," whistled the bird, carefully enunciating the P's for us.

"Really, we're fine," I called again, waving.

The bird hesitated, blinked, looked down to confirm its position atop the fence post, and then held its wings elevated once more, just to be on the safe side.

"Go on, take off," I cried.

"KIP-IP-IP—"

"Will you just get the hell *out* of here?!" I shouted, causing the bird to blink, turn its small pigeonish head around, raise its wings again, and then finally take off to accost some other birders in another part of the county.

Turning back to the roadside, we discovered that the Sedge Wren (or whatever it was) had seen us take up with that brazen hussy of a sandpiper—the very idea! Honestly, what kind of bird wants to be treated like that?—and was not coming back until we'd apologized properly and sent roses.

We returned to the Toyota. "I feel used," I said, sitting down heavily.

The morning went on in a rush of dark silhouettes, queued up on power lines or flitting across the road ahead, but we knew we were approaching the end of the birder's day. All the signs were there: the sun was well above the yardarm, bringing an unpleasant warmth to the backs of our necks as we craned them out the car windows—which, admittedly, I was doing a whole lot more than Jim. The dew was completely gone, and the pleasant, refreshingly cool squelching of my sneakers gone with it, replaced by a mere damp and deadening warmth, as if there were used tea bags between my toes. Fewer birds were singing, or perhaps it was simply that there were more cars moving around, the constant whir and rush and hum of them filling our ears with an auditory fog too thick to disclose any detail. The honeymoon was over, and now we were driving home from Niagara, wondering if either of us had thought to cancel the newspaper.

As he turned the car back toward Iowa City, Jim politely asked if I had any ideas where he might see a Bachman's Sparrow or a Swainson's Warbler.

"Other than in my field guide?" I responded.

He laughed, and explained that they were two of the few American birds he had yet to see, and knowing they turned up at least occasionally in North Carolina, he figured it couldn't hurt to ask. I was flattered, but these were not the birds of the roadside and suburbs that I knew well —these were deep-woods critters, the kind who live out there where a man who travels without insect repellent becomes an insect attractant, where men are men and beasts are beasts and each is occasionally food for the other. They were not birds of my world.

"Sorry, Jim," I replied sadly. "I've got no idea."

But as I sat, staring out into the forest alongside our perfectly straight road, I realized that my world—like all our worlds—is mutable through travel. By an act of will, I can fit my world out with new places, and with the birds inside them, for that matter. Hadn't I just grafted southeastern Iowa onto my Carolinian inner landscape without even the briefest of psychological protests?

We pulled up in front of the dorm, which was just as tall, just as rectangular as when I'd left. Jim dropped me off, leaned over to shake my hand, and buzzed away into a knot of church traffic. I looked at my watch; it was ten twenty-five.

I stood outside Slater Residence Hall, gazing into the improbably blue sky that itself touched the sky of my world, some thousand miles away. I had taken in four hours' worth of Iowa and was filled with an unlikely glee. As I took the stairs two at a time, it was all I could do not to yell "KIP-IP-IP-IP!" at the top of my lungs.

EPILOGUE

First-Person Plural

> *You must not know too much, or be too precise or scientific about*
> *birds and trees and flowers and watercraft; a certain free margin,*
> *and even vagueness–perhaps ignorance, credulity–helps your enjoy-*
> *ment of these things.*
>
> *—Walt Whitman, Specimen Days*

Maybe Walt's right. I've come to a boundary, and I'm
not happy about it. My life list sits at around two hundred
fifty birds, and may for some years. It seems I've reached a
certain age, and now only certain birds are left: the rare,
the out-of-the-way, and the very, very hard to find.

These are not identical categories. Rare birds are just
that—there aren't a lot of them. When there are fewer than
a hundred Bachman's Warblers or California Condors in
the entire world, you're talking about needles and haystacks;
Bachman's Warbler is probably extinct by now, and the
Condor barely exists in captivity, let alone in the wild. The
odds of my seeing one are therefore about the same as the
odds of my meeting the pope in the produce section of
the local I.G.A.

Out-of-the-way birds can be rare or common, but they're assuredly not local. I might have the chance to see the rare but spectacular Whooping Crane, for instance, if I can get from Virginia to its breeding ground: Wood Buffalo Park in Alberta. To see a more common but equally out-of-the-way bird in the wild, like maybe a Hoopoe, a Kookaburra, or a Scarlet Macaw, I have to renew my passport; the first is native to Africa and Europe, the second to Australia, and the third to Central America.

Finally, there are those local birds that exist in some numbers nearby, but which are very difficult to spot—those of the rail family, for instance. That there are "marsh hens" aplenty in the reeds around my parents' place in Beaufort is near certain; that I'm ever going to set eyes on these secretive fowl is a good deal less certain, especially since some of them are nocturnal. Without a great deal of effort, specialized equipment, and dumb luck, I may live near a number of bird species for years without seeing them.

To log the next few lifers on my list, therefore, I'll have to do some traveling. I got my first Hooded Warbler up in the Shenandoah National Park, which is only about an hour away; if I'm lucky, I can get a few more lifers there, but I'll have to go looking for them brazenly. Demurely waiting for a new bird to surprise me in the yard is no longer feasible. I'm no longer pure—I seek pleasure out. Hell, I *pay* for it.

And yet . . .

It's early March in Virginia, and winter's back is broken under the load of green shoots. Red maples are budding, their branches tipped with a scarlet never to be seen on any self-respecting Easter bonnet, and the yellow of the forsythia is joining in, turning my front yard from what is supposedly a prim, quiet, pastel concert into a glorious, full-blown pan-African reggae festival. And now, as if they sensed the deep soul of the land seeping up through the whiteness of the early year, the sky is full of black birds.

With a host of creaky, rusty, grating jeers, the foothills teem with Common Grackles. Their blackness mottles the telephone wires all the way from Orange to Culpeper, and the corners of my eyes are full of the smooth arc of their flight. Their tails are wedge-cut, longer in the center than at the edges, and when the birds fly, the center feathers drop down a bit, leaving a shallow V, as though they'd been folded—as if the birds had been made, in their thousands, through origami. When the sun hits them, the Grackles' feathers explode into bronzes, purples, greens, and indigos, and their yellow eyes wink, as if they know just how much beauty they're sneaking past the unobservant. In North Carolina I never noticed them, because they were always there; now, simply by removing themselves from my presence for five months, they've made me miss them. Every scrubby roadside cedar has a branchful of Grackles on it, and I welcome the sight. Maybe I can still be reached.

And then, a little past sundown, with a crescent moon just brighter than the redness in the west, I'm standing in my front yard with my sons. My wife is out of town, and I'm just realizing that a deadline for a fax is moments away, so I'm loading the kids into the car as quickly as any father can load a five-year-old and a three-year-old. I'm regretting having missed what must have been a spectacular sunset, and am preparing to ignore its remnants just for spite, when my elder son gasps.

"Look at all the birds!"

I turn and look up at the last pale blue patch overhead. Dipping, soaring, circling, and moving north is a vast column of birds, wings extended in silhouette.

"There must be a thousand of them!"

"There must be a thousand of them!"

Well, fifty or sixty, certainly, great birds flying almost overhead. I pick up my youngest and hold him up to see. As they pass against the reddish west, their blackness remains untouched and complete, their wings barely moving in the cool evening breeze of a new spring.

Part of me is noting the shallow V of the wings, the dihedral position that distinguishes the Turkey Vulture, even from miles away. Part of me is wondering what great dead animal this flock was settled upon a few minutes ago. Part of me is curious where the birds are off to, whether to roost in the trees by the river or nest in the shelter of the hills.

But most of me is just standing here under a near-dark moon, watching what ought to be an omen of death and gloom, with a great big grin on my face. Their eyes shining in the dim light, their voices the fierce whispers of childhood delight, my sons are with me. I bird. They bird. We bird.

Bibliography

Achenbach, Joel. "All Atwitter." *Washington Post*, May 14, 1997, sec. C, p. 1.

Audubon, John James. *Audubon's Birds of America*. Introduction and descriptive captions by Ludlow Griscom. New York: Macmillan, 1950.

———. *The Audubon Society Baby Elephant Folio: Audubon's Birds of America*. Edited by Roger Tory Peterson and Virginia Peterson. New York: Abbeville Press, 1981.

Austin, Oliver L., Jr. *Birds of the World*. New York: Golden Press, 1961.

Boucher, Norman, ed. *A Bird Lover's Life List and Journal*. Boston: Museum of Fine Arts and Bulfinch Press, 1992.

Burton, Robert. *National Audubon Society North American Birdfeeder Handbook*. London and New York: Dorling Kindersley, 1992.

CNN.com. "Weeks after eagle attack, dachshund near recovery." March 24, 2002. [Online]. Available: www.cnn.com/2002/US/03/24/eagle.dachshund/; accessed July 12, 2002.

Catesby, Mark. *Catesby's Birds of Colonial America*. Chapel Hill: University of North Carolina Press, 1985.

Catesby, Mark. *The Natural History of Carolina, Florida, and the Bahamas*. Savannah: Beehive Press, 1974.

267

Cokinos, Christopher. *Hope Is the Thing with Feathers: A Personal Chronicle of Vanished Birds.* New York: Warner Books, 2001.

Connor, Jack. *The Complete Birder: A Guide to Better Birding.* Boston and New York: Houghton Mifflin, 1988.

Ehrlich, Paul R., David S. Dobkin and Darryl Wheye. *Birds in Jeopardy.* Stanford, Cal.: Stanford University Press, 1992.

Forbush, Edward Howe. *A Natural History of American Birds of Eastern and Central North America.* Edited by John Birchard May. New York: Bramhall House, 1939.

Ford, Alice. *John James Audubon.* Norman: University of Oklahoma Press, 1964.

Garrett, Laurie. *The Coming Plague: Newly Emerging Diseases in a World Out of Balance.* New York: Farrar, Straus and Giroux, 1994.

Gould, Stephen Jay. *Bully for Brontosaurus.* New York: W.W. Norton, 1991.

The New Grolier Multimedia Encyclopedia, 1993.

Harriot, Thomas. *A Briefe and True Report of the New Found Land of Virginia.* New York: Dover Publications, 1972.

Heinzel, Hermann, and Martin Woodcock. *Collins Guide to the Birds of Britain and Europe.* London: William Collins Sons, 1978.

A Hornbook of Virginia History. Richmond: The Virginia State Library, 1965.

Jefferson, Thomas. *Notes on the State of Virginia.* Chapel Hill: University of North Carolina Press, 1955.

Limburg, Peter R. *What's-in-a-Names of Birds.* New York: Coward, McCann & Geoghegan, 1975.

Long, John L. *Introduced Birds of the World.* Sydney: Reed, 1981.

Martel, Brett. "Report Raises a Squawk." *Richmond (Va) Times-Dispatch,* November 5, 2000, p. A2.

Milne, Lorus and Margery. *The Audubon Society Field Guide to North American Insects and Spiders.* New York: Knopf, 1988.

Newsweek. "Periscope"/"Ecology: Good News," June 23, 1997, p. 6.

Pancake, John. "Appreciation." *Washington Post,* July 31, 1996, sec. F, p. 1.

Pearson, T. Gilbert, ed. *Birds of America.* Garden City, NY: Garden City Publishing Company, 1936.

Peterson, Roger Tory. *A Field Guide to the Birds of Eastern and Central North America.* Boston: Houghton Mifflin, 1980.

Peterson, Roger Tory, and the Editors of LIFE. *The Birds.* New York: Time Inc., 1963.

Peterson, Roger Tory, ed. *The Bird Watcher's Anthology.* New York: Harcourt, Brace, 1957.

Petras, Kathryn, and Ross Petras, eds. *Very Bad Poetry.* New York: Vintage Books, 1997.

Savory, Theodore. *Naming the Living World.* New York: John Wiley & Sons, 1962.

Scott, Shirley F., ed. *Field Guide to the Birds of North America.* 2d ed. Washington, DC: National Geographic Society, 1992.

Sill, Ben L., Cathryn P. and John C. *Another Field Guide to Little-Known & Seldom-Seen Birds of North America.* Atlanta: Peachtree Publishers, 1990.

Stokes, Donald and Lillian. *Stokes Field Guide to Birds: Eastern Region.* Boston: Little, Brown, 1996.

Webster's New Collegiate Dictionary. Springfield, Mass.: G.C. Merriam, 1981.

Wetmore, Alexander. *Song and Garden Birds of North America.* Washington, D.C.: National Geographic Society, 1964.

White, E.B. *Essays of E.B. White.* New York: Harper & Row, 1977.

Wilkinson, Tom. "Zebras Musseling In." *Washington Post*, May 14, 1997, sec. H, p. 1.

Wilson, Charles Reagan, and William Ferris, eds. *Encyclopedia of Southern Culture.* Chapel Hill: University of North Carolina Press, 1989.

Winokur, Jon. *Zen to Go.* New York: New American Library, 1989.

Acknowledgments

Producing a book is supposedly a lonely endeavor, so I have no good explanation for why this one required the help of so many people.

First, I should note that I'm luckier than most people in having *five* grandparents. The four who were directly involved in my becoming a birder and a writer are mentioned elsewhere, but I can't fail to mention the fifth, Marilyn Cashwell, whose love and support have meant so much to me and my family. If she wasn't directly involved in my becoming a birder or a writer, it's only because of my own tardiness in claiming her.

Thanks next to my many birding partners: Mary Stevens and Paul Hart; Gilly and Brenda Macknee; Jim Miller; Tom Parker, Wallace Hornady, Jim Reid, Karen Bond, Chris Sprouse, Arnulf Koehnke and Jacob Foster; Linda Cope; and the good folk at Back Bay NWR, the Chesapeake Bay Bridge-Tunnel, and Cape May. Your guidance, sharp eyes, and early morning patience have given me the fabric from which this book is woven.

Thanks also to those who have given me material for my studies: Joe and Lou Cashwell, whose shelves I raided early on in life; Lea Sutker, whose vigilance over the Beaufort Library's discarded-book sales has kept me supplied with classic bird books for decades; and my in-laws, Graham and Ruth Dalton, who gave me a Peterson guide for my twenty-fifth birthday and sent my birding down a very different track than it might have taken.

Lyrics from "I'm the Breeze" appear in the epigraph to Chapter 13 by gracious permission of the writers, Jim Wann and Bland Simpson. The song itself is taken from the musical *King Mackerel and The Blues Are Running: Songs and Stories of the Carolina Coast,* which is published and leased for stock and amateur theatrical productions, by Samuel French, Inc. The show's soundtrack is available on Sugar Hill Records and should be required listening for anyone who loves the Carolina coast.

For patience, support, and my continuing education, thanks to Woodberry Forest School and all its people; for long hours of thoughtful editing, thanks to Barbara Morrow and John Corenswet.

Thanks for encouragement, education, advice, and the occasional chance to see print: Doris Betts, Daphne Athas, the late Tim McLaurin, and the rest of English 99's writers, 1984–85; Gary Groth and *The Comics Journal;* WVTF Radio; Carey Amberger, Anthony Sgro and *Woodberry Forest Magazine & Journal;* Kaethe Douglas; Paul Clark, Randall Stickrod, and *The Readerville Journal.*

Thanks to those who offered practical suggestions and the occasional piece of pointed advice: Ted Blain, Bill Norris, Marta Randall, M.J. Rose, and Katharine Weber.

Digital thank-yous to Mignon and Karen at quietspace, whose excellence of design can be seen on the Web at both their own site (www.quietspace.com) and mine (www.

petercashwell.com), and to Sarah Rocklin for the photo that graces the latter.

For the greatest online support system a writer could ever want, I offer *big* digital thank-yous to the citizens of Readerville.com (with a nod to Kristjan Wager, who pointed me there in the first place) and its multi-talented proprietor, Karen Templer, who has offered encouragement, assistance, and generosity aplenty. I do not exaggerate in the slightest when I say that without them, you wouldn't be holding this book.

Thanks to those patient souls who have encouraged, or at least tolerated, my obsession with birds: my parents; my brother David; Uncalane; Mike Beard, Pete Rogers, and Carey Floyd (the Pros from Dover); and my sons, Ian and Dixon.

And of course, the biggest thanks of all to Kelly Dalton, my muse and polestar.

Birds first captured PETER CASHWELL's attention when his mother hung an avian mobile over his crib. He was born in Raleigh, N.C., grew up in Chapel Hill, and graduated from the University of North Carolina, where he took every creative writing course permitted by the English department (and one that wasn't). Cashwell has worked at lots of different jobs—radio announcer, rock musician, comic-book critic, improv comedy accompanist. Now he teaches English and speech at Woodberry Forest School in the foothills of Virginia's Blue Ridge Mountains, where he lives with his wife, Kelly Dalton, and their two sons, Ian and Dixon. He also co-writes "Loose Canons," a column for the *Readerville Journal.* You can learn all about him at www.petercashwell.com.

GRANT SILVERSTEIN is a Pennsylvania artist who specializes in etching. The illustrations for this book were done in pen-and-ink.